The Book of
PSALMS
F O R   W O R S H I P

Crown &
Covenant
PUBLICATIONS

www.crownandcovenant.com

**Crown &
Covenant**
PUBLICATIONS

Printed in the United States of America

ISBN 978-1884527-25-8 (pew edition)

Library of Congress Control Number: 2009927600

Music Engraving: Dolce & Nuit Productions
Cover Design: Eileen Bechtold
Copy editing: Linda Au Parker
Graphics: Ariana Davenport Stitzer
Project Manager: Lynne Gordon

Contents

Understanding the Psalms as Christian Worship

H OW DO WE OPEN UP THE MEANING OF THE PSALMS and see their connection to the rest of Scripture? Three important features of the book of Psalms help to guide us in this. They are a major part of what binds the book of Psalms into a unity, and they show us what makes the Book of Psalms especially appropriate for worship offered in the name of Christ Jesus.

The Psalms express a view of reality as well as of faith.

The Psalms show us the same kind of world that Jesus saw around Him, the kind of world in which He lived and in which He died. He had to walk carefully in that world if His mission was actually to be fulfilled without fatal compromise along the way. It is the same world in which we also must live, and where faith must be on the alert if it is to carry out its God-given work. The Psalms, recognizing the nature of this world, always speak from an underlying assurance of faith, but not necessarily from conditions of peace. The world is not a safe place, but a person can, nevertheless, find protection, meaning and fulfillment by trusting in the promises of the true and living God. Such is the message that Jesus preached in the Sermon on the Mount, a message with many ties to Psalm 37.

The worldview of the Psalms is actually the same that is found throughout Scripture. That is, the world of human society—however necessary and supportive and God-ordained is the role it plays in our lives—is regarded as a corrupt, deceitful, dangerous place where evil exists. And because the world is this way, the faith of the Christian needs to be awake and alert in it. It is because of this world-view that the Psalms are about more than human emotion or human piety. When David speaks about enemies, false friends, sickness, warfare and terrible devastations, he speaks about realities he has lived among. The Psalms might also be used to teach us how to pray about such things because harsh realities are often the means by which the kingdom of God comes into our world and into our lives. The workings of heaven, the judgments of the end times, are with us even now. Our own individual histories and struggles are played out—with God's help— upon this dangerous field.

Thus the Psalms are prayers that express faith rather than complacency. God's promises are not just to be taken for granted. Even for God's covenant people, peace and safety are not guaranteed. God's decisive help in bringing about such blessings will often involve great outward struggle on the part of the Christian as well as earnest prayer. The Psalms do not assume that inner peace is the natural state of the believer's heart—it is instead an achievement brought about through whole-hearted trust in the true and living God. And even so, such peace is not necessarily a once-for-all achievement: It may have to be prayed for again and again as new dangers and crises arise. Furthermore, it may happen that the way God deals with His people is difficult to understand—sometimes so difficult that when the Psalms touch on such things they become the most searching prayers of all. David shows us that such prayer and faith are costly.

The Psalms do not make our emotions and hopes their starting place. What they do for us is offer a way, through Spirit-given words, by which the worshiper can join himself both with the hopes and feelings of Israel's flawed but great king David, and also with those of David's divinely-great successor, the Messiah Jesus. The Psalms, as worship-songs and prayers, prepare us to take our place in the kingdom under various conditions in the world and in our lives. Comfort, indeed great comfort, is offered by the Psalms, but comfort is not usually their main point. The Psalms call us to faith and to work—to the work of prayer and self-discipline, of repentance and rededication—if we really want to see the goodness and beauty of God manifested. They also offer us a real experience of the presence of God along the way.

One more thing should be mentioned here. Although the world is dangerous, the Psalms are not teaching us to be afraid of the world but rather alert in it. The fear that the Psalms do point us to is not fear of the world but an appropriate fear of God—not the kind of fear that keeps us away from God, but the kind that draws us to Him. After all, He is the One who really matters. It is for this reason that the Psalms use such an amazing freedom and directness when speaking to God. This directness in prayer might look easy, yet there are definite pitfalls to try to avoid. The Psalms help us in this by giving us a model of boldness that we can build upon securely.

This boldness is not just something we can put on by our own effort, of course, but is really a matter of inward assurance in relation to God. The Psalms show us this assurance not for us to try and imitate it, but rather so we might believe in the grace and promises of God. Then we will have reason for assurance. In other words, the Psalms are calling us to faith in the God who calls us to Himself in grace. What David manifested in the Psalms was the absolute assurance of one who has his foundation in God. Even in David's greatest distress and misery he still has assurance to come before his God and know that his pleading will be heard. His faith is still alive, and so is his love toward God, even when comfort and hope may be far distant. David, imperfect as he was as a man, is in the Psalms a model of what true faith is. His prayers are rich in emotion, but the foundation of his pleading is nothing less than the promises of the God who cannot be unfaithful.

David's kingdom is the foundation of Jesus' claims.

The Psalms proclaim a new development of God's redemptive work that begins with David. The unique kingship of David, established upon the promised faithfulness of God, is the same kingship that Jesus would be born to inherit and fulfill. Christians, therefore, properly see in the Davidic character of the Psalms a rich manifestation of Christ Jesus.

First of all, we should recognize that the Book of Psalms itself was the sign that something new and permanent had come into being, it was not just a collection of songs. The beginning of the book of Psalms was the first indication in the history of Israel's worship since Moses that a new era had begun. The worship service established in the Law of Moses had been jealously defended by the Lord against any human innovations. But now something has been introduced into that Mosaic arrangement. Who authorized this change? It was David, the same man to whom God had promised an everlasting kingdom. What was this change? King David's own prayer-songs were from now on to be sung in the temple along with the offering up of sacrifices. The prayers and thanksgivings that David composed under the guidance and inspiration of the Spirit became part of the new form of Israel's acceptable worship of the Lord. The words and life of this person, David, are offered up to the Lord in the midst of Israel at worship, and the Lord is pleased. Thus we see a new era in the progress of God's redemptive work: the Davidic era has come into being.

The book of Psalms thus has a real and effective unity in David. The whole collection of Psalms in it is a continuation of what David began—and of what the Lord continued to direct. Though other inspired authors would make their contributions, these come into the book of Psalms through David and in service to the kingdom that had its beginning in David. These other authors do not give their names to an era or to a kingdom, nor do they bring a new order of temple worship into being. The unity of the book of Psalms is, therefore, more than just the unity of its inspiration, and more than just the predominance of David's actual authorship. David is the great patron of the book of Psalms, and his unique calling and authority stand behind everything in it.

The nature of the change is that the relatively impersonal system of law and worship that God had previously established through Moses now becomes something with a definite personal character through David. This is a progress in God's grace. God is becoming more and more personally recognizable among his people through His chosen representative. This progress is nowhere near complete in David, but it does indicate the kind of fulfillment that would eventually be accomplished in the person of Jesus.

David is not so much exalted by his Psalms becoming part of Israel's worship as transformed. His human character and experience—transcribed in words of the Spirit—have become wholehearted praise to the Lord. The unity of Israel with the Lord that it worships now takes place in the presence of another evident unity, that of a son and his heavenly Father. In the light of redemptive history, what we see here is a prefiguring of the incarnation. David knows that he was chosen by the Lord and even called His son. In the new service of worship offered in the temple, David has become, in a sense, the meaning of the sacrifices. Though both the kingdom and the temple would eventually come to a violent end, and God's chosen son would cease to have an earthly kingdom to his name any longer, the Psalms would continue to teach God's worshiping people the character and struggles of the king who was God's chosen one.

What, in general, does the book of Psalms contain? It is basically a collection of testimonies, both in thanksgiving and in concern, regarding the well-being of that unique institution that God established in David. It is David's kingdom, after all, that would, in the appointed time, in Jesus, come to embrace the whole of God's redemptive work—and as such would reach out with grace and power toward all the earth. The Psalms, reflecting the life of that chosen realm under many different circumstances and conditions, are prayers, celebrations, and pleadings lifted up to the Lord in terms of His faithful promises.

The Christian should note that in praying the prayers of the Psalms he is actually identifying with the king who is praying in them and through them. The Christian is not expected to be a nobody or to pray as a nobody. Even when David is most humble and wretched, most conscious of his guilt and shame, he is still the anointed king. As a Christian takes up David's words as his own words, he finds in them also the presence of Jesus. After all, David is not merely an accident of history, but a step in the unfolding of God's redemptive plan of which Jesus is the attainment. Jesus does not merely copy David as His pattern, but also fulfills that grace which David could only plead for. Therefore, even when David is at his lowest point, Jesus continues to uphold him as part of His own identity. After David's heinous deeds, God takes David's repentance and makes it a true model of what sorrow for sin is really about (see Psalms 51 and 32).

While the Psalms do not represent the whole range of valid prayer, they do show a well-constructed path of devotion already paved for us. And one of the significant consequences of looking at the Psalms through David in this way is that we can see Christ Jesus in all the Psalms, we are not limited to seeing Jesus just in the few Psalms that speak prophetically about a future time. Christians do, after all, know that the God they worship has shaped both Scripture and the special history of His people to conform to the unity of His unfolding plan. Therefore it does not seem impossible that the Psalms should be used in this interlocking way to manifest the Christ who is at the heart of that plan.

The Psalms belong to us as Christians because they are Davidic: that is the heart of the matter. God promised David an everlasting kingdom. David is called God's "son". David exercised authority over the services of the temple. And as Anointed King David was also under orders to purge from the kingdom and city of God all that was found unworthy or deceitful in them (see Psalm 101), the prayers and praises of this chosen man were thus appropriate to become the songs that would continually rise up to the Lord together with the sacrificial offerings of Israel. That is, even before the prophets introduce the figure of the coming greater Messiah, just in terms of David himself with all his flaws, we see a kingly and priestly authority in the Psalms that only Jesus would be able to unite and fulfill. When Christians sing the Psalms, they can recognize in David the earthly foundation on which Jesus built.

The intercessory voice in the Psalms pointed ahead to the burden that Jesus would take up.

God allowed the kingdom of David to perish after all, despite His promise to the contrary. Was God therefore unfaithful? The Psalms raise this painful question as one that cannot be explained away. And because it cannot be explained away, this question links the Psalms to the suffering that Jesus would have to embrace in order to satisfy God's justice and achieve the salvation of His people. The Psalms play a role not found elsewhere in Scripture in conveying a feeling of the burden of sin-bearing and of the Messiah's suffering.

If we were to take the Psalms specifically addressed to the condition of the Davidic kingdom and then arrange them in rough chronological order, we would see a clear development and be brought up against an unavoidable question. The earlier kingdom-Psalms are full of confidence and a sense of a glorious calling and destiny in the Lord (Psalms 2, 110 and 72, for instance). Then dark times come, as shown in later Psalms (such as Psalms 60, 80, 132, 77 and 89). And at last the unthinkable does actually happen: the kingdom comes to a violent end (described in Psalms 74 and 79). And although a Psalm from a yet later time (such as Psalm 126) does express hope in the goodness of God for the future, it does not answer the hard question about how the Lord let this devastation happen in the first place. No answer to this question is found in the Psalms—or indeed anywhere else in the Scriptures. The Davidic voice in the Psalms can do nothing but absorb the pain of the contradiction and wait for the Lord's answer.

What makes it especially heavy is that this question challenges what the Psalms most consistently celebrate about God: the way that He as a righteous God keeps His promises to His people. Affirmations of this kind are at the very heart of covenant faith. And yet, at the same time, we see in the Psalms that God's faithfulness and reliability are confronted with the most serious kind of challenge. What is happening to David's kingdom seems to contradict the faithfulness of God. This tension, found throughout the book of Psalms, is not there by accident.

God does not, of course, leave His people without giving them some kind of word to help them understand and accept the outworking of His will. In fact the Prophets began to speak of a new stage in the outworking of God's covenant. They said that God would in time send another man of David's line to be the Anointed King over Israel. This man would be a greater king than David. He would restore the fallen kingdom and triumph over all its enemies. This Messiah would rescue the people of David's fallen kingdom, and lead them to safety, peace and freedom from shame. This is indeed a more profound answer from God. But even so, can it be His whole answer? This Messiah could certainly bring them into victory and joy in the Lord. But how could He free them from shame? How could He free them from their unanswered questions concerning the Lord's faithfulness? How could restoration to prosperity be the answer to everything? Could the pain of broken promises simply be put aside and forgotten?

At this point we should turn to another side of the Prophets' teachings, and see how it links up with the tone and content found in some of the Psalms. The references in the Prophets to a Messiah that would deliver Israel with great power, are relatively few and brief in comparison with the space the Prophets devoted to warning about coming disasters. Even fewer in the Prophets are references to a suffering figure (such as in Isaiah 50 and 53). Who is this person? Can this also be the Messiah, or is it someone different? The Prophets do not make it clear. What is noteworthy, however, is that at the same time that the Prophets have begun speaking here and there about a righteous figure who endures great suffering, many of the Psalms speak in a voice appropriate to that suffering figure. The Davidic voice of the early Psalms (those written by David himself) that spoke with such great confidence has become in the later Psalms a voice of desperation. He upholds the justice and goodness of God at the same time that God's unexplainable actions are tearing him apart.

Here are two streams of revelation that are coming together. On the one hand in the Prophets, we see both a glorious future Messiah and also a person who is burdened with the sin and reproach that really belongs to Israel. On the other hand in the Psalms, we see David appear in two very different ways. Sometimes we see David radiant in the glory, dignity and authority that the Lord invested in him. And at another point we see David pleading desperately to the Lord—because of the shame and guilt of his own sin, and in behalf of God's people in their sin and need, and for the honor of God's own great and holy name. Thus the Psalms give a voice to a pleading Messiah, a Messiah who is not always triumphant. How appropriate it was, then, that Jesus would learn from the Psalms how to pray and to discipline His soul. He would have been preparing to take up the yoke of humiliation that He had to bear before there would be any glory to bestow on others. So it was that Jesus, who grew up singing the Psalms as a regular part of His worship and devotion to God, learned two things from them. He learned to see God's own Kingdom in terms of the kingdom that God had promised to David. And Jesus also learned to take hold of the voice speaking in the Psalms and find in it an expression of His own calling to glorify God. As the Son of David in the time when all things had to be fulfilled, Jesus would have a higher responsibility—and would bear a heavier burden—than His ancestor in the flesh ever knew.

Mere words cannot solve the problem. They cannot take away the sting of God's apparent unfaithfulness. Such reasoning is, in fact, likely to add another insult to God, likely to contain some insinuation that He is not entirely good, not entirely what He says He is. Yet this is God, the One who, despite all appearances and accusations, is wholly and irreproachably faithful. Therefore, the answer contained in the Psalms is not a chain of reasoning but something quite different: it is a person whose role and responsibility are revealed. As Israel slides downward toward its doom, the David who speaks in the Psalms becomes something more than a reminder of past glories. David expresses a concern over the sin of his people, the danger they are in, and their desperate need of God's promised grace. David's prayers show his awareness of his own sins but they are also deeply intercessory for those that God had placed in his care. God's answer is in the person of Jesus, who takes upon himself David's concerns, the sins of His people, the honor of the God who is faithful, and makes atonement upon the cross.

Of course, Christians are in a position to see that this way of reading of the Psalms is absolutely right. From the perspective of a divine Son of God, how would it be possible that the Psalms did not reflect Jesus as the Christ? How could the divine Messiah who came into the history of God's covenant people not have been reflected in David, His predecessor in that same history, both in glory and in suffering? To make these connections depends, of course, upon our having a high view of Scripture. But on the other hand, having a high view of Scripture forces us into making these connections. If Scripture is a work of the God who directs events within history, then God's design shines through, both in Scripture and in the outworking of His covenant in the course of time.

What we see, then, is that although the Psalms do not express every legitimate Christian prayer, they do serve as the God-given model of prayer forged in the heat of testing. And the voice that speaks in the Psalms is one with many layers of connection to Jesus, both in His glory and in His agony. It is this inspired voice, even more than the poetry of the Psalms, that makes this part of God's Word such an instrument of soul-searching power in His hands. It is part of our legacy in Christ. Even the hard questions that the Psalms raise are part of our legacy as Christians and still have disturbing power today. This is so because though Jesus, now the risen and glorified Christ, rules with authority over all things in heaven and earth, we do not always see events turning out favorably for His people or for the honor of His name. Can we explain this away with reasons? Or can we block such thoughts from our minds? The Psalms show us a different path, a path of prayer that faces hard truths and avoids easy wrong answers. The Psalms also point us back to the cross of Christ, that mystery above all, where questions of God's justice and God's faithfulness come to resolution.

By singing the Psalms in worship Christians trace again the way that Jesus took. It was from the Psalms that Jesus learned both the exaltation of His calling and the inescapable burden of His intercessory labor. The sonship of Jesus did not exempt Him either from suffering or from shame as He worked out the obedience required of Him. Jesus took the words and experiences of David and confirmed them, both by the way He made them into His own prayers and as He fulfilled them in His life and death.

—Rev. Dr. G. Duncan Lowe

The Experience of Singing the Psalms

M OVING FROM READING, STUDYING, AND MEDITATING on the Psalms from a prose translation of the Bible, to making them a rewarding singing experience for a gathering of believers, can be an enormous leap for those unfamiliar with the historical development of the practice. While this is not the place to explore the nature of Hebrew poetry in detail, a few words about it are essential. Hebrew poetry is characterized by parallelism; that is, most psalms consist of pairs of lines, of which the second either repeats in different words the ideas of the first, contrasts with them, or otherwise builds upon the first line. For example,

> Do not fret because of evil men
> or be envious of those who do wrong. (Ps. 37:1)

> For the Lord watches over the way of the righteous,
> but the way of the wicked will perish. (Ps. 1:6)

In both the Hebrew text and its translations, lines contain varying numbers of syllables. Some verses have three lines instead of two. There are no rhymes such as characterize poetry in English and many other European languages. Some Hebrew poetry is acrostic; that is, each verse begins with the next letter of the Hebrew alphabet. Psalm 119 is acrostic in a larger sense: every eight verses are a strophe beginning with the next letter of the alphabet. Thus, Hebrew poetry is sufficiently different from traditional European poetry that it cannot be used directly in a form recognizable to singers and listeners in those languages. A reader of the English Bible may well believe that the Psalms are prose and not musical at all.

The use of the Psalms in the temple and synagogue in biblical times is well attested in Scripture and in rabbinic sources. There, they were (and are) delivered in a heightened speech or a musical or semi-musical recitation known as cantillation. Such recitation requires either a soloist or that all who are participating know both the text and the melodic formulae thoroughly. The earliest Christians made use of the Psalms, both in corporate worship and in private devotion. Bishops in the early centuries were required to have memorized all 150 psalms. Throughout the ensuing centuries, all 150 psalms have been chanted weekly in monastic communities, and parts of them (versicles) are chanted or sung within the services in parish churches.

For many centuries, however, these were sung by the clergy and choir, and not by the congregation. In fact, it is not clear whether the congregation sang at all in the Old Testament synagogue. In the Apostolic era, both Paul and James commended the singing of psalms, and it is possible that Acts 4:24 refers to singing by the assembled saints, "lifting up their voices with one accord." The church fathers and other early Christian writings promote the use and the singing of the Psalms: Athanasius, Eusebius, Basil the Great, Augustine, Jerome, and others. Church Councils in the 4th and 5th centuries prohibited the singing of any extra-biblical materials, partly because many of the heresies plaguing the Church were spread through newly written hymns and imitation "psalms." Throughout the centuries we often call the "Middle Ages," the congregation did not sing in the service.

Efforts to involve large numbers of congregants in singing plainchant (which has no harmonies) and Anglican chant (which has) have not produced confident or hearty congregational singing, particularly in the absence of instrumental accompaniment to hasten the singers along. In the twentieth century there were a number of attempts to secure congregational participation in singing psalm texts — Gélineau style, that of the community of Taizé, and the use of some scattered psalm verses as praise choruses. Each of these has had some good effect, but none has met the need for confident congregational singing of complete psalms without dependence on accompaniment.

It was the genius of the Protestant Reformation, first, to make use of whole psalms and the complete Psalter, and second, to discover a way to make the Psalms not only singable but popular and influential. That way was to translate the Psalms into modern poetry and sing them to the same types of tunes that people were accustomed to singing elsewhere — that is, in stanzas and lines of predictable length and with a regular rhythmic organization, or meter. (Hence the term metrical.) For example, for some years before the Reformation, composers and clergymen encouraged the non-liturgical singing of uplifting "spiritual folk songs" or "laude" ("praise songs") instead of the bawdy popular songs of the day. It should come as no surprise that people whose hearts were ignited by the Gospel of Christ at the Reformation hungrily took up the singing of psalms as part of their new-found faith. *The Book of Psalms for Worship* stands heir to this long tradition.

During and since the Reformation, there have been three main currents of metrical Psalmody: the Continental, the English, and the Scottish.

Continental Metrical Psalms

At the time of the Reformation, Uldrich Zwingli in Zürich based his reformed liturgy not on the Mass but on a special late-Medieval form of preaching service which had no singing. For a time, several other Swiss cities, including Basel and Geneva, followed Zwingli's practice and allowed no music of any kind in worship. Most of the other Reformers, however, took as their starting-point the structure of the Mass and included music. One of the most important changes instituted by both Martin Luther and John Calvin was provision for the congregation to sing during the service. As early as 1523, Luther called for the singing of German hymns and of singing the word of God. As the Reformation unfolded, Luther expanded his concept of materials to be sung: loose paraphrases of the Psalms, newly written hymns, and German translations of Latin hymns. Calvin, because of his theology of sola scriptura, used only the Psalms for worship, and metrical psalmody became a hallmark of the Reformed faith.

Moreover, Calvin's experience as a refugee pastor in Strasbourg from 1538 through 1541 had shown him by experience the merits of singing psalms in metrical form rather than chanting the prose text — people learned them easily, sang them readily, and received great spiritual blessing from them. In 1539 Calvin produced his first metrical Psalter in French—six psalms translated by Calvin himself and thirteen by the poet Clément Marot. (Marot, in fact, had been versifying the Psalms in French to entertain the royal Court in Paris.) When he was recalled to Geneva in 1541, Calvin persuaded the authorities there to approve metrical psalmody in worship.

Over the course of the next two decades, Calvin oversaw the preparation of a series of interim psalters, each larger than the last, until the entire metrical psalter in French was complete in 1562. In order to accommodate meter and rhyme, it was sometimes necessary to add words to the psalm. The poets were not permitted to "pad" the translation with anything that was not there; words were added only to exegete the psalm in order to clarify the meaning. Thus, it is correct to describe these versions as "close paraphrases."

Most of the 125 tunes used in the *Genevan Psalter* were composed or edited by Louis Bourgeois. In style, many of them resemble popular tunes of the time, but there is no evidence that they were simply borrowed from secular songs such as bar tunes. There is, on the contrary, clear evidence of the influence of Plainchant as a source.

The result was a masterful blending of text and tune, the music serving to support the text rather than to interfere with the purpose of "sung prayer." The *Genevan Psalter* has been one of the most influential collections of worship music in the centuries since. It was the basis of psalter translations in Dutch, German, Hungarian, Czech, Hebrew (for mission work to Jews), and other languages— at least 24 in all. Although in Geneva the Psalms were sung in unison (octaves) and unaccompanied in worship services, numerous polyphonic settings of them were published in many of the countries where the psalter spread. These were originally for use only at home or social events, but today harmonized settings are widely used in church, and many of the Reformed denominations use instrumental accompaniment in services. *The Genevan Psalter* is still important today, especially in the churches of Dutch background. The Canadian Reformed Churches have published a new English version utilizing all of the Genevan tunes, in addition to a selection of other scriptural and post-scriptural materials, as *Book of Praise* (1974, 1984). Some of the 1562 tunes are found in current hymnals of other Reformed and Reformed-derivative denominations. The French, in contrast, have not modernized or revised their psalter, and in consequence the Psalms are little used in the Reformed churches in the Francophone world.

English Metrical Psalmody

The Reformation in England followed a different course from the Continent, being established by fiat of Henry VIII. While this was a process rather than a single event, the date most often attached to it is 1534, when the Act of Supremacy declared Henry "the supreme head in earth of the Church of England." King Henry vacillated about the doctrine, polity, and worship of his new church, and not until after his death in 1547 was it firmly steered in a Reformed direction.

Early attempts to follow the lead of Genevan psalmody failed, in part because the English were accustomed to songs with shorter lines and stanzas than were typical of the French psalter.

The first prayer-book in English was published in 1549, and in the same year an incomplete psalter by Thomas Sternhold and a complete one by Robert Crowley appeared. In succeeding years, Sternhold's versions were amended and supplemented by John Hopkins and several others, and in 1562 was published by John Day—but universally known as "Sternhold and Hopkins." Most of their versions were in "common" or ballad meter, and were widely popular and readily sung. This psalter was reprinted more than 200 times as a separate volume, and was also printed in most editions of both the *Geneva Bible* and *The Book of Common Prayer*.

Translations that were more literary were made by such English poets as Sir Thomas Wyatt (the "father of the English sonnet" translated six of the penitential psalms in terza rima, a technical tour de force), Sir Philip Sidney, and his sister the Countess of Pembroke. These were not intended for congregational singing, but stand as monuments to the qualities of the Psalms as literature.

The "Brownists" were a group of English Congregationalists who sang originally from the Sternhold and Hopkins version. Some years after emigrating to the Netherlands (1581), they produced a new version by Henry Ainsworth (1612). This was the version they continued to use after they famously relocated to the New World in 1620. The Puritans who established the Massachusetts Bay Colony in 1630 sang from Sternhold and Hopkins, but increasingly felt that it was not sufficiently faithful to the Hebrew. In 1650, they published what has ever since been known as the *Bay Psalm Book*, the first book to be published in English-speaking North America. (It was published in Cambridge, Massachusetts, in the basement of the President's house at Harvard College, on a press imported specifically for the purpose.) This psalter, with its 1651 revision called the *New England Psalm Book*, was in use for over a century among both Congregationalists and Baptists. The ninth edition (1698) included the first music printed in North America. In addition to its importance in American history, its influence can also be found in the *Scottish Psalter* of 1650.

In England, the aging Sternhold and Hopkins version was succeeded in 1696 by the "New Version" of Nahum Tate and Nicholas Brady, poets of the "Augustan Age" of English literature. (Tate later became Poet Laureate.) One of the Augustan goals was to "elevate" English poetry to the level of the poets of the age of the Emperor Augustus—Virgil and Horace. The attempt to make David sound like Horace served to lessen worshipers' attachment to the Psalms.

The Scottish Tradition

The first complete metrical psalter in Scotland appeared in 1564. It was well loved at the time, but within eighty years was generally thought archaic. One of the tasks assigned the Westminster Assembly of Divines (1643-1653) was to prepare a new version of the Psalms, suitable for use in England, Scotland, and Wales. The version they approved in 1646 was revised and emended by the General Assembly of the Church of Scotland and approved in 1650. That version embedded itself in the Scottish soul; it fortified and consoled them during the persecution and the "Killing Times," and has been sung by countless presbyterians of every stripe around the globe for 350 years. Its persistence is more than a habit of the familiar; at its best, the *Scottish Psalter* has an incomparable majesty of language which sinks deep into the heart. It continues to be used by various Presbyterian bodies in Scotland, Canada, the United States, Australia, and elsewhere. It has shaped the development of psalters in Turkish, Armenian, Modern Greek, Chinese, Japanese, and other world languages in the nineteenth and twentieth centuries.

A metrical psalter in Scottish Gaelic was published in 1694, and is still used in Gaelic services in psalm singing churches in the highlands and the Hebrides. A psalter in Irish Gaelic was published at least as early as 1836 for mission work among the Irish population.

The Eclipse of Metrical Psalmody

The last gasp of English metrical psalters came in 1719, with the effort of Isaac Watts titled *The Psalms of David Imitated in the Language of the New Testament*. The author's aim, as he famously summarized it, was "to make David speak like a Christian." In addition to these paraphrases, he also published a variety of hymns.

The long, dark night of metrical psalmody began, if a date can be fixed, with the publication of Watts's *Imitations*. The Church of England had not required the exclusive use of the Psalms by the congregation for some years; the Psalms were to be chanted, but the chief use of metrical psalters in the Church of England was for home and devotional use. The preference for songs of lighter theological weight figured heavily in the growing adoption of hymns, which were not bound to biblical texts. During the following century and a half, Watts's Imitations were the key to prising open the congregational repertoire in England, the United States, Canada, and even Scotland. Successive editions of hymnals displayed ever-declining numbers of psalm texts.

In the first half of the nineteenth century, hymnals included both psalms and hymns, usually with a large selection of psalms at the front of the book. Both Old School and New School Presbyterians published such hymnals (both in 1843), but by 1866 the hymnal of the Presbyterian Church included fewer psalms and made no distinction between biblical and extra-biblical materials. Nor did their hymnals published in 1873, 1895, 1911, and 1933, and in fact the Southern Presbyterian hymnal of 1927 seems to have included no Psalms at all. The Congregationalists and Baptists had largely abandoned psalms by 1801, and by the 1870s even Isaac Watts' paraphrases were no longer to be found.

Renewal and Revision in the Scottish Tradition

Several denominations have continued to sing metrical psalms exclusively or nearly so, and a number of revisions have been made, particularly in the United

States. Like the 1611 "King James" translation of the Bible, the *Scottish Psalter* eventually was found too difficult or distracting for the uninitiated, due to normal changes in the English language. What is a visitor to make, for example, of these lines from Psalm 18:26?

> Pure to the pure, thou froward kyth'st
> unto the froward wight.

By the mid-19th century, psalm-singing churches in the United States were increasingly on the defensive as the flood of extra-biblical hymns swept across Christendom and all but extinguished the book that had been the sung praise of the Church throughout eighteen centuries. An effort by Reformed Presbyterians in 1866 to improve the rhymes and modernize the vocabulary and syntax of the *Scottish Psalter* proved abortive, but in the following years the need became even more pressing. The United Presbyterians produced a version in 1870, the Reformed Presbyterians in 1889. The latter was available in the "split leaf" format popular in Great Britain at the time (and still in limited use). In this, the tunes are printed in the top portion of the page but separated from the texts in the lower portion. (This is also sometimes called "Dutch door binding.") In this way, tunes and texts can be chosen independently and matched as desired.

During the multiple revisions of this era, differences in the theology of translation surfaced, especially in regard to strict, loose, or free paraphrase. In 1893, several psalm singing denominations in America attempted to produce a "uniform version." Their final version was presented in 1909, but forthrightly valued elegance and aesthetics over fidelity to the Hebrew text. It simply omitted psalm portions the committee thought tasteless or sub-Christian. The Reformed Presbyterian Church had already withdrawn from the joint committee and rejected both the Uniform Version and the principles upon which it was based. Instead, it produced in 1911 a revision of its 1889 version. The 1909 Union Version lived on for a number of years in the 1912 United Presbyterian Psalter and was used in several denominations. Many of its texts were used in *The Hymnbook* (1955) and the *Trinity Hymnal* (1961, rev. 1990). Its influence remains in the current *Presbyterian Hymnal* and in the *Psalter Hymnal* of the Christian Reformed Church, which contain all or nearly all 150 psalms. This revival of interest in singing the Psalms is solid evidence that their abandonment in the nineteenth and twentieth centuries was, in the grand sweep of Christian history, an anomaly, one which many believers are slowly correcting.

The style of tunes used for psalm singing has also diverged. At the same time hymns were displacing psalms, most American and British denominations began to use organs in worship, making possible more variety of sound and style. While the "core repertory" of tunes in most hymnals and psalters remains accessible to worshipers, a growing number of tunes popular in denominations using accompaniment have proven too difficult for unaccompanied congregational singing. The simpler musical style demanded by unaccompanied congregations has been a determinative factor in many of the revisions of the psalter in the more conservative churches.

The Reformed Presbyterian Church produced revised psalters in 1929 and 1950, "to improve the English expression; to remove embarrassing or amusing expressions; to bring the meaning of the words nearer to the Hebrew." A simpler system of page layout made the 1950 psalter easier to use, although it still retained the British convention of printing only one stanza of text within the tune.

The 1973 version of the psalter, titled *The Book of Psalms for Singing*, was a more thorough-going revision than previous versions. The format was changed to reflect current American practice: up to five stanzas of text were placed within the music, with further text placed below. Psalms were divided into shorter sections, both to make the thematic structure of the psalm clearer and to encourage the singing of entire selections rather than excerpted stanzas.

Evangelical sentiment about the Psalms was changing significantly. Many hymn-singing churches felt a need for the greater depth of spiritual meaning in the Psalms, and found that psalms had been all but pushed out of the available hymnals. As Americans became more globally aware, they realized that the psalms of trouble which they had ignored in America's prosperity were often a major source of encouragement for Christians facing persecution elsewhere. They discovered in *The Book of Psalms for Singing* a usable, attractive, and biblically faithful collection.

During the same period, collections of metrical psalms for singing have been produced by individuals and congregations in several denominations and countries, and psalm singing churches in Northern Ireland, Scotland, and Australia which had hitherto remained faithful to the 1650 *Scottish Psalter* have produced new versions suited to their particular needs. Meanwhile, the *Scottish Psalter* remains in print.

The present edition of *The Book of Psalms for Worship* is thus one of a family of psalm versions which share the same goals: a collection that is faithful to the Hebrew text yet comprehensible to its generation of worshipers, and one whose texts and tunes invite the full and heart-felt participation of the people of God in singing His praises.

—Dr. Robert M. Copeland

Preface

A PSALTER REVISION COMMITTEE was appointed at the Reformed Presbyterian Church of North America's 167th Synod (1997) "to prepare and publish a revised version of *The Book of Psalms for Singing*." After the newly appointed Committee discussed the work at hand, established useful guidelines, and prepared a workable plan to accomplish the task, they set out to revise the text of *The Book of Psalms for Singing* (1973) into modern English. They consulted both the Old Testament Hebrew and modern English Bible translations (e.g., NASB, ESV, NIV, NKJV) throughout its work, seeking always to be sensitive to the wide array of matters that relate to such a revision project: accuracy, clarity, readability, singability, and various nuances of poetic genre. Revision work also entailed a removal, addition, or reuse of music selections. Given the vast heritage of tunes possessed by the Christian Church, the committee necessarily has been selective in its choices. The committee here presents *The Book of Psalms for Worship*.

This new manual of praise renders the covenantal name of God as "LORD," and no longer as "Jehovah." One exception, however, is Psalm 83, where the term "Yahweh" is used. In the three traditional versions that were preserved without change, Psalms 23, 24, and 100, "GOD" and "HIM" (all upper case) are also used for the divine name respectively. On the subject of rendering the divine name, *The Book of Psalms for Worship* reads in accord with most of those modern English versions of the Bible that have become accepted standards for use in Christian churches.

A New Testament verse accompanies each Psalm selection beneath its title. Each verse reflects some point or reference in the selection itself. The verse is not meant to be exhaustive of the entire selection, but primarily as a help to grasp the real correspondence between Old and New Testaments in the one person of Jesus Christ, who Himself sang the Psalms. Thus, the verses are meant to foster worship that is truly in Christ, in Spirit, and in truth.

Many of the tunes in this new Psalter are repeated from *The Book of Psalms for Singing*. Some of these are kept in their familiar place. Others are relocated or repeated elsewhere. Still other tunes are included that are known to and treasured by the Christian Church, but are not found in the 1973 version. Additionally, some new tunes are introduced here for the first time. The committee has sought for every psalm to be suitable to common congregational singing, having also weighed the "adjustment factor" of becoming familiar with new tunes. In this light, some Psalms have alternate selections.

The committee also has endeavored to achieve a balance in the outer vocal ranges of the music (i.e., soprano and bass lines). Tunes that generally have been considered "too high" now have been lowered. In most cases, a tune does not go above an E or E♭. Thus, psalm leaders should rarely need to adjust a selection's printed pitch.

The committee thanks those who have offered constructive criticism and useful suggestions, as well as those who have prayed for our work and us over the past decade. The committee's united hope and prayer is that the Lord would "confirm for us the work of our hands" (Ps. 90:17) for His greater glory among the praises of His people throughout the world. To Him be the glory in the Church and in Christ Jesus to all generations forever and ever. Amen.

Rev. Brian E. Coombs, *Chr.*
Dr. Robert M. Copeland
Ms. Franki Fuhrman
Rev. Dr. G. Duncan Lowe
Mr. Charles McBurney (*dec.*)

Mrs. Lori McCracken
Rev. Andrew K. Schep
Mr. Michael Tabon
Mrs. Elaine Tweed

That Man Is Blessed

For He Himself is our peace.
—Ephesians 2:14

1. [1] That man is blessed who does not walk As   wick-ed men   ad - vise,
2. [3] He's like a   deep - ly plant-ed tree Be - side a   wa - ter stream,
3. [5] The wick-ed   there - fore will not stand When time of judg-ment comes,

Nor stand where sin-ners meet, nor sit Where scorn - ers pose   as   wise.
Which in   its   sea-son bears its fruit, Whose leaves stay fresh and   green.
Nor   will   the sin-ners stand a-mong As - sem-bled righ-teous ones.

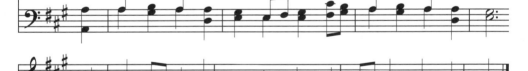

[2] In - stead he   is   the one who makes The LORD's law his de - light,
In   all   he does he will suc - ceed. [4] The   wick-ed   are not   so,
[6] Be - cause the LORD the righ-teous loves; The   path they walk He knows.

And   in that law he med - i - tates By   day and   in   the night.
But   they are like the scat-tered chaff Swept by   the winds that blow.
The   wick-ed walk a   dif-ferent path, That to   de - struc-tion goes.

Gesangbüch der Herzögl, 1784

ELLACOMBE CMD

How Blessed the Man

For in Him we live and move and have our being.
—Acts 17:28

1. ¹How blessed the man who does not walk Where wick-ed men would guide his feet, Nor stands in paths with sin-ful men, Nor sits up-on the scorn-er's seat. ²The LORD's law is his great de-light, His med-i-ta-tion day and night.

2. ³He shall be like a grow-ing tree That's plant-ed by the wa-ter-side, Which in its sea-son bears its fruit, And has a leaf that does not fade. In all that may his hands em-ploy, He will pros-per-i-ty en-joy.

3. ⁴But yet the wick-ed are not so; They are like chaff that blows a-way. They will not in the judg-ment stand, Nor sin-ners with the righ-teous stay. The LORD the way of just men knows; The wick-ed to de-struc-tion goes.

Gauntlett's Comprehensive Tune Book, 1851

GIESEN 88.88.88

Why Do Gentile Nations Rage?

To which of the angels did He ever say, "You are My Son"?
—Hebrews 1:5

1. [1] Why do Gen-tile na-tions rage, And their use-less plots de-sign?
2. [4] He who sits in heav-en laughs, For the Lord views them with scorn.
3. [7] "I the LORD's de-cree make known; This is what He had to say:
4. [10] There-fore kings now heed this word: Earth-ly judg-es, come and hear.

[2] Kings of earth in schemes en-gage, Rul-ers are in league com-bined.
[5] He will speak to them in wrath, And in an-ger He will warn:
He de-clared, 'You are My Son; I have brought You forth this day.
[11] Rev'-rent wor-ship give the LORD; With your joy mix trem-bling fear.

They speak out a-gainst the LORD; His Mes-si-ah they de-fy:
[6] "Yet ac-cord-ing to My will, I have set My King to reign;
[8] Ask of Me and You I'll make Heir to earth and na-tions all.
[12] Kiss the Son, His wrath to turn, Lest you per-ish in your stride,

[3] "Let us break their chains and cords, Let us cast them off," they cry.
And on Zi-on's ho-ly hill, My A-noint-ed will re-main."
[9] Them with i-ron rod You'll break, Smash-ing them in piec-es small.'"
For His an-ger soon may burn. Blessed are all who in Him hide.

Jakob Hintze, 1678; harm. J.S. Bach, 1685-1750

SALZBURG (Hintze) 77.77 D

Why Do Gentile Nations Rage?

God has fulfilled this for us their children,
in that He has raised up Jesus. —Acts 13:33

1. ¹Why do Gen-tile na-tions rage, And their use-less plots de-sign?
2. ⁴He who sits in heav-en laughs, For the Lord views them with scorn.
3. ⁷"I the LORD's de-cree make known; This is what He had to say:
4. ¹⁰There-fore kings now heed this word: Earth-ly judg-es, come and hear.

²Kings of earth in schemes en-gage, Rul-ers are in league com-bined.
⁵He will speak to them in wrath, And in an-ger He will warn:
He de-clared, 'You are My Son; I have brought You forth this day.
¹¹Rev'-rent wor-ship give the LORD; With your joy mix trem-bling fear.

They speak out a-gainst the LORD; His Mes-si-ah they de-fy;
⁶"Yet ac-cord-ing to My will, I have set My King to reign;
⁸Ask of Me and You I'll make Heir to earth and na-tions all.
¹²Hon-or Him, His wrath to turn, Lest you per-ish in your stride,

³"Let us break their chains and cords, Let us cast them off," they cry.
And on Zi-on's ho-ly hill, My A-noint-ed will re-main."
⁹Them with i-ron rod You'll break, Smash-ing them in piec-es small.'"
For His an-ger soon may burn. Blessed are all who in Him hide.

Joseph Parry, 1879

ABERYSTWYTH 77.77. D

Why Do Gentile Nations Rage?

*Truly in this city there were gathered together against
Your holy servant Jesus... —Acts 4:27*

1. ¹ Why do Gen-tile na-tions rage, And their use-less plots de-sign?
2. ⁴ He who sits in heav-en laughs, For the Lord views them with scorn.
3. ⁷ "I the LORD's de-cree make known; This is what He had to say:
4. ¹⁰ There-fore kings now heed this word: Earth-ly judg-es, come and hear.

² Kings of earth in schemes en-gage, Rul-ers are in league com-bined.
⁵ He will speak to them in wrath, And in an-ger He will warn:
He de-clared, 'You are My Son; I have brought You forth this day.
¹¹ Rev-'rent wor-ship give the LORD; With your joy mix trem-bling fear.

They speak out a-gainst the LORD; His Mes-si-ah they de-fy:
⁶ "Yet ac-cord-ing to My will, I have set My King to reign;
⁸ Ask of Me and You I'll make Heir to earth and na-tions all.
¹² Hon-or Him, His wrath to turn, Lest you per-ish in your stride,

³ "Let us break their chains and cords, Let us cast them off," they cry.
And on Zi-on's ho-ly hill, My A-noint-ed will re-main."
⁹ Them with i-ron rod You'll break, Smash-ing them in piec-es small.'"
For His an-ger soon may burn. Blessed are all who in Him hide.

John B. Dykes, 1861

HOLLINGSIDE 77.77 D

2D Why Do the Gentiles Rage?

Psalm 2

Behold, He is coming with clouds, and every eye will see Him.
—Revelation 1:7

1. ¹Why do the Gen - tiles rage and clam - or, And na - tions
2. ⁴Yet He shall laugh, en - throned in heav - en, The Lord will
3. ⁷I will de - clare the LORD's de - ci - sion, He said to
4. ¹⁰So now, you kings, take hold of wis - dom; Be warned, you

brood on fruit - less dreams? ²Kings of the earth are set and
scorn them in re - ply. ⁵For He will speak to them in
Me: "You are My Son, This day You are of Me be -
earth - ly judg - es here. ¹¹With rev' - rence serve the LORD in

read - y, And rul - ers meet to plan their schemes.
an - ger And in His wrath will ter - ri - fy.
got - ten, ⁸Your her - i - tage has now be - gun;
wor - ship, Re - joice— but trem - ble still with fear.

A - gainst the LORD they raise re - bel - lion, And His A -
⁶"This is the King whom I ap - point - ed, I con - se -
On You I will be - stow the na - tions, How - ev - er
¹²And be sin - cere in your de - vo - tion, Or per - ish

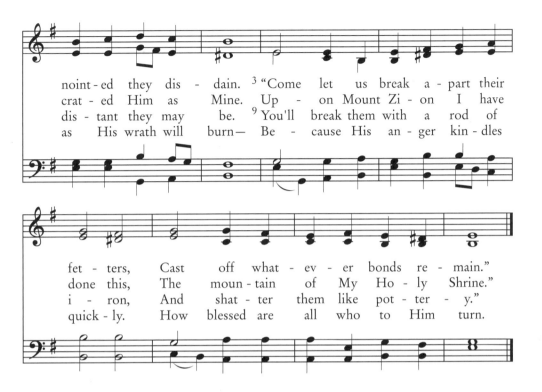

noint - ed they dis - dain. ³ "Come let us break a - part their
crat - ed Him as Mine. Up - on Mount Zi - on I have
dis - tant they may be. ⁹ You'll break them with a rod of
as His wrath will burn— Be - cause His an - ger kin - dles

fet - ters, Cast off what - ev - er bonds re - main."
done this, The moun - tain of My Ho - ly Shrine."
i - ron, And shat - ter them like pot - ter - y."
quick - ly. How blessed are all who to Him turn.

Brian E. Coombs, 2008

KENT 98.98 D

3A
Psalm 3

O LORD, My Foes Are Multiplied

But I have prayed for you, that your faith should not fail.
—Luke 22:32

1. [1] O LORD, my foes are mul - ti - plied; A -
2. [3] But You, my shield and glo - ry, LORD, My
3. [5] I lay down, slept, and woke a - gain; The

gainst me man - y rise! [2] They say of me, "He
head You lift - ed high. [4] And from His ho - ly
LORD sus - tains my life. [6] I will not fear ten

has no help, Though he on God re - lies."
hill the LORD Gave an - swer to my cry.
thou - sand strong Sur - round - ing me with strife.

4. [7] LORD, rise and save me, O my God;
   For You subdue my foes!
   You strike the jaw of wicked men,
   And smash their teeth with blows.

5. [8] Deliverance is of the LORD,
   To grant it as He will;
   O may the blessing that You give
   Be on Your people still.

Virginia Harmony, 1831   NEW BRITAIN CM

Lord, How My Foes Are Multiplied

*In this you greatly rejoice, though now you have been grieved
by various trials. —1 Peter 1:6*

1. ¹LORD, how my foes are mul - ti - plied; How man - y
   now a - gainst me rise! ²Man - y are those who
   say of me, "In vain he on his God re - lies."

2. ³You are my shield and glo - ry, LORD; You are the
   One who lifts my head. ⁴I cried out, "LORD!" His
   an - swer came, Yes, from His ho - ly hill it sped.

3. ⁵I lay down, slept, and woke a - gain, Be - cause the
   LORD sus - tains my life. ⁶I will not fear ten
   thou - sand strong Who would en - cir - cle me in strife.

4. ⁷LORD, rise and save me, O my God;
   For You subdue my every foe!
   You strike the jaw of wicked men,
   Smashing their teeth with mighty blows.

5. ⁸Deliverance comes from the LORD;
   He works salvation—as He will.
   O may the blessing You have shown
   Be granted to Your people still.

Kiernan J. Stringer, 2005; arr. Brian E. Coombs, 2005

TORONTO LM

4A

Psalm 4

Give Answer When I Call

Do not let the sun go down on your anger,
nor give the devil an opportunity. —Ephesians 4:26

1. ¹Give an - swer when I call, O God; You
2. ²How long will you, O sons of men, My
3. ³The LORD will hear me when I call. Know
4. ⁴When you are by your an - ger stirred, Be

are my righ - teous - ness. To me be gra - cious;
glo - ry turn to shame? How long will you love
this with cer - tain - ty; The LORD has claimed the
care - ful not to sin; In - stead be si - lent

hear my prayer; You freed me in dis - tress.
van - i - ty And make de - ceit your aim?
god - ly one His ver - y own to be.
on your bed, And med - i - tate with - in.

You freed me in dis - tress.
And make de - ceit your aim?
His ver - y own to be.
And med - i - tate with - in.

5. ⁵Present a righteous sacrifice,
   And make the LORD your trust.
   ⁶Since many say, "Who shows us good?"
   Your face, LORD, shine on us!

6. ⁷You fill my heart with joy beyond
   When wine and grain increase;
   ⁸Since You alone, LORD, keep me safe,
   I'll go to sleep in peace.

John K. Robb, 1929

WALLACE CM

Answer When I Call

You ought to say, "If the Lord wills,
we shall live and do this or that." —James 4:15

1. [1] An-swer when I call, O God who jus-ti-fies.
2. [3] Know the LORD His saints has set a-part in grace;
3. [5] Of-fer sac-ri-fic-es that are right and just;
4. [7] You have giv-en my heart great-er joy by far

In my stress You freed me; hear in grace my cries.
And the LORD will hear me when I seek His face.
On the LORD re-ly-ing, in Him place your trust.
Than when grain and new wine most a-bun-dant are.

[2] Sons of men, how long will you my glo-ry shame?
[4] Trem-ble in your an-ger, yet from sin de-part;
[6] "Who will show us good-ness?" man-y peo-ple say;
[8] So in peace I lie down; I will rest and sleep,

Will you love what's worth-less? Will lies be your aim?
On your bed, in si-lence, speak with-in your heart.
The light of Your face, LORD, lift on us, we pray.
For, O LORD, You on-ly will me safe-ly keep.

Spencer Lane

PENITENCE 11.11.11.11 (Trochaic)

5A

Psalm 5

Listen to My Words, O Lord

Let us offer to God acceptable worship, with reverence and awe.
—Hebrews 12:28

1. 1 Lis-ten to my words, O Lord; Know the whis-pered things I say.
2. 4 For I know that You, O God, Find in e-vil no de-light;
3. 7 Yet in Your a-bound-ing love, To Your house will I draw near,

2 Heed my cry-ing out for help— God, my King, to You I pray.
E-vil can-not dwell with You, 5 Nor the proud stand in Your sight.
Bow-ing to Your ho-ly place, Wor-ship-ing in rev'-rent fear.

3 Hear me in the morn-ing, Lord, When I lift my voice on high,
You hate all who prac-tice sin. 6 You de-stroy the one who lies;
8 Since, O Lord, my en-e-mies All a-round me lie in wait,

Set-ting forth my plea to You, Look-ing out with watch-ful eye.
For the Lord a-bom-i-nates Those who schemes of blood de-vise.
Lead me in Your righ-teous-ness; Make Your way be-fore me straight.

4. 9 In their mouth there is no truth;
All their heart destruction seeks,
Like an open grave their throat,
While their tongue with honey speaks.
10 Make them bear their guilt, O God;
Snare them in the things they planned!
Cast them out for all their sins:
Rebels who against You stand.

5. 11 Yet let all who trust in You
Sing for joy through all their days.
Guard all those who love Your name;
Let them give You joyful praise.
12 Blessing to the righteous one,
You, O Lord, will surely bring;
With Your favor, like a shield,
You will give him covering.

J. W. Bischoff

MORNING LIGHT 77.77 D

Listen to My Words, O Lord

Walk while you have the light, lest darkness overtake you.
—John 12:35

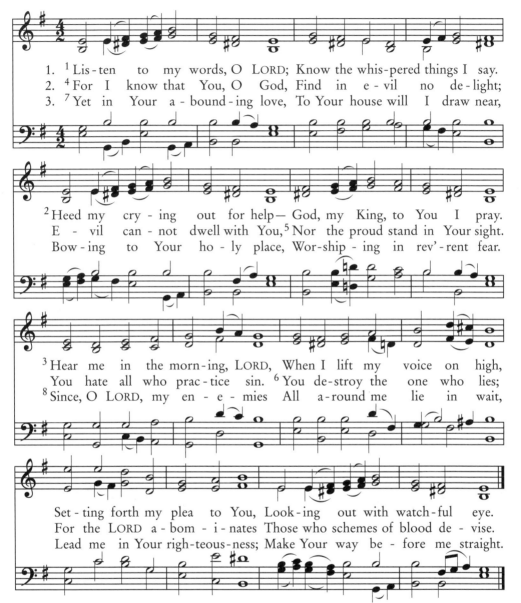

1. [1] Lis-ten to my words, O LORD; Know the whis-pered things I say.
2. [4] For I know that You, O God, Find in e-vil no de-light;
3. [7] Yet in Your a-bound-ing love, To Your house will I draw near,

[2] Heed my cry-ing out for help— God, my King, to You I pray.
E-vil can-not dwell with You, [5] Nor the proud stand in Your sight.
Bow-ing to Your ho-ly place, Wor-ship-ing in rev'-rent fear.

[3] Hear me in the morn-ing, LORD, When I lift my voice on high,
You hate all who prac-tice sin. [6] You de-stroy the one who lies;
[8] Since, O LORD, my en-e-mies All a-round me lie in wait,

Set-ting forth my plea to You, Look-ing out with watch-ful eye.
For the LORD a-bom-i-nates Those who schemes of blood de-vise.
Lead me in Your righ-teous-ness; Make Your way be-fore me straight.

4. [9] In their mouth there is no truth;
   All their heart destruction seeks,
   Like an open grave their throat,
   While their tongue with honey speaks.
   [10] Make them bear their guilt, O God;
   Snare them in the things they planned!
   Cast them out for all their sins:
   Rebels who against You stand.

5. [11] Yet let all who trust in You
   Sing for joy through all their days.
   Guard all those who love Your name;
   Let them give You joyful praise.
   [12] Blessing to the righteous one,
   You, O LORD, will surely bring;
   With Your favor, like a shield,
   You will give him covering.

Joseph Parry, 1879

ABERYSTWYTH 77.77 D

5C

Psalm 5:1-7

Listen to My Words, O Lord

Watch and pray, lest you enter into temptation.
— Matthew 26:41

1. ¹Lis-ten to my words, O Lord; Know the whis-pered things I say. ²Heed my cry-ing out for help— God, my King, to You I pray.

2. ³Hear me in the morn-ing, Lord, When I lift my voice on high, Set-ting forth my plea to You, Look-ing out with watch-ful eye.

3. ⁴For I know that You, O God, Find in e-vil no de-light; E-vil can-not dwell with You, ⁵Nor the proud stand in Your sight.

4. You hate all who practice sin.
   ⁶You destroy the one who lies;
   For the Lord abominates
   Those who schemes of blood devise.

5. ⁷Yet in Your abounding love,
   To Your house will I draw near,
   Bowing to Your holy place,
   Worshiping in rev'rent fear.

Traditional English melody

SCARBOROUGH FAIR 77.77

Lord, Do Not Chasten Me in Wrath

Shall I not drink the cup which My Father has given Me?
—John 18:11

6A
Psalm 6

1. ¹ LORD, do not chas-ten me in wrath. ² Be
2. ⁴ Now in Your stead-fast love, send help! Re-
3. ⁶ I'm wear-ied from my moans and cries; I

gra-cious, LORD— I waste a - way! ³ LORD, heal my bones and
turn, O LORD, to me and save! ⁵ For none re-mem-bers
flood my bed with tears each night. ⁷ Be - cause of all my

trou-bled soul; O LORD, how long will You de - lay?
You in death, And who will praise You in the grave?
foes and grief, My eyes grow weak and lose their sight.

4. ⁸ Depart from me, all evil men!
The LORD has heard my tearful cry,
⁹ The LORD has heard my pleading voice,
The LORD my prayer will not deny.

5. ¹⁰ My enemies will come to shame,
Upon them great dismay will fall;
They are turned back the way they came,
And shame will quickly seize them all.

William Bradbury, 1853

OLIVE'S BROW LM

6B

Psalm 6

Be Gracious, LORD

He had offered up prayers and supplications,
with vehement cries and tears. —Hebrews 5:7

1. [1,2] Be gra-cious, LORD, re-buke me not in wrath,
2. [4] O LORD, re-turn to lib-er-ate my soul!
3. [6] I have grown wear-y with my sighs and moans;
4. [8,9] The LORD has heard, the LORD has heard my cries;

Nor in Your an-ger, for I waste a-way;
And for Your stead-fast love come now to save!
I cry and flood my bed with tears each night.
All e-vil-do-ers, go, de-part from me!

My bones, my soul are trou-bled— heal me, LORD!
[5] For no one will re-mem-ber You in death,
[7] Due to my grief and all my en-e-mies,
The LORD re-ceives each prayer I make to Him.

[3] How long, O LORD, how long will You de-lay?
And who will glo-ri-fy You in the grave?
My weep-ing eyes grow weak and lose their sight.
[10] Trou-bled and shamed, my foes leave sud-den-ly.

Frederick C. Atkinson, 1870

MORECAMBE 10.10.10.10

O Lord, My God, I Take Refuge

All the churches shall know that I am He
who searches the minds and hearts. —Revelation 2:23

7A
Psalm 7:1-9

1. ¹O LORD, my God, I take refuge in You;
2. ³O LORD my God, if my hands were un-just,
3. ⁶LORD, rise in an-ger, and be my de-fense

O save me from all those who have pur-sued.
⁴Harm-ing my foes or my friends in their trust,
A-gainst my en-e-my's rage so in-tense;

²Lest they should tear me like li-ons with prey;
⁵Let my pur-su-er come near and sur-round,
Rise, bring the judg-ment that You have de-creed.

With none to res-cue, they'd drag me a-way.
Tramp-ling my life in the dust of the ground.
⁷Let peo-ples come and with You gath-ered be.

4. Come back to rule over them from on high.
   ⁸The LORD will judge as the nations draw nigh.
   My cause is right, LORD, O vindicate me;
   Judge me as You my integrity see.

5. ⁹O let the evil of wicked men cease,
   And all the righteous establish in peace;
   God who is righteous examines and finds
   All of the depths of men's hearts and their minds.

Traditional Irish melody; adapt. from Erik Routley, 1917–1982 and Daniel Evans, 1874–1948   SLANE 10.10.10.10

7B God Is My Shield

Psalm 7:10-17

The following night the Lord stood by and said, "Be of good cheer."
— Acts 23:11

6. ¹⁰God is my shield, yes, He is my de - fense,
7. ¹²He whets His sword if one does not re - pent;
8. ¹⁴Look at the man in la - bor with his sin:
9. ¹⁷I will give thanks to Him who is the LORD

For He will sure - ly save the right in heart.
He has His bow al - read - y strung and bent.
Con - ceiv - ing e - vil, he gives birth to lies.
Ac - cord - ing to His per - fect right - teous - ness;

¹¹A righ - teous judge, God judg - es righ - teous - ly;
¹³His dead - ly wea - pons He has now pre - pared;
¹⁵He digs a pit, but falls in it him - self;
And I will sing to Him for - ev - er - more.

The wrath of God is burn - ing ev - ery day.
He makes His ar - rows fi - ery, dead - ly shafts.
¹⁶His vi - cious plans come down on his own head.
I'll praise His name; He is the LORD Most High.

George William Warren, 1892

NATIONAL HYMN 10.10.10.10

O LORD, Our Lord

I tell you that if these should keep silent,
the stones would immediately cry out. — Luke 19:40

1. [1] O LORD, our Lord, in all the earth How
2. [2] From in-fants' and from chil-dren's lips You
3. [3] When I re-gard the heav'ns You made, Your
4. [4] I ask my-self, "What then is man That

glo-rious is Your name! For You have set a-
or-dered praise to sound To si-lence all Your
fin-gers' work I trace; I see the moon and
You should give him thought— The son of man, that

bove the heav'ns Your glo-ry and Your fame.
en-e-mies, The wick-ed to con-found.
shin-ing stars Which You have set in place.
You to him Such gra-cious care have brought?"

5. [5] Yet You created him to be
Just less than one divine;
You gave him honor as a crown,
And made his glory shine.

6. [6] You made him ruler of the works
Created by Your hand;
You placed all things beneath his feet
To be in his command:

7. [7, 8] All sheep and oxen, birds and fish,
All beasts both wild and tame.
[9] O LORD, our Lord, in all the earth
How glorious is Your name!

Scottish Psalter, 1615

DUNFERMLINE CM

8B

LORD, Our Lord

Psalm 8

But we see Jesus, who was made a little lower than the angels, for the
suffering of death crowned with glory and honor. —Hebrews 2:9

1. [1] LORD, our Lord, in all the earth How ex-cel-lent Your name!
2. [3] When I view the skies a-bove Which Your own fin-gers made,
3. [5] You made man just less than God With ra-diant glo-ry crowned.

You a-bove the heav'ns have set The splen-dor of Your fame.
When I see the moon and stars Which You in or-der laid,
[6] You placed him a-bove Your works; Be-neath him all is found:

[2] From the mouths of in-fants young You the pow'r of praise com-pose
[4] What is man so frail and weak That You should re-mem-ber him?
[7] Ox-en, sheep, and all wild beasts, [8] Birds, and fish the o-ceans claim.

In the face of en-e-mies To stop a-veng-ing foes.
What can be the son of man That You should care for him?
[9] LORD, our Lord, in all the earth How ex-cel-lent Your name!

Freylinghausen Gesangbüch, 1704; arr. John Wesley, 1742 AMSTERDAM 76.76.77.76

O Lord, Our Lord

8C
Psalm 8

They were utterly astonished, saying, "He has done all things well!"
— Mark 7:37

1. ¹ O LORD, our Lord, in all the earth How
2. ² From in - fants' and from chil - dren's lips You
3. ³ When I re - gard the heav'ns You made, Your
4. ⁴ I ask my - self, "What then is man That

glo - rious is Your name! For You have set a -
or - dered praise to sound To si - lence all Your
fin - gers' work I trace; I see the moon and
You should give him thought— The son of man, that

bove the heav'ns Your glo - ry and Your fame.
en - e - mies, The wick - ed to con - found.
shin - ing stars Which You have set in place.
You to him Such gra - cious care have brought?"

5. ⁵ Yet You created him to be
   Just less than one divine;
   You gave him honor as a crown,
   And made his glory shine.

6. ⁶ You made him ruler of the works
   Created by Your hand;
   You placed all things beneath his feet
   To be in his command:

7. ⁷, ⁸ All sheep and oxen, birds and fish,
   All beasts both wild and tame.
   ⁹ O LORD, our Lord, in all the earth
   How glorious is Your name!

Matthew Wilkins, *A Book of Psalmody*, c. 1730   STROUDWATER CM

9A

I Now Will Give Wholehearted Thanks

Psalm 9:1-10

Now out of His mouth goes a sharp sword,
that with it He should strike the nations. —Revelation 19:15

1. ¹I now will give whole-heart-ed thanks to the LORD,
2. ³When back-ward my foes were all turned in de-spair,
3. ⁵You chas-tened the na-tions, the wick-ed de-stroyed;

And all of Your mar-vel-ous works will re-cord.
They stum-bled and per-ished be-cause You were there.
Their names You e-rased and for-ev-er made void.

²In You will be glad and ex-ult-ing-ly cry;
⁴For You have de-fend-ed my judg-ment and cause;
⁶The foe is con-sumed and com-plete-ly e-rased;

And praise to Your name will I sing, O Most High.
En-throned, You judge right-ly, en-forc-ing the laws.
Their cit-ies de-stroyed and their mem-'ry ef-faced.

4. ⁷The LORD will eternally sit on His throne,
   Establishing it for His judgment alone.
   ⁸In righteousness He'll judge the world
   here below;
   And to every people shall equity show.

5. ⁹The LORD is a stronghold to help the oppressed;
   A stronghold of safety in times of distress.
   ¹⁰Those knowing Your name, LORD, their trust
   in You place;
   You have not forsaken those seeking Your face.

Ira. D. Sankey, 1887

SANKEY 11.11.11.11

Sing Praise to the Lord

The light shines in the darkness,
and the darkness did not overcome it. —John 1:5

9B

Psalm 9:11-20

6. [11] Sing praise to the LORD, who in Zi-on does dwell;
   A-mong all the peo-ples His great do-ings tell.
   [12] When blood He a-ven-ges, His mem-'ry is clear;
   The cry of the poor nev-er fades from His ear.

7. [13] LORD, see what I suf-fer from mal-ice and hate;
   Have mer-cy! O lift me a-way from death's gate;
   [14] In gates of the daugh-ter of Zi-on I'll praise,
   Re-joic-ing in Your might-y pow-er to save.

8. [15] The na-tions are sunk in the pit they pre-pared;
   Their foot in the net that they hid is en-snared.
   [16] The LORD by His judg-ment has made Him-self known;
   He catch-es the wick-ed in snares of their own.

9. [17] The wicked to death's realm of darkness are brought;
   All nations who would not keep God in their thoughts.
   [18] Forgotten no longer the cause of the weak,
   Nor perished forever the hope of the meek!

10. [19] Arise, LORD, that man may not make himself strong;
   Let nations be judged in Your presence for wrong.
   [20] O LORD, put Your fear and Your terror in them;
   Let nations know truly that they are mere men.

Traditional Welsh melody; arr. John Roberts, 1839

JOANNA (St. Denio) 11.11.11.11

10A

Psalm 10:1-11

Why Do You Stand So Far Away?

I guarded them, and not one of them was lost
except the one destined to be lost. —*John 17:12*

1. ¹Why do You stand so far a-way, O LORD?
2. ⁴The wick-ed proud-ly does not choose to seek;
3. ⁷His mouth is full of curs-es, lies, and threats;
4. He hides him-self that he may seize the poor;

Why do You hide Your-self in trou-bled times?
In all his thoughts he says, "There is no God."
Be-neath his tongue are e-vil thoughts and deeds.
To seize the poor he traps him in his net.

²In pride the wick-ed chase and trap the poor;
⁵He can-not see Your judg-ments, yet He thrives;
⁸He lurks and hides a-long the vil-lage streets,
¹⁰He crouch-es, wait-ing for his chance to pounce;

Let them be caught in schemes they have de-vised.
He sneers with scorn at all his en-e-mies.
The in-no-cent he mur-ders se-cret-ly.
He o-ver-pow'rs the help-less with his claws.

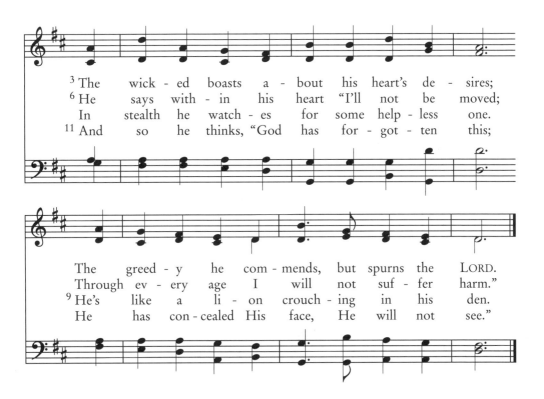

³ The wicked boasts about his heart's de - sires;
⁶ He says with - in his heart "I'll not be moved;
In stealth he watch - es for some help - less one.
¹¹ And so he thinks, "God has for - got - ten this;

The greed - y he com - mends, but spurns the LORD.
Through ev - ery age I will not suf - fer harm."
⁹ He's like a li - on crouch - ing in his den.
He has con - cealed His face, He will not see."

William H. Monk, 1875   UNDE ET MEMORES 10.10.10.10.10.10

10B
Psalm 10:12-18

Rise Up, O Lord

The Lord is not slow about His promise,
as some think of slowness, but is patient with you. —2 Peter 3:9

5. ^{12} Rise up, O LORD! O God, lift up Your hand!
6. ^{14} But You indeed see evil and distress,
7. ^{15} O break the arms of brutal, evil men;
8. ^{17} You hear, O LORD, the longing of the meek;

Do not forget the ones who are oppressed.
You see, and with Your hand You set things right.
Search out their wickedness till You find none.
Their heart You strengthen; You incline Your ear.

^{13} Why has the wicked proudly scoffed at God?
The helpless can commit himself to You;
^{16} The LORD is King through all eternity;
^{18} O vindicate the crushed and fatherless,

He thinks that You will never take account.
You are the helper of the fatherless.
The Gentile nations perished from His land.
That men of earth may terrify no more.

Alfred M. Smith, 1879–1971; arr. Brian E. Coombs, 2008

SURSUM CORDA 10.10.10.10

My Trust Is in the LORD

In the last time there will be scoffers,
indulging their own ungodly lusts. —Jude 1:18

11A
Psalm 11

1. ¹ My trust is in the LORD; How can you say to me: "Now quick - ly, like a bird es - cape, And to your moun - tain flee!
2. ² The wick - ed bend the bow With ar - row fixed for flight, To shoot it at the righ - teous one In cov - er of the night!
3. ³ What can the righ - teous do If the foun - da - tions fall?" ⁴ The LORD is in His ho - ly place; The LORD rules o - ver all.
4. His eyes will sure - ly see; His eye - lids test men's sons. ⁵ The LORD tries just and wick - ed men; His soul hates cru - el ones.

5. ⁶ Upon all wicked men
   He'll rain entangling snares;
   Brimstone and fire and burning wind
   He for their cup prepares.

6. ⁷ For righteous is the LORD,
   And He loves righteous ways;
   And everyone who upright is
   Will look upon His face.

Gregorian Chant; arr. Lowell Mason, 1824

OLMUTZ SM

11B

Psalm 11

My Trust Is in the LORD

Tribulation and distress for all who do evil...
glory and honor to all who do good. —Romans 2:9-10

1. ¹ My trust is in the LORD; How
2. ² The wick - ed bend the bow With
3. ³ What can the righ - teous do If
4. His eyes will sure - ly see; His

can you say to me: "Now like a bird make
ar - row fixed for flight, To shoot it at the
the foun - da - tions fall?" ⁴ The LORD is in His
eye - lids test men's sons. ⁵ The LORD tries just and

your es - cape, And to your moun - tain flee!
righ - teous one In cov - er of the night!
ho - ly place; The LORD rules o - ver all.
wick - ed men; His soul hates cru - el ones.

5. ⁶ Upon all wicked men
   He'll rain entangling snares;
   Brimstone and fire and burning wind
   He for their cup prepares.

6. ⁷ For righteous is the LORD,
   And He loves righteous ways;
   And everyone who upright is
   Will look upon His face.

Samuel Howard, 1762

ST. BRIDE SM

Help, Lord

*But as for these enemies of mine...bring them here
and slaughter them in my presence.* —Luke 19:27

1. [1]Help, LORD, be - cause the god - ly man now ceas - es;
2. [3]O may the LORD cut off all lips that flat - ter,
3. [5]"In My con - cern, be - cause the poor are plun - dered,

The faith - ful van - ish from the sons of men.
And ev - ery boast - ing tongue that speaks great things—
For the af - flict - ed groan - ing in des - pair—

[2]They emp - ty false - hood speak to one an - oth - er;
[4]Those who have said, "With our tongue we will con - quer;
Now," says the LORD, "I will a - rise to save him,

With flat - t'ring lips and dou - ble heart they speak.
Our lips are ours; what lord rules o - ver us?"
I'll place him in the safe - ty he de - sires."

4. [6]The words proceeding from the LORD are flawless,
   Words pure as silver tested in the fire;
   Like silver that is molten in a furnace,
   It then emerges seven times as pure.

5. [7]O LORD, You will preserve Your people always,
   And from this generation keep them safe.
   [8]On every side the wicked strut and swagger,
   When people glorify the vilest things.

Israeli folk tune   LINDESFARNE 11.10.11.10

13A
Psalm 13

How Long Will You Forget Me, Lord?

The Son of Man has come to seek and save that which was lost.
— Luke 19:10

1. [1]How long will You for - get me, LORD? For -
2. [2]How long must I ad - vise my soul, And
3. [3]Con - sid - er me, O LORD, my God; Give

ev - er will it be? How long un - til You
con - stant sad - ness know? How long must I be
an - swer to my cry. Let me see light, or

show Your face Which You've con - cealed from me?
sub - ject to The tri - umph of my foe?
I will sleep In death with those who die.

4. [4]"See, I have overcome him now!"
My enemy will call;
My adversaries will rejoice
When I begin to fall.

5. [5]But Your unfailing love I trust;
Your saving pow'r I praise.
[6]The LORD in bounty dealt with me;
My songs to Him I raise.

John H. Gower, 1890

MEDITATION CM

O How Long, Lord?

"Behold, he is praying."
—Acts 9:11

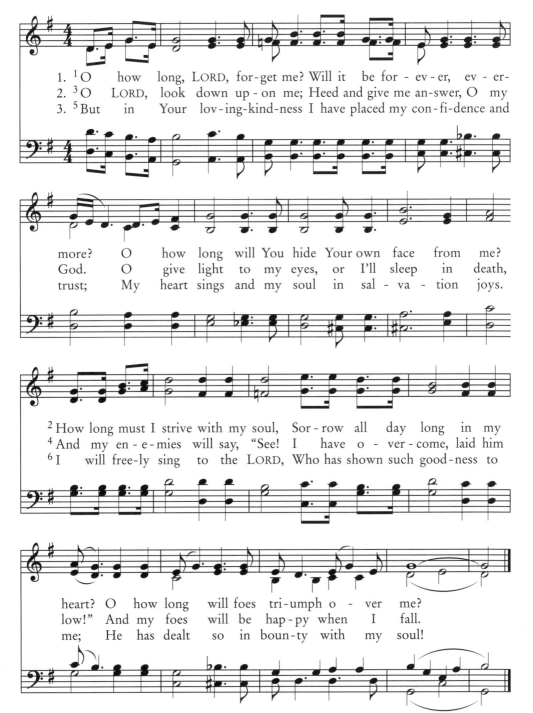

1. ¹O how long, LORD, for-get me? Will it be for - ev - er, ev - er-
2. ³O LORD, look down up-on me; Heed and give me an-swer, O my
3. ⁵But in Your lov-ing-kind-ness I have placed my con-fi-dence and

more? O how long will You hide Your own face from me?
God. O give light to my eyes, or I'll sleep in death,
trust; My heart sings and my soul in sal - va - tion joys.

²How long must I strive with my soul, Sor - row all day long in my
⁴And my en - e - mies will say, "See! I have o - ver - come, laid him
⁶I will free-ly sing to the LORD, Who has shown such good-ness to

heart? O how long will foes tri-umph o - ver me?
low!" And my foes will be hap-py when I fall.
me; He has dealt so in boun-ty with my soul!

African-American melody; arr J. Jefferson Cleveland, 1937–1986; alt. Michael Tabon   CLEVELAND (Irr.)

14A

Psalm 14

Within His Heart the Fool Spoke

Rise and pray, lest you enter into temptation.
—Luke 22:46

1. ¹With - in his heart the fool spoke, And said, "There is no God!"
2. ³To - geth - er they're cor - rupt - ed; They all have turned a - side.
3. ⁵There they will be in ter - ror, For God is with the just.

De - struc - tive in their vile deeds, Not one of them does good.
Not one for good has la - bored, Not e - ven one has tried.
⁶Though you would shame the wretch - ed, The LORD re - mains his trust.

²The LORD looks down from heav - en Up - on the hu - man race:
⁴Have all of them no knowl - edge Whose deeds are so ab - horred?
⁷From Zi - on, send sal - va - tion, And help to Is - r'el bring!

Has an - y - one shown wis - dom, Does an - y seek God's face?
Like bread they eat My peo - ple, And call not on the LORD.
The LORD re - stores His cap - tives: Let Ja - cob— Is - r'el— sing!

Hans Leo Hassler, 1564–1612; harm. J.S. Bach, 1685–1750   PASSION CHORALE 76.76 D

Within His Heart the Fool Speaks

14B
Psalm 14

*They said among themselves, "This is the heir.
Come, let us kill him and seize his inheritance." — Matthew 21:38*

1. [1] With - in his heart the fool speaks, He says, "There is no God."
2. [3] They all have strayed and wan - dered, Cor-rupt they have be - come;
3. [5] There they will be in ter - ror, For God is with the just.

In mal - ice, they do vile deeds; Not one of them does good.
Not one shows an - y good - ness, No, not a sin - gle one.
[6] Though you would shame the need - y, The LORD re - mains his trust.

[2] The LORD looks down from heav - en To see the sons of men,
[4] With - in such e - vil - do - ers, Is there no knowl-edge stored?
[7] May res - cue come from Zi - on, And joy to Is - r'el bring!

If one for God is seek - ing, If an - y un - der - stands.
Like bread they eat My peo - ple, Not call - ing on the LORD.
The LORD will free His cap - tives, With joy will Ja - cob sing!

Louis Bourgeois, 1547; arr. Robert M. Copeland, 1971

OLD 128TH 76.76 D

15A

Psalm 15

Within Your Tent Who Will Reside?

Then Jesus called a little child to Him,
and set him in the midst of them. —Matthew 18:2

1. ¹O LORD, with - in Your tent who will re - side?
2. ³He will not harm his friend, nor him de - fame;
3. He keeps his prom - ise, though it brings him pain.

And on Your ho - ly hill who may a - bide?
He will not seek to spread his neigh - bor's shame.
⁵His gold no prof - it earns from wrong - ful gain.

²Who walks in blame - less - ness, Who acts with righ - teous - ness,
⁴But vile men he ab - horred, And rath - er would a - ward
No bribes will he re - ceive, The guilt - less to ag - grieve;

His heart will truth ex - press— It is his guide.
To those who fear the LORD, An hon - ored name.
Those who such things a - chieve Un - moved re - main.

Robert Lowry, 1826–1899

LOWRY 64.64.66.64

Within Your Tent Who Will Reside?

15B
Psalm 15

Love does no wrong to a neighbor;
therefore love is the fulfillment of the law. —Romans 13:10

1. ¹O LORD, with-in Your tent who will re-side?
2. ³He will not harm his friend, nor him de-fame;
3. He keeps his prom-ise, though it bring him pain.

And on Your ho-ly hill who may a-bide?
He will not seek to spread his neigh-bor's shame.
⁵His gold no prof-it earns from wrong-ful gain.

²Who walks in blame-less-ness, Who acts with righ-teous-ness,
⁴But vile men he ab-horred, And rath-er would a-ward
No bribes will he re-ceive, The guilt-less to ag-grieve;

His heart will truth ex-press— It is his guide.
To those who fear the LORD, An hon-ored name.
Those who such things a-chieve Un-moved re-main.

Thomas H. Ingham, 1878–1948; arr. Brian E. Coombs, 2008

DAWN 64.64.66.64

16A

Psalm 16:1-6

Keep Me, O God

But after I have been raised, I will go before you to Galilee.
— Matthew 26:32

1. [1] Keep me, O God, I trust in You. [2] O
2. [3] The ho - ly and ma - jes - tic ones Up -
3. I'll not join in their gifts of blood, Such

LORD, I this con - fess: "You are my Lord; a -
on the earth I prize. [4] But those who choose an -
of - f'rings I'll not make; Nor will I ev - er

part from You No good do I pos - sess."
oth - er god, Their sor - rows mul - ti - ply.
on my lips The names of i - dols take.

4. [5] The LORD's the portion of my cup,
   And my inheritance;
   You've given me the lot I have,
   Kept in Your providence.

5. [6] The bound'ries You have set for me,
   Enclose a pleasant site;
   My beautiful inheritance
   Is truly my delight.

William Mather, c. 1806

MEDFIELD CM

I'll Bless the LORD Who Counsels Me

16B

I and the Father are one.
—John 10:30

Psalm 16:7-11

6. [7] I'll bless the LORD who coun - sels me,
7. [8] I've set the LORD be - fore my face
8. [9] Be - cause of this my heart is glad,

That I may know what's right;
That Him I'll al - ways see.
My glo - ry cel - e - brates;

In - deed, my mind has giv - en me
Be - cause He is at my right hand,
In - deed, my bod - y e - ven now

In - struc - tion in the night.
Un - shak - en I will be.
In hope se - cure - ly waits,

9. [10] Because You will not leave my soul
Consigned to depths below;
Corruption You will not allow
Your Godly One to know.

10. [11] The path of life You'll show to me;
With You is joy untold.
And pleasures that will have no end,
In Your right hand You hold.

Isaac Smith, c. 1770

ABRIDGE CM

16C
Psalm 16

Preserve Me, O God

He looked ahead and spoke of the resurrection of the Christ.
—Acts 2:31

1. ¹Preserve me, O God, for I'm trusting in You.
2. ⁴Those running to idols will multiply griefs.
3. You care for my lot, ⁶where the lines fell to me,

²"Yes, You are my Master," I said to the LORD;
I will not pour out their drink offrings of blood,
My pleasant and lovely inherited land.

Besides You I do not possess any good.
Nor will I confess their vain names with my lips.
⁷The LORD who gives counsel to me I will bless,

³In Your holy messengers I take delight.
⁵The LORD's my inherited portion and cup.
For surely my mind teaches me through the night.

4. ⁸The LORD ever present before me I keep.
He stands at my right hand; I shall not be
moved.
⁹My glory rejoices, my heart is made glad;
And also my flesh will live safely at ease.

5. ¹⁰For You'll not abandon my soul to the grave,
Your Godly One You will preserve from decay.
¹¹Life's path You will show me; full joy is with
You;
Your right hand holds pleasures for me evermore.

Traditional American melody; harm. Carlton R. Young, b. 1926   FOUNDATION 11.11.11.11

Preserve Me, O God

"I have food to eat that you do not know about."
—John 4:32

1. ¹Pre - serve me, O God, for I'm trust-ing in You.
2. ⁴Those run - ning to i - dols will mul-ti-ply griefs.
3. You care for my lot, ⁶where the lines fell to me,

²"Yes, You are my Mas-ter," I said to the LORD;
I will not pour out their drink of-f'rings of blood,
My pleas-ant and love-ly in - her-it-ed land.

Be - sides You I do not pos-sess an-y good.
Nor will I con - fess their vain names with my lips.
⁷The LORD who gives coun-sel to me I will bless,

³In Your ho-ly mes-sen-gers I take de - light.
⁵The LORD's my in - her-it-ed por-tion and cup.
For sure - ly my mind teach-es me through the night.

4. ⁸The LORD ever present before me I keep.
He stands at my right hand; I shall not be moved.
⁹My glory rejoices, my heart is made glad;
And also my flesh will live safely at ease.

5. ¹⁰For You'll not abandon my soul to the grave,
Your Godly One You will preserve from decay.
¹¹Life's path You will show me; full joy is with You;
Your right hand holds pleasures for me evermore.

Don McCrory, b. 1952   STERLING 11.11.11.11

16E
Keep Me, O God

Psalm 16

The Holy Spirit…who is given as a pledge of our inheritance.
—Ephesians 1:13-14

1. ¹Keep me, O God, I trust in You. ²O LORD, I
2. I'll not join in their gifts of blood, Such of-f'rings
3. ⁶The bound-'ries You have set for me En - close a

this con-fess: "You are my Lord; a-part from You No good do
I'll not make; Nor will I ev - er on my lips The names of
pleas-ant site; My beau-ti - ful in-her - i-tance Is tru - ly

Up -
And
That

I pos-sess." ³The ho - ly and ma - jes - tic ones Up -
i - dols take. ⁵The LORD's the por - tion of my cup, And
my de - light. ⁷I'll bless the LORD who coun-sels me, That

But
You've
In -

on the earth I prize. [4] But those who choose an-oth-er god,
my in-her-i-tance; You've giv-en me the lot I have,
I may know what's right; In-deed, my mind has giv-en me

Their
Kept
In -

Their sor-rows
Kept in Your
In-struc-tion

Their sor-rows mul-ti-ply.
Kept in Your prov-i-dence.
In-struc-tion in the night.

sor-rows
in Your
struc-tion

4. [8] I've set the LORD before my face
   That Him I'll always see.
   Because He is at my right hand,
   Unshaken I will be.
   [9] Because of this my heart is glad,
   My glory celebrates;
   Indeed, my body even now
   In hope securely waits,

5. [10] Because You will not leave my soul
   Consigned to depths below;
   Corruption You will not allow
   Your Godly One to know.
   [11] The path of life You'll show to me;
   With You is joy untold.
   And pleasures that will have no end,
   In Your right hand You hold.

Robert M. Copeland, 1978

CONSERVA ME CMD

17A
Consider, LORD, a Righteous Cause

Psalm 17:1-7

Now he is comforted and you are tormented.
—Luke 16:25

1. ¹Con - sid - er LORD, a righ-teous cause; O lis - ten to my cry!
2. ³You came by night and test - ed me, You searched my heart with-in;
3. ⁶On You, O God, my soul has called, For You will an-swer me.

Give Your at - ten-tion to my prayer, For my lips do not lie.
You probed and found no wrong in - tent, I'll keep my mouth from sin.
O lis - ten to my ear-nest words! In - cline Your ear to me!

²Let jus-tice from Your pres-ence come By vin - di - ca - ting me;
⁴I'm kept from vio-lence by the word As spo-ken from Your lips.
⁷In won-drous and a - maz-ing ways Your lov-ing-kind-ness show;

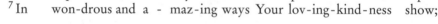

So let Your eyes see ev - ery-thing With per-fect eq - ui - ty.
⁵My foot I've kept up - on Your path, And so it nev - er slips.
Your right hand saves those trust-ing You, To hide them from the foe.

Andre Gretry, 1741–1831; arr. William J. Kirkpatrick, 1891

LANDAS CMD

Keep Me the Focus of Your Eye

17B

Psalm 17:8-12

"Behold, I cast out demons and perform cures today and tomorrow, and the third day I shall be perfected." —Luke 13:32

4. ⁸Keep me the fo - cus of Your eye;
5. ¹⁰These men have closed their hard - ened hearts;
6. ¹²My foe is like a li - on strong

Be - neath Your wings me hide
Their boast - ful words a - bound.
That craves to tear his prey;

⁹From wick - ed men and dead - ly foes
¹¹Sur - round - ing us, they close - ly watch
A li - on young pre - pared to pounce,

Who press on ev - - ery side.
To cast us to the ground.
He lurks a - long the way.

William Tans'ur, *New Harmony of Sion, II*, 1764

ST. ANDREW CM

17C
Psalm 17:13-15

Arise, Confront My Foe

These are wells without water, clouds carried by a tempest, for whom is reserved the blackness of darkness forever. —2 Peter 2:17

7. [13] A - rise, con - front my foe, And bring him down, O LORD; De - liv - er me from wick - ed hands, And free me by Your sword.

8. [14] Save me from world - ly men By Your own hand, O LORD, From men who have be - yond this life No vi - sion or re - ward.

9. You fill them with good things; Their sons are sat - is - fied. They leave their chil - dren all the wealth Which they have set a - side.

10. [15] But I in righ - teous - ness Your face will sure - ly see; And with Your like - ness, when I wake, I sat - is - fied will be.

W.J. Evans, 1866–1947   ARFRYN SM

I Love You, Lord

18A
Psalm 18:1-6

Therefore you are no longer a slave but a son,
and if a son, then an heir of God. —Galatians 4:7

1. ¹ I love You, Lord! You are my strength:
2. ³ I call up - on the Lord for help,
3. ⁴ I was en - cir - cled by death's ropes,
4. ⁶ In my dis - tress I cried for help,

² The Lord, my rock, my fort, my pow'r,
For wor - thy of all praise is He;
And at de - struc - tion's flood, I feared.
And begged the Lord, my God, to hear.

My God, my hid - ing place, my shield,
And in this way I will be saved
⁵ The ropes of She - ol wrapped a - round;
He from His tem - ple heard my voice;

My horn of safe - ty, and my tow'r.
And res - cued from my en - e - my.
Be - fore me snares of death ap - peared.
My cry for help had reached His ear.

Lowell Mason, 1830

UXBRIDGE LM

18B
Psalm 18:7-15

Earth Shook and Quivered

To execute judgment on all, to convict all who are ungodly
among them of all their ungodly deeds. —Jude 1:15

5. [7] Earth shook and quiv-ered to its depths;
6. [8] His nos-trils smoked, His mouth blew fire;
7. [10] He swift-ly on a cher-ub flew;
8. [12] Then through the clouds His bril-liance burst

The moun-tains rocked with trem-bling frame.
Coals kin-dled in con-su-ming flame.
On wings of wind He rushed in flight.
With hail-stones and with coals of fire.

Foun-da-tions of the whole world shook,
[9] Thick dark-ness was be-neath His feet;
[11] He hid Him-self in dark-ness deep,
[13] The LORD Most High then thun-dered forth;

Be-cause He in His an-ger came.
He bent the heav-ens when He came.
Thick clouds a-bout Him black as night.
He spoke with hail and coals of fire.

9. [14] He shot His arrows at His foes,
And made them scatter in retreat;
He made abundant lightning flash,
And sent them fleeing in defeat.

10. [15] Deep channels of the sea lay bare,
With earth's foundations deep and vast
When Your rebuke went forth, O LORD,
The power of Your nostrils' blast.

Traditional Bohemian melody

FREUEN WIR UNS LM

From Heaven He Took Hold of Me

18C

*We know that we are of God, and the whole world
lies under the power of the wicked one. —1 John 5:19*

Psalm 18:16-24

11. [16] From heav-en He took hold of me
12. [18] They came at me in my dis-tress;
13. [20] Ac-cord-ing to my righ-teous-ness

And lift-ed me as wa-ters rose;
The LORD was my se-cu-ri-ty.
I am re-ward-ed by the LORD;

[17] From those who hat-ed me, He saved,
[19] To lib-er-ty He brought me forth,
And as my hands have been found clean,

From all my o-ver-pow-'ring foes.
Be-cause He took de-light in me.
He gives to me a just re-ward.

14. [21] I've kept the pathways of the LORD,
And from my God I did not stray.
[22] I've kept His judgments in my thoughts,
And did not cast His laws away.

15. [23] I have been blameless in His sight,
Abstained from all iniquity.
[24] He found me righteous, with clean hands,
And so the LORD rewarded me.

Robert Schumann, 1839; alt.

CANONBURY LM

18D

Psalm 18:25-29

With Men of Kindness You Are Kind

The lamp of the body is the eye. If therefore your eye is good,
your whole body will be full of light. — Matthew 6:22

16. ²⁵ With men of kind - ness You are kind;
17. ²⁷ For You a suf - f'ring peo - ple save,
18. ²⁹ With help from You I can ad - vance

To blame - less ones You're blame - less, too.
But bring the proud eyes from their height.
A - gainst a troop and rout them all;

²⁶ And with the pure You, too, are pure;
²⁸ O LORD, my God, You light my lamp.
And with the help my God will give,

But with the crook - ed You are shrewd.
He turns my dark - ness in - to light.
I have the strength to leap a wall.

William Boyd, 1847–1928

PENTECOST LM

How Perfect Is the Way of God

18E

Psalm 18:30-36

Jesus…said to them, "You are mistaken, not knowing the Scriptures nor the power of God." — Matthew 22:29

19. ³⁰ How per - fect is the way of God!
20. ³¹ For who is God ex - cept the LORD?
21. ³³ He makes my feet as swift as deer's,
22. ³⁵ You gave me Your sal - va - tion's shield;

The LORD's word has been prov - en sound;
Be - sides our God, who is a Rock?
And sets me on the heights to stand.
I am up - held by Your right hand.

He is a shield to ev - ery - one
³² The God who arms me with all strength,
³⁴ My arms can bend a bow of bronze;
Your gen - tle - ness has made me great;

Who has in Him a ref - uge found.
He makes me per - fect in my walk.
In skills of war He trains my hand.
³⁶ You clear my way, se - cure I stand.

James William Elliot, 1833–1915

CHURCH TRIUMPHANT LM

18F
I Chased and Overtook My Foes

Psalm 18:37-45

It is a fearful thing to fall into the hands of the living God.
—Hebrews 10:31

23. ³⁷ I chased and o - ver - took my foes;
24. ³⁹ With strength You armed me for the fight,
25. ⁴¹ They cried for help, but none could save;

I did not turn till they were slain.
Sub - dued my foes be - neath my feet.
The LORD with si - lence met their shout.

³⁸ I crushed them all be - neath my feet;
⁴⁰ Those hat - ing me You put to flight;
⁴² I beat them fine as wind - blown dust;

They fell and could not rise a - gain.
Their slaugh - ter I then made com - plete.
Like ref - use I have dumped them out.

26. ⁴³ You set me over many lands;
You saved me from my enemy.
A people whom I did not know
Are in subjection now to me.

27. ⁴⁴ And when they hear and know my voice,
These strangers say they will obey.
⁴⁵ In fear they tremble, losing heart;
They leave their strongholds in dismay.

Traditional Bohemian melody

FREUEN WIR UNS LM

Blessed Be My Rock

He will destroy those wicked men miserably,
and lease his vineyard to other vinedressers. — *Matthew 21:41*

18G
Psalm 18:46-50

28. [46] Blessed be my Rock, the LORD who lives! My
29. [48] You save me from my en - e - mies, Ex -
30. [49] And so a - mong the na - tions, LORD, My
31. [50] He gives His king de - liv - er - ance, His

Sav - ior, God, ex - alt - ed be! [47] For
alt - ing me a - bove my foes; You
thank - ful - ness I will pro - claim; Be -
love on Da - vid He will pour, Up -

God brought ven - geance on my foes, Sub - du - ing na - tions
res - cue me from vio - lent men, From reb - els who a -
fore the peo - ples of the world, I will sing prais - es
on His own a - noint - ed one, And his de - scen - dants

un - der me, Sub - du - ing na - tions un - der me.
gainst me rose, From reb - els who a - gainst me rose.
to Your name, I will sing prais - es to Your name.
ev - er - more, And his de - scen - dants ev - er more.

William Bradbury, 1816–1868

ANDRE LM

19A

Psalm 19:1-6

The Skies Above

His invisible attributes are clearly seen…
even His eternal power and Godhead. —Romans 1:20

1. ¹The skies a-bove de-clare the glo-ry of our God;
2. ³Al-though they do not speak, and ut-ter not a word,
3. In heav'n He pitched a tent; He gave the sun its place.
4. ⁶The heav-ens are its course— at one end it will rise

The fir-ma-ment dis-plays His han-di-work a-broad.
Though they no lan-guage use, or voice that can be heard,
⁵And with an ath-lete's joy, it thrills to run its race.
Till to the oth-er end it runs a-cross the skies;

²From day to day they pour out speech;
⁴Their mes-sage to the world they send,
It ris-es, glo-rious, like a groom
Its rays ex-tend on ev-ery side,

Their knowl-edge ev-ery night they teach.
Their word to earth's re-mot-est end.
When he e-merg-es from his room.
And noth-ing from its heat can hide.

Their knowl-edge ev-ery night they teach.

William Bradbury, 1816–1868

CLARKSVILLE 66.66.88

The Lord's Most Perfect Law

*All spoke well of Him, and were amazed at the
gracious words that came from His mouth.* —Luke 4:22

5. [7]The LORD's most per-fect law Will make the soul re-vive;
6. The LORD's com-mand is pure, En-light-'ning eyes to see.
7. [10]They're more to be de-sired Than stores of fin-est gold;

The LORD's firm wit-ness makes The sim-ple-mind-ed wise.
[9]Fear of the LORD is clean, And lasts e-ter-nal-ly.
Than hon-ey from the comb More sweet-ness far they hold.

[8]The pre-cepts of the LORD are right,
The judg-ments of the LORD ex-press
[11]With warn-ings they Your ser-vant guard;

And fill the heart with great de-light.
His truth and per-fect righ-teous-ness.
In keep-ing them is great re-ward.

8. [12]His errors who can know?
   Cleanse me from hidden stain.
   [13]Your servant keep from sins;
   Let them not in me reign.
   Completely blameless then I'll be,
   From guilt of great transgression free.

9. [14]O let the words I speak
   Be pleasing in Your sight;
   And may my inmost thoughts
   Be in Your judgment right.
   O LORD, You are a Rock to me;
   You have redeemed and set me free.

English melody, 1826

MILLENNIUM 66.66.88

20A

Psalm 20

The LORD Reply in Your Distress

I say to you, inasmuch as you did it to one of the least of these
My brethren, you did it to Me. — Matthew 25:40

1. 1The LORD re - ply in your dis - tress;
2. 5In Your sal - va - tion we'll re - joice,
3. 7A trust in char - iots some pro - claim,

May Ja - cob's God de - fend you then.
In our God's name our ban - ners raise;
And some in hors - es take their pride;

2And from His place of ho - li - ness
May the LORD al - ways hear your voice,
But we will boast and praise this Name:

Both strength and help from Zi - on send.
Grant all you ask through all your days.
The LORD our God, and none be - side.

3 May He ac - cept your sac - ri - fice,
6 I know now that the LORD de - fends
8 While we are raised and up - right stand,

And all your of - f'rings bear in mind.
And saves His own a - noint - ed king.
Our foes are made to bow and fall.

4 May He grant all your heart's de - lights,
From ho - ly heav'n He an - swer sends;
9 O save the king, LORD, by Your hand,

4 May He grant all your heart's de - lights,
From ho - ly heav'n He an - swer sends;
9 O save the king, LORD, by Your hand,

Ful - fill - ing all
His right hand sav - - - - -
And an - swer us

Ful fill ing all you have de signed.
His right hand sav - ing pow er bring.
And an swer us the day we call.

Thomas Campbell, 1825–1876   SAGINA LMD

20B

Psalm 20

The Lord Reply in Your Distress

I knew that You always hear me.
—John 11:42

1. [1]The Lord re - ply in your dis - tress;
2. [3]May He ac - cept your sac - ri - fice,
3. [5]In Your sal - va - tion we'll re - joice,
4. [6]I know now that the Lord de - fends

May Ja - cob's God de - fend you then.
And all your of - f'rings bear in mind.
In our God's name our ban - ners raise;
And saves His own a - noint - ed king.

[2]And from His place of ho - li - ness
[4]May He grant all your heart's de - lights,
May the Lord al - ways hear your voice,
From ho - ly heav'n He an - swer sends;

Both strength and help from Zi - on send.
Ful - fill - ing all you have de - signed.
Grant all you ask through all your days.
His right hand sav - ing pow'r will bring.

5. [7]A trust in chariots some proclaim,
And some in horses take their pride;
But we will boast and praise this Name:
The Lord our God, and none beside.

6. [8]While we are raised and upright stand,
Our foes are made to bow and fall.
[9]O save the king, Lord, by Your hand,
And answer us the day we call.

William Leighton, c. 1614

LEIGHTON LM

The King in Your Great Strength, O Lord

Worthy is the Lamb who was slain to receive power and riches and wisdom, and strength and honor and glory and blessing! —Revelation 5:12

21A
Psalm 21:1-6

1. [1] The king in Your great strength, O LORD, Has joy a-bun-dant-ly;
2. [3] For You have wel-comed him with gifts, With bless-ings man-i-fold;
3. [5] In Your sal-va-tion he is great, And glo-ri-fied is he;

In Your sal-va-tion he de-lights With joy ex-ceed-ing-ly,
And You have placed up-on his head A crown of pur-est gold.
And You up-on him have be-stowed Most glo-rious maj-es-ty.

[2] What he de-sired with-in his heart You ful-ly have sup-plied;
[4] When he re-quest-ed life from You, You life to him did give;
[6] For You will ev-er set on him The bless-ings of Your grace;

What he re-quest-ed with his lips, You nev-er have de-nied.
Such length of days You gave to him: For-ev-er he will live.
And You will cause him to be filled With joy be-fore Your face.

English melody; arr. Arthur S. Sullivan, 1871   NOEL CMD

21B
Because the King Trusts in the LORD

Psalm 21:7-13

*...When the Lord Jesus is revealed from heaven
with His mighty angels. —2 Thessalonians 1:7*

4. ⁷ Be - cause the king trusts in the LORD His con - fi - dence is sure;
5. ⁹ In an - ger You will burn them up At Your ap - point - ed hour;
6. ¹² For You will make them all re - treat— Your ar - rows are in place—

And through the love of Him Most High, The king is kept se - cure.
The LORD will swal - low them in wrath, In fi - ery flames de - vour.
And on Your bow - string they are aimed To strike them in the face.

⁸ Your hand will search for en - e - mies And find out all Your foes,
¹⁰ Their fruit You will re - move from earth, Their chil - dren from man - kind.
¹³ In Your al - might - y strength, O LORD, Ex - alt Your - self on high;

And all who har - bor hate for You Your right hand will op - pose.
¹¹ Their e - vil plots will not suc - ceed, Nor schemes they have de - signed.
Then we will sing with psalms of praise, Your pow - er glo - ri - fy.

Gesangbüch der Herzögl, 1784

ELLACOMBE CMD

My God, My God

Then He said to them, "My soul is exceedingly sorrowful,
even to death. Stay here and watch with Me." — Matthew 26:38

22A

Psalm 22:1-11

1. ¹My God, my God, to You I cry, O why have You for-
2. ³But still You are the Ho-ly One; On Is-r'el's praise You
3. ⁶Re-proached of men, by all de-spised, A worm, and not a
4. ⁹You brought me safe-ly from the womb, Gave faith when on my

sak-en me? Why are You far from giv-ing help, And
are en-throned. ⁴Our fa-thers put their trust in You; You
man, am I. ⁷All they who see me laugh in scorn; They
moth-er's breast, ¹⁰Since birth en-trust-ed to Your care. You've

from my ag-o-niz-ing plea? ²All day, my God, I
saved them when to You they groaned. ⁵To You they cried, and
shake their heads and taunt-ing, cry: ⁸"He trusts the LORD! Let
been my God, in You I rest. ¹¹Be not far off, for

cry in vain; By night, yet no re-lief I gain.
res-cue came; They trust-ed, and were free from shame.
Him de-fend And save him, if He is his friend!"
grief is near; No oth-er help-er will ap-pear.

Jeremiah Ingalls, 1764–1828

FILLMORE 88.88.88

22B

Psalm 22:1-11

My God, My God

*Jesus cried out with a loud voice, "My God, My God,
why have You forsaken Me?" — Matthew 27:46*

1. ¹My God, my God, to You I cry, O why have You forsaken me? Why are You far from giving help, And from my agonizing plea? ²All day, my God, I cry in vain; By night, yet no relief I gain.

2. ³But still You are the Holy One; On Is-r'el's praise You are enthroned. ⁴Our fathers put their trust in You; You saved them when to You they groaned. ⁵To You they cried, and rescue came; They trusted, and were free from shame.

3. ⁶Reproached of men, by all despised, A worm, and not a man, am I. ⁷All they that see me laugh in scorn; They shake their heads and taunting, cry: ⁸"He trusts the LORD! Let Him defend And save him, if He is his friend!"

4. ⁹You brought me safely from the womb, Gave faith when on my mother's breast, ¹⁰Since birth entrusted to Your care. You've been my God, in You I rest. ¹¹Be not far off, for grief is near; No other helper will appear.

French Plainsong (Processionale), 13th cent.; arr. Thomas Helmore, 1856   VENI EMMANUEL 88.88.88

Be Not Far Off

Then two robbers were crucified with Him,
one on the right and another on the left. — Matthew 27:38

5. [11]Be not far off, for dan - ger's near! With none to
6. [14-15]My life like wa - ter is poured out. My bones have
7. [16]Like dogs, the wick - ed cir - cle me; And they have
8. [19]But be not far from me, O LORD; Hur - ry, my

help, I face my foes. [12]Like man-y bulls they cir - cle me;
all been pulled a - part. My thirst-y tongue clings to my jaws.
pierced my hands and feet. [17]I now can num - ber all my bones;
Strength, send help to me! [20-21]My soul de - liv - er from the sword;

Strong bulls of Ba - shan me en - close. [13]They o - pen
With - in me melts, like wax, my heart. My strength is
With star - ing eyes they look at me. [18]My clothes a -
From dogs and li - ons set me free. Though by the

wide their mouths at me, Like li - ons roar-ing hun - gri - ly.
dried like bro - ken clay; And in death's dust my soul You lay.
mong them they di - vide, And for my robe with dice de - cide.
ox I'm near - ly torn, Your an - swer saved me from its horn.

William Shore, 1840

WAVERTREE 88.88.88

22D

Psalm 22:22-26

I'll Praise You in the Gathering

And I, when I am lifted up from the earth,
will draw all people to Myself. —*John 12:32*

9. 22 I'll praise You in the gath-er-ing, Tell-ing my broth-ers
10. 24 For He has not de-spised the poor; He has not scorned their
11. 25 With-in the con-gre-ga-tion great I of-fer praise You

of Your name; All you who hold the LORD in awe,
wretch-ed state. He has not turned a-way His face
have sup-plied; I'll pay my vows with those who fear.

23 To Him Your prais-es now pro-claim. Give Him the glo-ry,
From an-y-one in trou-ble great. When an-y cried to
26 With food the meek are sat-is-fied; Those seek-ing Him will

Ja-cob's seed; All Is-r'el's sons, fear Him in-deed!
Him in grief, He heard his prayer and sent re-lief.
praise the LORD. May your heart live for ev-er-more!

William H. Doane, 1832–1915

VISION 88.88.88

All Ends of Earth Will Turn to Him

22E
Psalm 22:27-31

Go therefore and make disciples of all the nations, baptizing them in the name of the Father and of the Son and of the Holy Spirit. — Matthew 28:19

12. ²⁷All ends of earth will turn to Him; The LORD they will again recall. The nations' fam-'lies all will come, To wor - ship and be - fore Him fall, ²⁸Be - cause the LORD the king-dom owns And rules a - bove all earth-ly thrones.

13. ²⁹All those who pros - per in the earth Will eat and low be - fore Him bend; And in His pres-ence all will bow, Who help - less to the dust de - scend, Who e - ven though they vain - ly strive, Can nev - er keep their souls a - live.

14. ³⁰A seed will rise to do His will, And of the Lord be made a - ware. ³¹The gen - er - a - tion that will come Will then His righ - teous - ness de - clare To peo - ple who are yet to be, That He has done this; it was He.

Franz. J. Haydn, 1798; arr. Isaac B. Woodbury, 1819–1858   CREATION 88.88.88

23 A

Psalm 23

The LORD's My Shepherd

What man of you, having a hundred sheep, if he loses one of them,
does not go after the one which is lost until he finds it? — Luke 15:4

1. ¹ The LORD's my Shep-herd, lead-ing me;
2. ³ And He re-stores my soul a-gain;
3. ⁴ Though in a val-ley dark as death,

I will not be in need.
He guides the steps I take
No e-vil will I fear;

² He'll make me lie in pas-tures green;
To walk a-long a righ-teous path,
Your rod and staff, they com-fort me,

By qui-et wa-ters lead.
All for His own name's sake.
For You are al-ways near.

4. ⁵ A feast You have prepared for me
   In sight of all my foes;
   And You anoint my head with oil,
   My full cup overflows.

5. ⁶ What love and goodness all my life
   Will follow after me;
   And in the LORD's house evermore
   My dwelling place will be.

Traditional Irish melody

ST. COLUMBA CM

The Lord's My Shepherd

I am the good shepherd. The good shepherd
lays down His life for the sheep. —John 10:11

Descant

5. 6Good - ness and mer - cy all my life Shall

1. 1The LORD's my Shep - herd, I'll not want; 2He
2. 3My soul He doth re - store a - gain; And
3. 4Yea, though I walk in death's dark vale, Yet
4. 5A ta - ble Thou hast fur - nished me In
5. 6Good - ness and mer - cy all my life Shall

sure - ly fol - low me; And in GOD's house for

makes me down to lie In pas - tures green; He
me to walk doth make With - in the paths of
will I fear no ill; For Thou art with me,
pres - ence of my foes; My head Thou dost with
sure - ly fol - low me; And in GOD's house for

ev - er - more My dwell - ing place shall be.

lead - eth me The qui - et wa - ters by.
righ - teous - ness, Ev'n for His own name's sake.
and Thy rod And staff me com - fort still.
oil a - noint, And my cup o - ver - flows.
ev - er - more My dwell - ing place shall be.

Jesse S. Irvine, 1872; desc. W. Baird Ross, 1871–1950

CRIMOND CM

23C
Psalm 23

The Lord's My Shepherd

I am the good shepherd. I know My own and they know Me.
—John 10:14

1. ¹The LORD's my shep - herd; I will lack noth - ing.
2. ⁴Al - though I trav - el Through death's dark val - ley,
3. ⁵You've set my ta - ble Where foes are watch - ing;

²He makes me lie down In pas - tures green.
No threat or dan - ger There will I fear,
My head a - noint - ed, My cup You've filled.

He leads by calm streams, ³And He re - vives me;
Since You will al - ways Stay close be - side me;
⁶Such love and good - ness Through life pur - sue me;

He guides in right ways For His name's sake.
Your rod and staff give Com - fort to me.
I'll live for - ev - er In the LORD's house.

Traditional Gaelic melody; arr. Brian E. Coombs, 2004   BUNESSAN 55.54 D

The Lord Is My Shepherd

You were straying like sheep, but have now returned to the Shepherd and Guardian of your souls. —1 Peter 2:25

1. ¹The LORD is my Shep-herd, lack noth-ing shall I.
2. For His name, He leads me on paths that are right.
3. ⁵You set me a ta-ble in front of my foes.

²In lush, ver-dant pas-tures He there makes me lie;
⁴Though I walk the val-ley where death hides the light,
My head You a-noint, and my cup o-ver-flows.

Be-side tran-quil wa-ters He leads me a-long;
Since You are there with me, no e-vil I fear;
⁶Your good-ness and love will pur-sue me each day,

³Be-cause He re-stores me, my soul is made strong.
Your rod and Your staff give me com-fort and cheer.
And I in the LORD's house for-ev-er will stay.

Traditional English melody

WASSAIL WASSAIL 11.11.11.11

24A

Psalm 24

The Earth and the Riches

For the Son of Man will come in the glory of His Father.
— Matthew 16:27

1. ¹The earth and the rich-es that in it are stored, The
2. ⁵Yes, he from the LORD shall a bless-ing ob-tain, And

world and its dwell-ers be-long to the LORD. ²For
from God his Sav-ior he'll righ-teous-ness gain. ⁶Thus

He is the One who first caused it to stand, And
look-ing to Him is a whole bless-ed race; All

up from the seas He es-tab-lished the land.
those who, like Ja-cob, are seek-ing Your face.

³O who can the path to the LORD's mount as-
⁷O gates, lift your heads! An-cient doors, lift them

cend? And who in the place of His ho-li-ness
high! The great King of glo-ry to en-ter draws

William H. Doane, 1875

TO GOD BE THE GLORY 11.11.11.11

24B

Psalm 24:7-10

Ye Gates, Lift Up Your Heads

*Jesus...led them up a high mountain apart, by themselves.
And He was transfigured before them.* —Mark 9:2

1. [7] Ye gates, lift up your heads on high; Ye doors that last for aye;
2. [9] Ye gates, lift up your heads; ye doors, Doors that do last for aye,

Be lift-ed up that   so the King Of glo-ry en-ter   may.
Be lift-ed up that   so the King Of glo-ry en-ter   may.

[1]
[8] But   who   of   glo-ry is the   King? The might-y LORD is   this.

[2]
[10] But   who   is   he that is the King, The King of glo-ry? Who is   this?

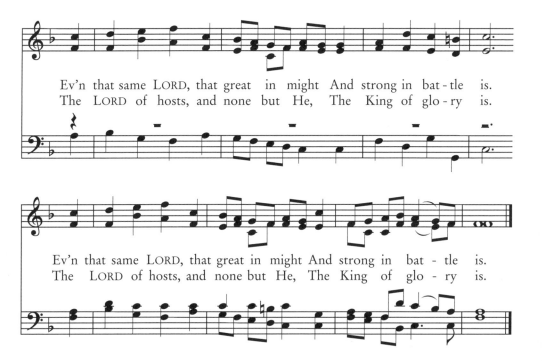

Ev'n that same LORD, that great in might And strong in bat-tle is.
The LORD of hosts, and none but He, The King of glo-ry is.

Ev'n that same LORD, that great in might And strong in bat - tle is.
The LORD of hosts, and none but He, The King of glo - ry is.

Andrew Mitchell Thomson, 1778–1831   ST. GEORGE'S EDINBURGH CMD

24C

Psalm 24

The Earth and the Riches

All things have been created through Him and for Him.
—Colossians 1:16

1. [1] The earth and the rich-es that in it are stored,
2. [3] O who can the path to the LORD's mount as-cend?
3. [5] Yes, he from the LORD shall a bless-ing ob-tain,

The world and its dwell-ers be-long to the LORD.
And who in the place of His ho-li-ness stand?
And from God his Sav-ior he'll righ-teous-ness gain.

[2] For He is the One who first caused it to stand,
[4] The man of pure heart and of hands with-out stain,
[6] Thus look-ing to Him is a whole bless-ed race;

And up from the seas He es-tab-lished the land.
Who swears not to i-dols nor wor-ships what's vain.
All those who, like Ja-cob, are seek-ing Your face.

4. [7] O gates, lift your heads! Ancient doors, lift them high!
   The great King of glory to enter draws nigh!
   [8] O who is the King that in glory draws near?
   The LORD, mighty LORD of the battle, is here!

5. [9] O gates, lift your heads! Ancient doors, lift them high!
   The great King of glory to enter draws nigh!
   [10] This great King of glory, O who can He be?
   The LORD God of hosts, King of glory is He!

S.A. Sterrett Metheny, 1909

GREYFRIARS 11.11.11.11

To You I Lift My Soul

It is I; do not be afraid.
— Matthew 14:27

25A

Psalm 25:1-7

1. ¹To You I lift my soul; LORD God, in You I trust.
2. ⁴In - struct me in Your paths; LORD, make me know Your way.
3. ⁶Your ten - der mer - cies, LORD, Your stead - fast love re - call,

²O do not let me suf - fer shame; And let my foes not boast.
⁵Teach me and make me fol - low You, That in Your truth I'll stay;
For these are things that have en - dured Through - out the ag - es all.

³Yes, those who wait on You No shame will ev - er see;
Since You have been my God, The One who res - cues me,
⁷My youth - ful sins, my faults, Do not bring these to mind;

Let shame be theirs who with - out cause Be - have with treach - er - y.
For You I'm wait - ing all the day; I wait ex - pect - ant - ly.
O LORD, re - mem - ber me in love, For You are good and kind.

George W. Martin; arr. Arthur S. Sullivan, 1862

LEOMINSTER SMD

25B
Psalm 25:8-15

The LORD Is Good and Just

For God is not unjust to forget your work and labor of love.
—Hebrews 6:10

4. ⁸The LORD is good and just; The way He'll sin-ners show.
5. ¹¹My sin-ful-ness is great, And great, O LORD, my blame;
6. ¹⁴Close friend-ship with the LORD Will all who fear Him know;

⁹He guides the meek in what is just, That they His path will know.
O par-don my in-iq-ui-ty, To glo-ri-fy Your name.
The knowl-edge of His cov-e-nant He un-to them will show.

¹⁰To those who keep His word, His cov-e-nant o-bey,
¹²To him who fears the LORD The path to choose is shown.
¹⁵My eyes up-on the LORD Con-tin-ual-ly are set;

The lov-ing-kind-ness of the LORD And truth will be their way.
¹³His soul will have pros-per-i-ty; The land his seed will own.
For He it is that shall bring forth My feet out of the net.

Louis Hartsough, 1828–1919

CALVARY (Welcome Voice) SMD

Be Gracious, Turn to Me

25C

Psalm 25:16-22

For Demas has forsaken me, having loved this present world.
—2 Timothy 4:10

7. ¹⁶Be gra - cious, turn to me,
8. ¹⁸Look on my grief and pain,
9. ²⁰Guard and pro - tect my life;
10. ²¹Since I up - on You wait

Des - o - late and op - pressed.
For - giv - ing all my sin.
Save and de - liv - er me!
Let truth and right de - fend.

¹⁷The trou - bles of my heart have grown;
¹⁹See how my en - e - mies in - crease,
O let me not be put to shame,
²²Re - demp - tion, God, for Is - ra - el

Re - lieve me from dis - tress.
How fierce their hate has been.
In You my trust will be.
From all his trou - bles send.

Robert Jackson, 1888

TRENTHAM SM

26A
Psalm 26

LORD, Vindicate Me

Which of you convicts Me of sin? And if I tell the truth,
why do you not believe Me? —John 8:46

1. ¹ LORD, vin - di - cate me; I have walked In my in - teg - ri - ty.
2. ⁴ I will not be with worth - less men, Nor with the hyp - o - crite.
3. ⁸ O LORD, I love Your dwell - ing place; Your house is my de - light.
4. ¹¹ But I have set my - self to walk In my in - teg - ri - ty;

And I have trust - ed in the LORD; I've been un - wa - ver - ing.
⁵ I hate the crowd of wick - ed men; With e - vil I'll not sit.
The place in which Your glo - ry dwells Is love - ly in my sight.
O deal with me in gra - cious - ness, Re - deem and set me free.

² Ex - am - ine me and prove me, LORD; Test heart and mind, I pray.
⁶ I'll guilt - less wash my hands and come Be - fore Your al - tar, LORD.
⁹ With sin - ners do not take my soul, With men who blood have spilled.
¹² My foot now stands on lev - el ground, A place of up - right - ness;

³ Since I be - hold Your stead - fast love; Your truth has led my way.
⁷ And I will shout with thank - ful voice; Your won - ders I'll re - cord.
¹⁰ Their hands per - form a wick - ed scheme; Their hands with bribes are filled.
And where the con - gre - ga - tion meets, The LORD I there will bless.

Lucy Broadwood; harm. Ralph Vaughan-Williams, 1906

KINGSFOLD CMD

Lord, Vindicate Me

I always take pains to have a clear conscience
toward both God and man. — Acts 24:16

26B
Psalm 26

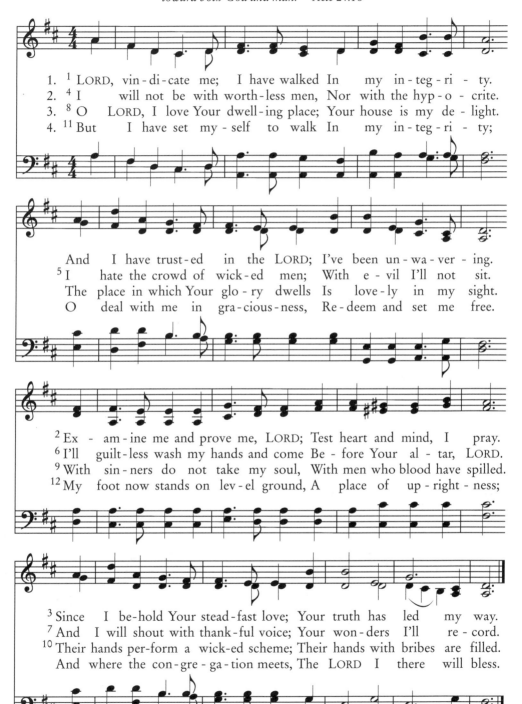

1. ¹ LORD, vin-di-cate me; I have walked In my in-teg-ri-ty.
2. ⁴ I will not be with worth-less men, Nor with the hyp-o-crite.
3. ⁸ O LORD, I love Your dwell-ing place; Your house is my de-light.
4. ¹¹ But I have set my-self to walk In my in-teg-ri-ty;

And I have trust-ed in the LORD; I've been un-wa-ver-ing.
⁵ I hate the crowd of wick-ed men; With e-vil I'll not sit.
The place in which Your glo-ry dwells Is love-ly in my sight.
O deal with me in gra-cious-ness, Re-deem and set me free.

² Ex-am-ine me and prove me, LORD; Test heart and mind, I pray.
⁶ I'll guilt-less wash my hands and come Be-fore Your al-tar, LORD.
⁹ With sin-ners do not take my soul, With men who blood have spilled.
¹² My foot now stands on lev-el ground, A place of up-right-ness;

³ Since I be-hold Your stead-fast love; Your truth has led my way.
⁷ And I will shout with thank-ful voice; Your won-ders I'll re-cord.
¹⁰ Their hands per-form a wick-ed scheme; Their hands with bribes are filled.
And where the con-gre-ga-tion meets, The LORD I there will bless.

Felix B. Mendelssohn, 1809–1847

PEACE CMD

27A

Psalm 27:1-3

The Lord Is My Light and My Salvation

When the time had come for Him to be received up...
He steadfastly set His face to go to Jerusalem. —Luke 9:51

1. ¹The Lord is my light and my sal - va - tion;
2. ²For when e - vil - do - ers came up - on me,
3. ³An ar - my may camp out to be - siege me;

By whom am I dis - mayed?
Seek - ing my flesh to eat,
Fear will not fill my heart.

The Lord is my life's de - fense and strong - hold;
My foes and my ad - ver - sar - ies stum - bled,
I will yet with con - fi - dence con - tin - ue,

Of whom am I a - fraid?
Fall - ing to their de - feat.
Though war a - gainst me start.

Andrew K. Schep, 2006

WILLARD 10.6.10.6

I Ask the LORD and Seek

*How much more will your heavenly Father give the
Holy Spirit to those who ask Him? — Luke 11:13*

27B

Psalm 27:4-6

4. ⁴ I ask the LORD and seek This
5. To gaze up - on the LORD, His
6. ⁵ He'll hide me in His tent When
7. ⁶ My head shall high - er be Than

one thing to ob - tain: That in the LORD's house
beau - ty to ad - mire; And in His tem - ple
comes the e - vil day. He'll set me high up -
all my foes a - round; I'll in the LORD's tent

I may live, And ev - er there re - main,
I would stay To pon - der and in - quire.
on a rock; I'll in His shel - ter stay.
sac - ri - fice, And sing with joy - ful sound.

French-Genevan Psalter, 1551

ST. MICHAEL SM

27C

Psalm 27:7-10

O Hear My Voice, Lord

At my first defense no one stood with me, but all forsook me.
—2 Timothy 4:16

8. [7] O hear my voice, LORD, when I cry, And
9. [9] O do not cause Your face to be Con-
10. For You have sure - ly been my help, Do
11. [10] My fa - ther and my moth - er both May

an - swer me in grace. [8] When You said, "Seek my
cealed from me, I pray. Treat me, Your ser - vant,
not a - ban - don me; Do not for - sake me
leave me all a - lone, But sure - ly then the

face," my heart Said, "LORD, I'll seek Your face."
with - out wrath; Do not turn me a - way.
now, I pray, O God who res - cues me.
LORD Him - self Will take me as His own.

Alexander R. Reinagle, c. 1836

ST. PETER CM

O LORD, Teach Me to Follow You

And they watched the gates day and night, to kill him.
— Acts 9:24

27D

Psalm 27:11-14

12. ¹¹ O LORD, teach me to fol - low You; In - struct me in Your way, And lead me on a lev - el path Be - cause of foes, I pray!

13. ¹² Give me not to my foes' de - sire; False wit - ness - es a - rise A - gainst me, breath - ing vi - o - lence And seek - ing my de - mise.

14. ¹³ Oh! What if I had not be - lieved! I am, by faith, as - sured That in the land of life I'll see The good - ness of the LORD.

15. ¹⁴ With pa - tience wait up - on the LORD, O let your strength be great; And so let cour - age fill your heart As on the LORD you wait.

Robert M. Copeland, 1972

LOUISE CM

28A

Psalm 28

Lord, I Call on You

*...Esteeming the reproach of Christ greater riches
than the treasures in Egypt. —Hebrews 11:26*

1. ¹LORD, I call on You to help me;
2. ³Drag me not a - way with sin - ners,
3. ⁶Bless - ed be the LORD who heard me,

O my Rock, do not be deaf;
Those who work in - i - qui - ty;
⁷For the LORD's my strength and shield.

If You're si - lent, un - re - spond - ing,
Peace - ful - ly they speak to neigh - bors,
I am helped when my heart trusts Him;

I'll sink in the pit of death.
As they're plot - ting treach - er - y.
Glad - ly sing - ing, thanks I yield.

2 When I voice my sup - pli - ca - tion,
4 Re - com - pense, re - pay them just - ly
8 For the LORD's their strength, their pow - er,

And I cry for help, O hear,
For the e - vil of their hands.
For His king a shield is He.

When I toward Your ho - ly tem - ple
5 They the LORD's works dis - re - gard - ed!
9 Save Your her - i - tage and bless them;

Lift my hands to You in prayer.
He de - stroys them; they'll not stand.
Shep - herd them e - ter - nal - ly.

Wolfgang Mozart, 1756–1791

AMADEUS 87.87 D

28B
Psalm 28:1-5

I Cry to You, O Lord

*The Lord knows how to deliver the godly out of temptations
and to reserve the unjust under punishment. —2 Peter 2:9*

1. [1] I cry to You, O LORD, my Rock To me do not be deaf; If You are si-lent I'll de-scend In-to the pit of death.
2. [2] O hear my sup-pli-ca-ting voice When un-to You I cry, When to Your ho-ly dwell-ing place I lift my hands up high.
3. [3] O drag me not a-way with those Who work in-i-qui-ty, Who to their neigh-bors speak of peace While plot-ting treach-er-y.

4. [4] Repay them justly for their deeds,
   The evil of their way;
   And for the things their hands have done
   A due reward repay.

5. [5] Since they do not regard the works
   And actions of His hand,
   The LORD will surely tear them down,
   He will not let them stand.

Scottish Psalter, 1615

DUNDEE (French) CM

The LORD Be Blessed

For the Lamb who is in the midst of the throne will shepherd them
and lead them to living fountains of waters. —Revelation 7:17

6. ⁶ The LORD be blessed, He heard my voice When
7. I have been helped; my heart is glad; My
8. ⁹ O save Your peo - ple; give them help; And

un - to Him I cried. ⁷ The LORD's my strength, He
joy - ous praise I'll sing. ⁸ The LORD's His peo - ple's
bless Your her - i - tage. Be their own Shep - herd,

is my shield; On Him my heart re - lied.
strength, He saves His own a - noint - ed king.
car - ry them Se - cure through ev - ery age.

William B. Bradbury, 1816–1868

BROWN CM

29A

Psalm 29

You Sons of the Gods

And I heard a voice from heaven, like the voice of many waters,
and like the voice of loud thunder. —Revelation 14:2

1. [1] You sons of the gods, give the LORD as His right,
2. [3] The LORD's voice is o - ver the wa - ters a - broad;
3. [5] The voice of the LORD splits the ce - dars in two;

As - cribe to the LORD both great glo - ry and might.
And thun - der pro - ceeds from the glo - ri - ous God.
The LORD shat - ters trees that in Leb - a - non grew.

[2] And un - to the LORD's name its glo - ry ac - cord;
A - bove the great wa - ters the LORD from His height!
[6] Then Leb - a - non's hills and Mount Si - ri - on reeled

In splen - dor of ho - li - ness wor - ship the LORD.
[4] The LORD's voice of splen - dor! The LORD's voice of might!
When He made them skip like young calves in the field.

4. [7] The LORD's voice in flashes of lightning exclaims,
The places it strikes all burst out into flames;
[8] The voice of the LORD makes the wilderness quake;
The LORD makes the desert of Kadesh to shake.

5. [9] The LORD's voice induces the deer to give birth,
And strips bare the forests that cover the earth;
But inside His temple all things will exclaim,
And everything found there will "Glory!" proclaim.

6. [10] The LORD ruled as King as the floodwaters raged,
And still shall the LORD rule throughout every age.
[11] The LORD will the strength of His people increase;
The LORD gives His people the blessing of peace.

Traditional Welsh melody; arr. John Roberts, 1839

JOANNA (St. Denio) 11.11.11.11

You Sons of the Gods

His voice was like the sound of many waters.
— Revelation 1:15

1. [1] You sons of the gods, give the LORD as His right, As-cribe to the LORD both great glo-ry and might. [2] And un-to the LORD's name its glo-ry ac-cord; In splen-dor of ho-li-ness wor-ship the LORD.

2. [3] The LORD's voice is o-ver the wa-ters a-broad; And thun-der pro-ceeds from the glo-ri-ous God. A-bove the great wa-ters the LORD from His height! [4] The LORD's voice of splen-dor! The LORD's voice of might!

3. [5] The voice of the LORD splits the ce-dars in two; The LORD shat-ters trees that in Leb-a-non grew. [6] Then Leb-a-non's hills and Mount Si-ri-on reeled When He made them skip like young calves in the field.

4. [7] The LORD's voice in flash-es of light-ning ex-claims; The pla-ces it strikes all burst out in-to flames; [8] The voice of the LORD makes the wil-der-ness quake; The LORD makes the des-ert of Ka-desh to shake.

[1, 2, 3, 4, 5]

[6] bless-ing of peace.

5. [9] The LORD's voice induces the deer to give birth,
And strips bare the forests that cover the earth;
But inside His temple all things will exclaim,
And everything found there will "Glory!" proclaim.

6. [10] The LORD ruled as King as the floodwaters raged,
And still shall the LORD rule throughout every age.
[11] The LORD will the strength of His people increase;
The LORD gives His people the blessing of peace.

Traditional Normandy carol

NORMANDY CAROL 11.11.11.11

30A
Psalm 30

O Lord, I Will Exalt You

Therefore humble yourselves under the mighty hand of God,
that He may exalt you in due time. —1 Peter 5:6

1. ¹O LORD, I will ex-alt You, For You have lift-ed me;
2. ⁴Sing prais-es, O you god-ly, Who to the LORD be-long;
3. ⁶When pros-p'rous, I once boast-ed, "Un-moved I shall re-main."

My foes You kept from boast-ing, De-nied them vic-to-ry.
And to His name most ho-ly Show grat-i-tude in song.
⁷But You, LORD, by Your fa-vor My moun-tain's strength main-tain;

²O LORD, my God, I plead-ed That You might heal and save;
⁵His an-ger lasts a mo-ment, His grace through life goes on;
For when Your face was hid-den, I then be-came dis-mayed.

³LORD, You from death have ran-somed, And kept me from the grave.
Though through the night tears lin-ger, Great joy comes with the dawn.
⁸O LORD, to You I cried out, And to the Lord I prayed:

4. ⁹"O where is the advantage
If my blood should be shed?
Will dust declare You faithful,
Can praise come from the dead?
¹⁰O LORD, to me be gracious,
And hear me as I've prayed.
To You, O LORD, I cry out
O be my help, my aid."

5. ¹¹You turned my grief to dancing,
From sackcloth set me free.
You wrapped me up in gladness;
I shall not silent be.
¹²Indeed, my soul, my glory,
Will praise You and adore;
O LORD, my God, I'll thank You
Both now and evermore.

Arthur H. Mann, 1881

ANGEL'S STORY 76.76 D

O Lord, I Will Exalt You

If you have been raised up with Christ,
keep seeking the things above, where Christ is. —Colossians 3:1

1. ¹O LORD, I will ex-alt You, For You have lift-ed me;
2. ⁴Sing prais-es, O you god-ly, Who to the LORD be-long;
3. ⁶When pros-p'rous, I once boast-ed, "Un-moved I shall re-main."

My foes You kept from boast-ing, De-nied them vic-to-ry.
And to His name most ho-ly Show grat-i-tude in song.
⁷But You, LORD, by Your fa-vor My moun-tain's strength main-tain;

²O LORD, my God, I plead-ed That You might heal and save;
⁵His an-ger lasts a mo-ment, His grace through life goes on;
For when Your face was hid-den, I then be-came dis-mayed.

³LORD, You from death have ran-somed, And kept me from the grave.
Though through the night tears lin-ger, Great joy comes with the dawn.
⁸O LORD, to You I cried out, And to the Lord I prayed:

4. ⁹"O where is the advantage
    If my blood should be shed?
    Will dust declare You faithful,
    Can praise come from the dead?
   ¹⁰O LORD, to me be gracious,
    And hear me as I've prayed.
    To You, O LORD, I cry out
    O be my help, my aid."

5. ¹¹You turned my grief to dancing,
    From sackcloth set me free.
    You wrapped me up in gladness;
    I shall not silent be.
   ¹²Indeed, my soul, my glory,
    Will praise You and adore;
    O LORD, my God, I'll thank You
    Both now and evermore.

Melchoir Teschner, c. 1615   ST. THEODULPH 76.76 D

31A In You, O Lord, I Put My Trust

Psalm 31:1-5

And Jesus cried out with a loud voice, and breathed His last.
— Mark 15:37

1. ¹ In You, O Lord, I put my trust;
2. ² Bow down Your ear to my re - quest
3. ³ Since You my rock and for - tress are,
4. ⁵ I to Your hand with con - fi - dence

A - shamed let me not be;
And swift - ly res - cue me;
For Your name's sake now guide.
My spir - it do com - mend;

Ac - cord - ing to Your righ - teous - ness,
Be - come for me a rock of strength,
⁴ And res - cue me from se - cret nets;
So now I pray, Lord God of truth,

O do de - liv - er me.
A strong - hold sav - ing me.
My ref - uge You a - bide.
To me re - demp - tion send.

Charles H. Gabriel, 1856–1932

AVONDALE (Gabriel) CM

In You, Lord, I Take Refuge

Be renewed in the spirit of your mind.
— Ephesians 4:23

31B
Psalm 31:1-8

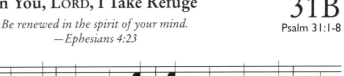

1. [1]In You, Lord, I take ref-uge; Let shame not come to me.
2. [3]You are my rock and for-tress; For Your name lead and guide.
3. [6]I hate those serv-ing i-dols; But in the Lord I rest.

In righ-teous-ness give an-swer; Set me at lib-er-ty.
[4]Be-cause You are my strong-hold, Free me from nets they hide.
[7]Your love gives me great glad-ness; You saw me when op-pressed.

[2]O has-ten to my res-cue, And to my plea give heed;
[5]In-to Your hand my spir-it I now en-trust to You;
You knew my soul's af-flic-tion, [8]And kept me from my foe.

O be my rock and ref-uge, A for-tress in my need.
Be-cause You have re-deemed me, Lord God whose word is true.
My feet You have es-tab-lished, Where they can safe-ly go.

Henry Smart, 1836

LANCASHIRE 76.76 D

31C
Psalm 31:9-18

O Lord, Be Gracious to Me

Therefore most gladly I will rather boast in my infirmities,
that the power of Christ may rest upon me. —2 Corinthians 12:9

4. ⁹O Lord, be gra-cious to me, Be-cause of my tra-vail;
5. ¹¹My ad-ver-sar-ies mock me, My neigh-bors look with dread,
6. ¹⁴I say, "You are my God," Lord; With faith in You I stand.
7. ¹⁷O put me not to shame, Lord, I trust in You to save;

My eye from grief is with-ered, My soul and bod-y fail.
My friends did not come near me, They turned a-round and fled.
¹⁵Save me from per-se-cu-tors; My times are in Your hand.
Let shame con-found the wick-ed, Brought speech-less to the grave.

¹⁰My life is spent with sor-row, My years with sigh-ing fade,
¹²For-got-ten like a dead man, I'm like a bro-ken pot.
¹⁶O may light from Your pres-ence Up-on Your ser-vant shine;
¹⁸Let ly-ing lips be si-lenced, So in-so-lent and vain,

My strength fails in af-flic-tion, My bones be-come de-cayed.
¹³Their whis-pers ter-ri-fy me— Be-cause my death they plot.
And in Your lov-ing-kind-ness Make Your sal-va-tion mine.
That speak a-gainst the righ-teous, With words of proud dis-dain.

Traditional Welsh melody

LLANGLOFFAN 76.76 D

How Great the Good

The solid foundation of God stands, having this seal:
"The Lord knows those who are His." — 2 Timothy 2:19

31D

Psalm 31:19-24

8. ¹⁹How great the good You've gath-ered For those re-ver-ing You,
9. ²¹The LORD be blessed for-ev-er, He showed His love to me;
10. ²³O love the LORD, you god-ly! The LORD the faith-ful keeps.

Stored up for all who trust You Where sons of men may view.
Be-sieged once like a cit-y, I faced the en-e-my.
But one whose deeds are haugh-ty, Full re-com-pense he reaps.

²⁰With-in Your se-cret pres-ence, There You pre-serve their life,
²²I said when filled with pan-ic, "I'm cast out from Your sight."
²⁴So then, be strong and stead-fast, And let your heart be brave;

A-way from whis-pered schem-ing, And far from tongues of strife.
But still You heard my plead-ing, When I cried out in fright.
All you who wait with pa-tience, Wait on the LORD to save.

John K. Robb, 1949

SAINTS' PRAISE 76.76 D

32A

Psalm 32:1-7

What Blessedness

How much more shall the blood of Christ...cleanse your conscience
from dead works to serve the living God? —Hebrews 9:14

1. [1] What bless - ed - ness be - longs to him
2. [2] Blessed is the one for whom the LORD
3. [3] I lan - guished, si - lent in my guilt;
4. [5] My sin I then con - fessed to You,

Who has for - giv - en been,
Counts no in - iq - ui - ty,
My days were filled with groans.
Not hid - ing guilt - i - ness;

For whom trans - gres - sions have been cleared,
And in whose spir - it is no taint
[4] On me Your hand pressed day and night,
I said, "I will be - fore the LORD

And cov - ered is his sin.
Of in - sin - cer - i - ty.
And heat dried up my bones.
Trans - gres - sions now con - fess."

5. Then You released me from my sin,
   And took its guilt away.
   [6] And therefore while You may be found,
   Let all the godly pray.

6. They'll not be harmed by rising floods.
   [7] In You I hide in peace;
   You keep me safe, surrounding me
   With songs of my release.

E.H. Frost

TABLER CM

Instruction I Will Give to You

You turned to God from idols to serve the living and true God.
—1 Thessalonians 1:9

32B

7. [8] In - struc - tion I will give to you,
8. [9] Be not like sense - less horse or mule,
9. [10] How man - y griefs the wick - ed earns
10. [11] Be glad and shout, you righ - teous ones,

And teach the way to go.
Which if you would sub - due,
As part of his re - ward;
And in the LORD re - joice;

My watch - ful eye will guide your steps;
You must with bit and bri - dle hold
But cov - 'nant love sur - rounds the one
And let all those with up - right hearts

My coun - sel you will know.
To bring him close to you.
Whose trust is in the LORD.
Sing out with joy - ful voice.

Adapt. from Johann G. Nageli, 1773–1836

MAIN CM

32C

Psalm 32:1-7

What Blessedness

*David also describes the blessedness of the man to whom God
imputes righteousness apart from works. —Romans 4:6*

1. ¹What bless-ed-ness be-longs to him Who has for-giv-en been,
2. ³I lan-guished, si-lent in my guilt; My days were filled with groans.
3. Then You re-leased me from my sin, And took its guilt a-way.

For whom trans-gres-sions have been cleared, And cov-ered is his sin.
⁴On me Your hand pressed day and night, And heat dried up my bones.
⁶And there-fore while You may be found, Let all the god-ly pray.

²Blessed is the one for whom the LORD Counts no in-iq-ui-ty,
⁵My sin I then con-fessed to You, Not hid-ing guilt-i-ness;
They'll not be harmed by ris-ing floods. ⁷In You I hide in peace;

And in whose spir-it is no taint Of in-sin-cer-i-ty.
I said, "I will be-fore the LORD Trans-gres-sions now con-fess."
You keep me safe, sur-round-ing me With songs of my re-lease.

John B. Dykes, 1868

VOX DILECTI CMD

Instruction I Will Give to You

*But you were washed, but you were sanctified, but you were
justified in the name of the Lord Jesus Christ. —1 Corinthians 6:11*

4. [8] In - struc - tion I will give to you, And teach the way to go.
5. [10] How man - y griefs the wick-ed earns As part of his re - ward;

My watch - ful eye will guide your steps; My coun - sel you will know.
But cov - 'nant love sur - rounds the one Whose trust is in the LORD.

[9] Be not like sense - less horse or mule, Which if you would sub - due,
[11] Be glad and shout, you righ - teous ones, And in the LORD re - joice;

You must with bit and bri - dle hold To bring him close to you.
And let all those with up - right hearts Sing out with joy - ful voice.

Source unknown

CAMPBELL CMD

33A

Psalm 33:1-5

With Gladness in the Lord

Take My yoke upon you and learn from Me,
for I am gentle and lowly in heart. — Matthew 11:29

1. ¹With glad - ness in the LORD, O let the
2. ²So give the LORD your thanks, With harp your
3. ³And as you sing and play, Your skill - ful -

righ - teous sing! For when the up - right
mu - sic raise; And with a ten - stringed
ness em - ploy. O sing a new song

give Him praise, It is a fit - ting thing.
in - stru - ment, Sing out to Him your praise.
un - to Him; With shouts ex - press your joy.

4. ⁴For upright is the word
   The LORD has given us,
   And all the works that He has done
   Were done in faithfulness.

5. ⁵For He seeks righteousness,
   And all that's just and fair;
   The LORD's love is throughout the earth,
   Abundant everywhere.

Johann G. Nageli, 1773–1836; arr. Lowell Mason, 1845

DENNIS SM

With Gladness in the Lord

33B

Rejoice in the Lord always; again I say, rejoice.
—Philippians 4:4

Psalm 33:1-5

1. [1] With glad-ness in the LORD, O let the righ-teous sing! For when the up-right give Him praise, It is a fit-ting thing. It is a fit-ting thing.

2. [2] So give the LORD your thanks, With harp your mu-sic raise; And with a ten-stringed in-stru-ment, Sing out to Him your praise. Sing out to Him your praise.

3. [3] And as you sing and play, Your skill-ful-ness em-ploy. O sing a new song un-to Him; With shouts ex-press your joy. With shouts ex-press your joy.

4. [4] For upright is the word
   The LORD has given us,
   And all the works that He has done
   Were done in faithfulness.

5. [5] For He seeks righteousness,
   And all that's just and fair;
   The LORD's love is throughout the earth,
   Abundant everywhere.

John Zundel, 1815-1882

LOUISVILLE SM

33C

Psalm 33:6-22

The Lord by His Word Has Created

Oh, the depth of the riches both of the wisdom and knowledge of God!
How unsearchable are His judgments! —Romans 11:33

6. [6] The LORD by His word has cre - at - ed the heav - ens;
7. [10] The LORD brings to noth - ing the plans of the na - tions;
8. [13] The LORD looks from heav - en to see all of man - kind,
9. [18] Be - hold, the LORD's eye is up - on all who trust Him,

And He by His breath made the stars come to be.
He frus - trates their coun - sel and makes their schemes fail.
[14] He looks from His throne on all dwell - ing on earth—
Who hope in His love and, in awe, Him re - vere.

[7] The depths of the o - cean He heaps up to - geth - er,
[11] But all that the LORD in His heart has in - tend - ed,
[15] The same One who made them, who all their hearts fash - ioned,
[19] They trust that from death He will res - cue and save them,

And puts in a store - house the waves of the sea.
The plans He has made will for - ev - er pre - vail.
Who knows what they do and con - si - ders its worth.
And keep them all liv - ing when fam - ine comes near.

8 So let all the earth and its peo-ple re - vere Him,
12 The na - tion the LORD has em - braced is most bless - ed,
16 The king is not saved by the strength of his ar - my;
20 The LORD we a - wait is our help and pro - tec - tion,

And in the LORD's pres - ence with awe let them stand.
Where He is ac - knowl-edged to be God a - lone,
The sol - dier as well should not trust his own might.
21 Our heart is glad trust - ing in His ho - ly name.

9 He spoke, it was done, and con - tin - ues to stand fast;
This peo - ple He claims, His in - her - it - ed por - tion,
17 The strength of a horse does not make res - cue cer - tain;
22 O LORD, let Your cov - e - nant love be up - on us,

It all was ac - com-plished when He gave com - mand.
The ones He has cho - sen and calls as His own.
A horse is a false hope for win - ning the fight.
As we hold to You and the hope that we claim.

Traditional Welsh melody

ASH GROVE 12.11.12.11 D

34 A

Psalm 34:1-10

At All Times I Will Bless the Lord

*Were there not any found who returned to give glory to God
except this foreigner? —Luke 17:18*

1. ¹ At all times I will bless the LORD, In praise my mouth em - ploy.
2. ⁵ They looked to Him and ra - diant were, A - shamed they shall not be.
3. ⁸ O taste and see the LORD is good; Those trust-ing Him are blessed.

² My soul is boast - ing in the LORD; The poor will hear with joy.
⁶ The LORD heard when this poor man cried, From trou - ble set him free.
⁹ O fear the LORD, saints; none who fear Will be with need op - pressed.

³ O glo - ri - fy the LORD with me, Let us ex - alt His name!
⁷ The An - gel of the LORD en - camps A - round those fear - ing Him;
¹⁰ The li - ons young may hun - gry be, And they may lack their food;

⁴ In all my fears I sought the LORD, From Him my res - cue came.
Those trust - ing Him He safe - ly guards, And He de - liv - ers them.
But they who tru - ly seek the LORD Will not lack an - y good.

Traditional French melody

CHAMPS ELYSEES CMD

I Will At All Times Bless the LORD

34B

Psalm 34:1-10

He did not waver at the promise of God through unbelief,
but was strengthened in faith, giving glory to God. —Romans 4:20

1. ¹I will at all times bless the LORD; His
2. ³Come, let us mag - ni - fy the LORD, And
3. ⁵How ra - diant, those who looked to Him! Their

praise my mouth will al - ways voice. ²And in the LORD my
praise His name in u - ni - ty! ⁴I sought the LORD, and
fac - es free from shame shall be. ⁶The LORD heard when this

soul shall boast; The poor will hear it and re - joice.
in re - ply, From all my fears He res - cued me.
poor man cried, And from all trou - ble set him free.

4. ⁷Encircling those who fear the LORD
His angel camps, and rescues them.
⁸O taste and see the LORD is good;
How blessed are those who trust in Him.

5. ⁹⁻¹⁰Revere the LORD, all you His saints.
Young lions may at times lack food;
But none who fears and seeks the LORD
Shall be deprived of any good.

Musikalisches Handbüch, Hamburg, 1690   WINCHESTER NEW LM

34C

Psalm 34:11-22

O Sons and Daughters, Come

Preaching peace through Jesus Christ—He is Lord of all.
—Acts 10:36

6. [11] O sons and daugh - ters, come! Give ear! And
7. [15] The LORD on just men keeps His eyes; His
8. [19] Though righ - teous men great trou - bles see, The

learn from me the LORD to fear. [12] Who,
ears are o - pen to their cries. [16] The
LORD from all will set them free. [20] And

seek - ing good, long life de - sires? Or who to man - y
LORD on vile men turns His face, From earth their mem - 'ry
all his bones He'll keep se - cure, No bro - ken ones will

days as - pires? [13] From e - vil make your
to e - rase. [17] The righ - teous cried; the
he en - dure. [21] But e - vil slays all

tongue re - frain; From speak - ing lies your lips re - strain.
LORD gave heed, And then from all their trou - bles freed.
wick - ed men; Those hat - ing just men are con - demned.

14 From ev - ery wick - ed way de - part; Do
18 To bro - ken hearts the LORD is near, To
22 The LORD re - deems those serv - ing Him, None

good; seek peace with all your heart.
save the con - trite He'll ap - pear.
trust - ing Him will He con - demn.

William B. Bradbury, 1859

SWEET HOUR LMD

35A

Psalm 35:1-6

Strive, Lord

This is your hour, and the power of darkness.
— Luke 22:53

1. ¹ Strive, LORD, with those who strive with me.
2. ³ Take up the spear and block the way,
3. ⁴ Those who de - sire to take my life
4. ⁵ Let them be chaff be - fore the wind,

And fight with those who fight with me.
Stop - ping the men who me pur - sue;
Hum - bled and shamed let them all be;
With the LORD's An - gel driv - ing them.

² Take up the buck - ler and the shield;
And to my soul in mer - cy say,
Let them be thwart - ed and turned back,
⁶ Make their way dark and slip - per - y,

Rise up and my De - fend - er be.
"I am sal - va - tion un - to you."
Those who plot e - vil things for me.
With the LORD's An - gel chas - ing them.

Gregorian Chant; arr. Lowell Mason, 1824

HAMBURG LM

Without a Cause Their Net They Hid

35B

Psalm 35:7-10

...Filled with all unrighteousness, sexual immorality, wickedness, covetousness, maliciousness; full of envy, murder... —Romans 1:29

5. [7] With - out a cause their net they hid
6. [8] Let him the un - ex - pect - ed meet;
7. [9] My soul shall in the LORD re - joice,
8. You give the poor de - liv - er - ance

To take me in the pit pre - pared;
Let him be caught with - in the snare
And boast in His sal - va - tion, too.
From one who is for him too strong;

With - out a cause they laid a trap
Which he has spread for oth - er feet,
[10] My bod - y will ex - ult and say,
The need - y and op - pressed You spare

In which my soul might be en - snared.
And fall to ut - ter ru - in there.
"O LORD, who can there be like You?
From those who steal and do them wrong."

William Bradbury, 1853

OLIVE'S BROW LM

35C

Now Men Arise to Bear False Witness

Psalm 35:11-18

Woe to that man by whom the offense comes!
— Matthew 18:7

9. ¹¹Now men a - rise to bear false wit - ness; They ask me
10. ¹⁴As if they were my friend or broth - er, I went a -
11. ¹⁶Like god - less jest - ers at a par - ty, They with their

things I do not know. ¹²My good they pay back with their
bout and grieved a - loud; As though in mourn - ing for my
teeth have gnashed at me. ¹⁷How long, O Lord, will You al -

e - vil; It fills my heart with grief and woe. ¹³When they were
moth - er, With deep - est sor - row I was bowed.¹⁵But at my
low this? How long look on and let this be? De - liv - er

sick I dressed in sack - cloth; I fast - ed with hu - mil - i -
stum - bling they were joy - ful— As - sail - ants all un - known to
me from their de - struc - tions, And save my life from li - ons

ty; But all the prayers I of-fered for them
me; To - geth - er they con - spire a - gainst me,
strong. [18] I'll thank You in the great as - sem - bly,

Would keep re - turn - ing back to me.
They slan - der me con - tin - ual - ly.
And praise You in the might - y throng!

Traditional American melody
WAYFARING STRANGER 98.98 D

35D

Let Not Those

Psalm 35:19-23

*Outside are dogs and sorcerers and sexually immoral and murderers
and idolaters, and whoever loves and practices a lie.* —Revelation 22:15

12. ¹⁹Let not those wrong - ful - ly my foes
13. ²⁰Of peace they will not speak at all,
14. ²²LORD, You have seen; do not be still.

Raise o - ver me their joy - ful cries;
Toward peace - ful neigh - bors scheme with lies.
O Lord, be not far from my sight.

And those who hate me with - out cause,
²¹With bra - zen words ac - cus - ing me,
²³O rouse Your - self, to judg - ment wake!

Let not with mal - ice wink their eyes.
They say, "We saw this with our eyes."
My God, my Lord, up - hold my right.

William Knapp, 1738

WAREHAM LM

With Justice Judge Me, LORD

35E
Psalm 35:24-28

For there stood by me this night an angel of God
to whom I belong and whom I serve. —Acts 27:23

15. 24 With jus - tice judge me, LORD, my God;
16. 26 Let them be hum - bled and a - shamed
17. 27 But let them shout a - loud with joy
18. Be - cause it brings to Him de - light

Let not my foes gloat o - ver me.
Who gloat at my ca - lam - i - ty;
Who long to see me jus - ti - fied;
To see His ser - vant pros - per - ing."

25 Let them not think, "We've swal - lowed him!
Clothe them with shame and with dis - grace
And let them nev - er cease to say,
28 I'll speak a - bout Your righ - teous - ness;

At last, our soul's de - sire we see!"
Who proud - ly rise up o - ver me.
"O let the LORD be mag - ni - fied.
Through - out the day Your praise I'll sing.

William Leighton, c. 1614

LEIGHTON LM

36A
Psalm 36:1-4

About the Wicked

Raging waves of the sea, foaming up their own shame; wandering stars
for whom is reserved the blackness of darkness forever. —Jude 1:13

1. ¹A - bout the wick - ed and his sin,
2. ²With flat - ter - y he views him - self
3. ³The words he ut - ters with his mouth
4. ⁴He med - i - tates up - on his bed,

My heart with - in me cries:
As good in his own eyes;
Are wick - ed - ness and lies;
Some e - vil to in - vent;

There sure - ly is no fear of God
His sin he's cer - tain no one will
He ceased from do - ing what is good,
He sets him - self in ways not good,

At all be - fore his eyes.
Dis - cov - er and de - spise.
A - ban - doned be - ing wise.
From e - vil won't re - pent.

Arr. Henry W. Greatorex, 1851

MANOAH CM

Your Love, Lord

But He said to them, "I have food that you do not know about."
—John 4:32

36B

Psalm 36:5-12

5. ⁵ Your love, LORD, reach-es up to heav'n, Your faith-ful-ness the skies.
6. ⁸ From all the boun-ty of Your house, They feast till sat-is-fied;
7. ¹⁰ To all those who ac-knowl-edge You, Your love for-ev-er show;

⁶ Your jus-tice is like moun-tains great, Like depths Your judg-ments wise.
From riv-ers full of Your de-lights, You will their drink pro-vide.
On those who up-right are in heart, Your righ-teous-ness be-stow.

LORD, You pre-serve both man and beast, ⁷ How pre-cious, God, Your grace!
⁹ Be-cause the flow-ing spring of life Is sure-ly found with You;
¹¹ By proud feet let me not be crushed, Nor led by e-vil hand

Be-neath the shad-ow of Your wings, Man-kind their trust will place.
And in that shin-ing light of Yours, We have the light in view.
¹² To where the e-vil-do-ers fell; Thrust down, they can-not stand.

Felix B. Mendelssohn, 1809–1847

PEACE CMD

36C

Psalm 36

About the Wicked

For by grace you have been saved through faith; and that
not of yourselves, it is the gift of God. —Ephesians 2:8

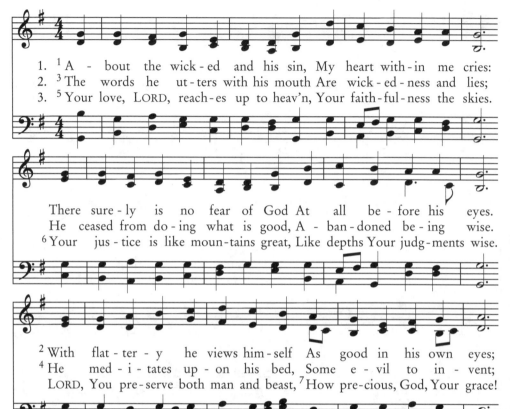

1. [1] A - bout the wick - ed and his sin, My heart with - in me cries:
2. [3] The words he ut - ters with his mouth Are wick - ed - ness and lies;
3. [5] Your love, LORD, reach - es up to heav'n, Your faith - ful - ness the skies.

There sure - ly is no fear of God At all be - fore his eyes.
He ceased from do - ing what is good, A - ban - doned be - ing wise.
[6] Your jus - tice is like moun - tains great, Like depths Your judg - ments wise.

[2] With flat - ter - y he views him - self As good in his own eyes;
[4] He med - i - tates up - on his bed, Some e - vil to in - vent;
LORD, You pre - serve both man and beast, [7] How pre - cious, God, Your grace!

His sin he's cer - tain no one will Dis - cov - er and de - spise.
He sets him - self in ways not good, From e - vil won't re - pent.
Be - neath the shad - ow of Your wings, Man - kind their trust will place.

4. [8] From all the bounty of Your house,
   They feast till satisfied;
   From rivers full of Your delights,
   You will their drink provide.
   [9] Because the flowing spring of life
   Is surely found with You;
   And in that shining light of Yours,
   We have the light in view.

5. [10] To all those who acknowledge You,
   Your love forever show;
   On those who upright are in heart,
   Your righteousness bestow.
   [11] By proud feet let me not be crushed,
   Nor led by evil hand
   [12] To where the evildoers fell;
   Thrust down, they cannot stand.

Louis Bourgeois, 1510–1561

OLD 44TH CMD

Do Not Be Angry

And the light shines in the darkness,
and the darkness did not overcome it. —John 1:5

1. ¹Do not be an-gry or out-raged When e-vil men you see.
2. ³Trust in the LORD and cul-ti-vate The good that you pos-sess.
3. ⁶He'll man-i-fest your righ-teous-ness As clear-ly as the light,

Do not be en-vi-ous of those Who do in-iq-ui-ty.
Be set-tled in the land and choose To live in faith-ful-ness.
And show the jus-tice of your cause Like noon-day shin-ing bright.

²For they like grass will quick-ly change, Will with-er and de-cay.
⁴En-joy the LORD and He will give Your heart's de-sire to you.
⁷Be-fore the LORD be still and wait, For Him wait ear-nest-ly.

Just like a green and ten-der plant They soon will fade a-way.
⁵Com-mit your path-way to the LORD; Trust Him; He will be true.
Do not let schem-ers an-ger you With their pros-per-i-ty.

4. ⁸Let anger cease to be in you,
And turn away from wrath.
For only evil will result
With anger's aftermath.
⁹For evildoers will not last;
Cut off, they cannot stand.
But those whose hope is in the LORD,
These will possess the land.

5. ¹⁰And so in just a little while
The wicked will not be.
You may seek out where once he lived,
But him you will not see.
¹¹As for the humble patient ones,
The land they will possess,
And there will savor the delights
Of peaceful blessedness.

D. Bruce Martin, 1929

REWARD CMD

37B
Psalm 37:12-22

Wicked Men Against the Righteous

*Let him show by good conduct that his works are done
in the meekness of wisdom.* —James 3:13

6. ¹² Wick - ed men a - gainst the righ - teous Plot and
7. ¹⁶ Bet - ter is the just one's pit - tance, Than the
8. ²⁰ Flow - ers fill the fields, then with - er; Smoke may

gnash their teeth at him. ¹³ But the Lord laughs at the
wick - ed's man - y gains. ¹⁷ Wick - ed arms will soon be
rise, but quick - ly clear. So will all the wick - ed

wick - ed, Know - ing that his day will come.
bro - ken, But the LORD the just sus - tains.
per - ish, And the LORD's foes dis - ap - pear.

¹⁴ Swords and bows the wick - ed read - y To de -
¹⁸ Days of blame - less men the LORD knows, And their
²¹ Sin - ners bor - row, not re - turn - ing, While the

stroy the poor and just. [15] But their bows will all be
her - i - tage en - dures. [19] Un - a - shamed in times of
righ - teous free - ly give. [22] Those He bless - es, earth in -

bro - ken, In their hearts their swords be thrust.
e - vil, They in fam - ine feast se - cure.
her - it; Those He curs - es will not live.

Luxemburg Kyriale, 1768   OMNI DIE 87.87 D

37C

Psalm 37:23-31

Steps a Man Takes

Indeed we count them blessed who endure....
The Lord is very compassionate and merciful. —James 5:11

9. ²³Steps a man takes are es-tab-lished By the
10. ²⁶His de-scen-dants are a bless-ing; Through the
11. ²⁹In the land the righ-teous set-tle, Dwell-ing

LORD for His de-light. ²⁴If he stum-bles, he'll not
day he lends and gives. ²⁷Turn from e-vil; prac-tice
in it end-less-ly, For the whole land in the

fall down, By the LORD his hand's held tight.
good-ness That you may for-ev-er live.
fu-ture Their in-her-i-tance shall be.

²⁵Though once young, I am quite old now, Yet through-
²⁸For the LORD, who loves true jus-tice, Will not
³⁰Words of wis-dom speaks the righ-teous, Jus-tice

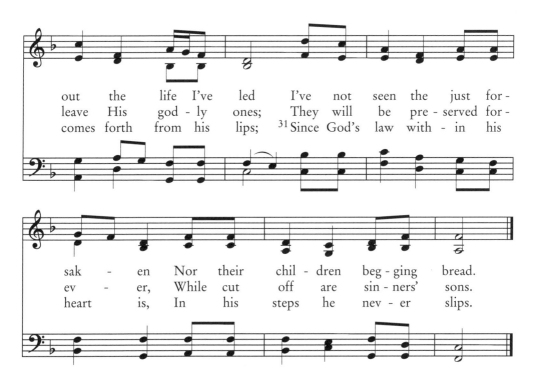

out the life I've led I've not seen the just for-
leave His god - ly ones; They will be pre - served for-
comes forth from his lips; ³¹ Since God's law with - in his

sak - en Nor their chil - dren beg - ging bread.
ev - er, While cut off are sin - ners' sons.
heart is, In his steps he nev - er slips.

The Sacred Harp, 1844; harm. Covenant Press, 1972   BEACH SPRING 87.87 D

37D Though the Wicked Hound the Righteous

Psalm 37:32-40

You also be patient. Establish your hearts,
for the coming of the Lord is at hand. —James 5:8

12. ³² Though the wick - ed hound the righ - teous
13. ³⁴ Wait up - on the LORD ex - pec - tant,
14. ³⁵ I have seen the ruth - less flour - ish

And his life they seek to end, ³³ In their hands the
Walk the way of His com - mand; As earth's heir He
Like a tree in fer - tile ground. ³⁶ But he passed on,

LORD won't leave him, He'll not let him be con - demned.
will ex - alt you, You will see the wick - ed banned.
gone for - ev - er; Though I searched, he was not found.

15. ³⁷ See the blameless; watch the upright,
   For his future there is peace.
   ³⁸ But all sinners face destruction;
   Future hopes for them will cease.

16. ³⁹ By the LORD the just are rescued;
   He's their strength in troubled days.
   ⁴⁰ From the wicked He delivers;
   All who trust the LORD He saves.

S.A. Sterrett Metheny, 1910

COMPASSION 87.87

Lord, Do Not in Hot Displeasure Speak

And behold, a leper came and worshiped Him, saying,
"Lord, if you are willing, You can make me clean." — Matthew 8:2

38A

Psalm 38:1-8

1. [1] LORD, do not in hot dis - pleas - ure
2. [2] For Your hand up - on me press - es;
3. [4] For my man - i - fold trans - gres - sions

Speak in stern re - proof to me;
Deep Your ar - rows sink with - in.
Have gone up a - bove my head;

Let Your chas - t'ning be in meas - ure,
[3] Wrath my flesh and bones dis - tress - es,
Like a bur - den, their op - pres - sions

And Your stroke from an - ger free.
Gives no rest be - cause of sin.
Weigh me down with con - stant dread.

4. [5] Loathsome are my wounds neglected;
My own folly makes it so;
[6] Bowed with pain, with grief dejected,
All day long I mourning go.

5. [7] For my loins are filled with burning;
There's no soundness in my flesh.
[8] Feeble, crushed, I'm ever groaning
In my spirit's restlessness.

John B. Dykes, 1862

ST. SYLVESTER 87.87

38B

Psalm 38:9-14

My Desire and Ceaseless Wailing

And they lifted up their voices and said,
"Jesus, Master, have mercy on us!" — Luke 17:13

6. ⁹My de - sire and cease - less wail - ing,
7. ¹¹Friends and loved ones whom I cher - ish
8. ¹²They who for my life are seek - ing,
9. ¹³I am like one deaf and speech - less,

Lord, un - veiled be - fore You lie.
From my plague now stand a - loof.
For me snares in se - cret lay,
I am mute, and nev - er speak.

¹⁰My heart throbs; my strength is fail - ing;
My own kins - men, though I per - ish,
Hurt - ful things a - gainst me speak - ing,
¹⁴I'm as one their words not hear - ing,

All the light has left my eye.
Come no more be - neath my roof.
Plots de - vis - ing through the day.
No de - fense my mouth will make.

Traditional Russian melody; arr. Brian E. Coombs, 2001

KATUSHKA 87.87

You, O Lord, I Have Been Trusting

38C

Psalm 38:15-22

Then Jesus answered and said to her, "O woman,
great is your faith! Let it be to you as you desire." —Matthew 15:28

10. 15 You, O Lord, I have been trust - ting;
11. 17 For I am a - bout to stum - ble;
12. 19 Great in num - ber, full of vig - or,
13. 21 Lord, I pray, do not for - sake me;

Lord, my God, You'll an - swer me 16 Lest they gloat and
Grief has ev - er with me been. 18 I in - iq - ui -
Strong the foes who me with-stood! 20 E - vil they for
O my God, stay near to me. 22 Hur - ry! Come at

start re - joic - ing, When my slip - ping feet they see.
ty ac - knowl-edge; Deep - ly troub - led by my sin.
kind - ness ren - der, Hat - ing me for do - ing good.
once to help me! O my Lord, my Sav - ior be!

Lowell Mason, 1792–1872

MOUNT VERNON 87.87

39A

Psalm 39:1-6

I Said, "I Will Keep Watch"

Let your speech always be with grace, seasoned with salt.
—Colossians 4:6

1. ¹I said, "I will keep watch and guard my ways,
2. ²Si - lent, I ceased from speak-ing e - ven good;
3. ⁴"LORD, make me know my end, my num-bered days;
4. Each man at best is but a fleet - ing breath.

And I will keep my tongue from sin - ful stain.
My heart with - in was hot, my sor - row stirred.
And let me know how fleet - ing is my life;
⁶Man, like a shad - ow, wan - ders to and fro;

As with a bri - dle I will keep my mouth,
³And while I mused a fire be - gan to burn;
⁵For You have made my days a hand-breadth long;
Sure - ly an up - roar he cre - ates in vain;

While in my pres - ence wick - ed men re - main."
Then with my tongue I spoke this ear - nest word:
My life - time is as noth - ing in Your sight.
He nev - er knows to whom his rich - es go."

James Langran, 1861

LANGRAN 10.10.10.10

And Now, O Lord

Nevertheless you have done well that you shared in my distress.
—Philippians 4:14

5. ⁷ "And now, O Lord, what am I wait-ing for?
6. ⁹ I held my tongue; I o-pened not my mouth,
7. ¹¹ With Your re-bukes You chas-ten man for sin;
8. ¹² LORD, hear my prayer, and heed my cry and tears;

My ex-pec-ta-tion You have sure-ly been.
For this af-flic-tion came at Your com-mand.
His beau-ty fades be-neath the touch of death.
I am Your pil-grim as my fa-thers were.

⁸ De-liv-er me from all my sin-ful-ness,
¹⁰ But now re-move Your plague a-way from me;
You, like a moth, con-sume his pre-cious things;
¹³ O turn Your gaze, let me be glad a-gain,

O make me not the scorn of fool-ish men.
I am con-sumed be-neath Your chas-t'ning hand.
Oh, sure-ly ev-er-y man is but a breath.
Be-fore I go a-way and am no more."

William H. Monk, 1861   EVENTIDE 10.10.10.10

40A

Psalm 40:1-9

I Waited for the LORD

Who shall separate us from the love of Christ? Shall tribulation, or distress, or persecution, or famine, or nakedness, or peril, or sword?" —Romans 8:35

1. ¹ I wait-ed for the LORD; He stooped and heard my cry.
2. Man-y will see with awe, And so will trust the LORD.
3. ⁶ You seek no of-fer-ing, De-sire no sac-ri-fice;
4. ⁸ To do Your will, O God, Is sure-ly my de-light;

²He brought me from a pit, Out of the dun-geon mire,
⁴Blessed he who trusts the LORD, And turns not to false men.
But You have giv-en me An o-pened, read-y ear.
Your law is part of me, Set deep with-in my heart."

My feet set on a rock, My foot-steps made se-cure.
⁵LORD, none com-pares to You, Your thoughts and works, my God!
You seek no of-f'rings burnt, Nor sac-ri-fice for sin.
⁹Good news I have pro-claimed, De-clared Your righ-teous-ness

³My lips He gave a song, A song to praise our God.
Should I de-clare each one, Their num-ber is too great.
⁷I said, "Be-hold I come, As in the book fore-told.
In the as-sem-bly great; You know, LORD, I spoke out.

Traditional Irish melody; arr. Leopold L. Dix, 1933

FINGAL 66.66 D

I Hid Not in My Heart

He trusted in God; let Him deliver Him now if He will have
Him; for He said, "I am the Son of God." — Matthew 27:43

40B
Psalm 40:10-17

5. ¹⁰I hid not in my heart Your truth and sav-ing help;
6. ¹²E-vils too great to count Have tak-en hold of me.
7. ¹³Come to my res-cue, LORD; O LORD, make haste to help.
8. ¹⁶Let all those seek-ing You Glad-ly re-joice in You,

In the as-sem-bly great I preached Your faith-ful-ness.
My sins close in on me So that I can-not see.
¹⁴Let all who seek my life Be shamed and be con-fused.
Who Your sal-va-tion love Say, "Glo-ry to the LORD!"

¹¹You'll not with-hold from me Your ten-der mer-cies, LORD;
They are more nu-mer-ous Than hairs up-on my head.
Let them fall back in shame Who want to see my hurt.
¹⁷May the Lord think of me; I suf-fer pain and want.

And Your un-fail-ing love Will ev-er keep me safe.
My heart now fails in me; My cour-age melts a-way.
¹⁵Let them be put to shame Who taunt and jeer at me.
My Help, my Sav-ior, come! My God, do not de-lay!

Traditional Spanish melody; arr. David Evans, 1927   MADRID 66.66 D

41A How Blessed the Man Who Guides the Poor

Psalm 41:1-6

For your sakes He became poor, that you
through His poverty might become rich. — 2 Corinthians 8:9

1. [1] How blessed the man who guides the poor By coun-sel strong and clear;
2. [3] The LORD sus-tains him on his bed Of sick-ness and of pain.
3. [5] My foes speak e-vil things of me And to each oth-er say,

The LORD will sure-ly res-cue him When e-vil days draw near.
And from his bed You make him rise; He will his health re-gain.
"When will he die; when will his name Com-plete-ly pass a-way?"

[2] The LORD will guard him in the land; His life is blessed in-deed;
[4] Now as for me, I said, "O LORD, Have mer-cy on my soul.
[6] And when he comes to vis-it me His words are all de-ceit;

Nor will You let him fall be-fore His ad-ver-sar-ies' greed.
Be-cause a-gainst You I have sinned, Re-store and make me whole."
He gath-ers e-vil in his heart, And tells it in the street.

Lucy Broadwood; harm. Ralph Vaughan-Williams, 1906

KINGSFOLD CMD

All Those Who Hate Me

41B

Psalm 41:7-13

We are hard pressed on every side, yet not crushed;
we are perplexed, but not in despair. —2 Corinthians 4:8

4. [7] All those who hate me whis-per ill, A - gainst me harm de - vise:
5. [10] But You, O LORD, be mer - ci - ful, Be gra - cious, make me strong;
6. [12] But as for me, You hold me up In my in - teg - ri - ty;

[8] "An e - vil scourge has come on him; Brought down he will not rise."
O raise me up so that I may Re - pay them for their wrong.
And in Your pres - ence ev - er-more My dwell-ing place shall be.

[9] And e - ven my fa - mil-iar friend, In whom my trust was real,
[11] My foes do not a - gainst me lift A cry of vic - to - ry;
[13] The LORD, the God of Is - ra - el, Be blessed and blessed a - gain

The one who ate my bread has turned, And lift - ed up his heel.
Be - cause of this I am as-sured That You are pleased with me.
From age to ev - er - last-ing age. A - men, and yes, A - men.

Franki Fuhrman, 2002

DONNELLY CMD

41C
Psalm 41:13

Book One Doxology

And the glory which You gave Me I have given them,
that they may be one just as We are one. —John 17:22

¹³Bless - ed be the LORD, the God of Is - ra -
el, from ev - er - last - ing to ev - er -
last - ing. A - men and A - men!

Eleanor Hutcheson, 1972

ALPHA (Irr.)

As Pants the Deer

You would have asked Him,
and He would have given you living water. —John 4:10

42A
Psalm 42:1-5

1. ¹ As pants the deer for wa-ter brooks, So pants my soul for
2. ⁴ My soul's poured out as I re-call How to God's house I

You, O God. ² I thirst for God, the liv-ing God;
led the crowds With joy-ful songs to keep the feast.

When will I see the face of God? ³ Tears are my food both
⁵ My soul, why so cast down, dis-turbed? Hope now in God; I'll

day and night. All day men say, "Where is your God?"
praise Him still. He is my help. He is my God.

Henry F. Hemy, 1864; arr. James G. Walton, 1874

ST. CATHERINE 888.888

42B

My God, My Soul Is in Despair

"He saved others, but He cannot save Himself."
— Matthew 27:42

Psalm 42:6-11

3. [6] My God, my soul is in de-spair; I there-fore will re-
4. [8] The LORD sends forth His love by day, At night His song will
5. [10] As if to shat-ter all my bones, My foes have cut me

mem - ber You From lands where riv-er Jor - dan flows From
be with me, My prayer to God who makes me live. [9] Then
with their words. All day they scoff, "Where is your God?" [11] O

Her-mon's peaks and Mi - zar's hill. [7] There deep calls deep, Your
I will say to God my Rock: "Did You for - get? Why
why, my soul, do you de - spair? Hope now in God, I'll

wa - ter-falls, There all Your waves rolled o - ver me.
must I mourn Be - cause I see the foe op-press?"
praise Him still. He is my Help. He is my God.

French Plainsong (Processionale), 13th cent.; arr. Thomas Helmore, 1856   VENI EMMANUEL 888.888

As Deer for Streams, I Pant for God

42C

Psalm 42:1-5

The water I give him will become in him a spring of living water,
welling up to eternal life. —John 4:14

1. ¹As deer for streams, I pant for God; I pant for
2. ³In stead-y streams, tears from my eyes Have been my
3. ⁴My yearn-ing soul turns to the past; To keep the
4. ⁵O why, my soul, do you grow ill? And why are

You so long-ing - ly. ²I thirst for God, the liv-ing
food each night and day; While those a-round, with mock-ing
feast I led the crowd. Up to God's house we'd come at
you cast down in me? Hope now in God. I'll praise Him

God; How long un - til God's face I see?
cries, "Where is your God?" to me they say.
last; With joy - ful thanks we'd shout a - loud.
still, My help - er and my God is He.

Appalachian Folk melody; arr. Brian E. Coombs, 2001

APPALACHIA LM

42D
Psalm 42:6-11

O God, My Soul Is in Despair

"He trusts in God; let God rescue Him now, if He will have Him."
— Matthew 27:43

5. [6] O God, my soul is in de-spair; So I re-mem-ber You
6. [8] The LORD com-mands His stead-fast love To be with me each day;
7. [10] As if to shat-ter all my bones My ad-ver-sar-ies say,

From Jor-dan's land, from Miz-ar's hill, And from Mount Her-mon too.
By night His song will be with me; To God, my Life, I'll pray.
"O tell us now, where is your God?" They taunt me all the day.

[7] Your wa-ter-falls, like thun-der, roar And deep to deep will call.
[9] I say to God, my on-ly rock, "O why for-get me so?
[11] O why, my soul, do you de-spair? Why so dis-cour-aged be?

Your waves have all rolled o-ver me; On me Your break-ers fall.
Why must I grieve at all the harm Com-mit-ted by the foe?"
Hope now in God, I'll praise Him still. My help, my God is He.

Lori McCracken, 2000

STEADFAST CMD

Before a Wicked Nation, God

We have an altar from which those who minister in the tabernacle have no right to eat. —Hebrews 13:10

43A
Psalm 43

1. [1] Be - fore a wick - ed na - tion, God, My
2. [2] For You are God who gives me strength; Why
3. [3] O send Your light forth and Your truth, And

in - no - cence de - fend; O vin - di - cate and
have You cast me off? Why must I go a -
let them be my guide, To lead me to Your

res - cue me From cruel, de - ceit - ful men.
bout in grief While foes op - press and scoff?
ho - ly hill, The place where You a - bide.

4. [4] Then to God's altar I will go,
   To God my boundless joy;
   And in Your praise, O God, my God,
   The harp I will employ.

5. [5] O why are you cast down, my soul?
   Why so discouraged be?
   Hope now in God, I'll praise Him still.
   My help, my God is He.

Carl G. Glaser, 1839

AZMON CM

43B

Psalm 43

O Vindicate Me

...So that you may eat and drink at My table in My kingdom.
—*Luke 22:30*

1. ¹O vin-di-cate me, plead my cause A-gainst a thank-less na-tion, God; From him who works de-ceit-ful-ly To bring a-bout his un-just ends, Now grant de-liv-er-ance to me. ²You are the God who gives me strength.

2. Why have You now a-ban-doned me? Griev-ing, op-pressed by en-e-mies, Send out Your light and truth to me ³That they may clear-ly guide my way, To lead me to Your ho-ly hill And to Your dwell-ing plac-es there.

3. ⁴Then I will to God's al-tar go, To God, the great-est of my joys. With harp I'll praise You, God, my God. ⁵My soul, why so cast down, dis-turbed? Hope now in God. I'll praise Him still. He is my help. He is my God.

Joseph Barnby, 1871

ST. CHRYSOSTOM 888.888

O God, We Have Heard of Your Works

44A

Psalm 44:1-8

They took the land from the nations God drove out before them.
—Acts 7:45

1. ¹O God, we have heard of Your works with our ears;
2. ³Suc - cess did not come from the sword in their hand,
3. ⁴O God, You a - lone are for - ev - er my King;
4. ⁶No trust will I place in my sword or my bow.

Our fa - thers have told what You did in past years:
Nor by their arm's strength did they con - quer the land.
Com - mand, and for Ja - cob de - liv - er - ance bring.
⁷⁻⁸We'll boast in the God who saved us from the foe;

²How na - tions were crushed and cast out by Your hand;
But rath - er it was by the light of Your face,
⁵Through You we will sure - ly push back all our foes,
All those hat - ing us You have brought down in shame,

You plant - ed our fa - thers to live in the land.
Your right hand and arm, for You showed them Your grace.
Through Your name we'll tram - ple on those who op - pose.
And so we will ev - er give thanks to Your name.

Traditional American melody; harm. Carlton R. Young, b. 1926

FOUNDATION 11.11.11.11

44B

But You Have Forsaken

Psalm 44:9-19

"I find no basis for a charge against this man."
—Luke 23:4

5. ⁹ But You have for-sak-en, to shame brought our boasts;
6. ¹¹ You sell us like sheep to be slaugh-tered for food,
7. ¹³ You make all our neigh-bors re-proach us in pride,
8. ¹⁵ Now all the day long I be-hold my dis-grace,
9. ¹⁷ This came on us but we did not for-get You;

No more in-to bat-tle You go with our hosts.
A-mong all the na-tions dis-persed and pur-sued.
And cause those a-round us to scoff and de-ride.
And feel deep with-in me the shame of my face.
But al-ways have been to Your cov-e-nant true.

¹⁰ You make us turn back from our foes in dis-may,
¹² In sell-ing Your peo-ple, no pay-ment You sought;
¹⁴ Our name a-mong na-tions a by-word You've made;
¹⁶ Be-cause the blas-phem-er and scof-fer I hear,
¹⁸ Our heart is not turned, and our steps have not strayed,

And spoil-ers who hate us have made us their prey.
Their price to Your treas-'ry no prof-it has brought.
The peo-ple all laugh at us, shak-ing their head.
As foe and a-ven-ger be-fore me ap-pear.
¹⁹ Though crushed a-mong ru-ins and un-der death's shade.

Traditional Welsh melody

MALDWYN 11.11.11.11

If We Have Forgotten

*In all these things we are more than conquerors
through Him who loved us. —Romans 8:37*

10. 20 If we have for-got-ten the name of our God,
11. 22 Through-out all the day for Your sake we're con-sumed;
12. 24 O why are You hid-ing the light of Your face,

Or have to an i-dol our hands spread a-broad,
We're count-ed as sheep that to slaugh-ter are doomed.
For-get-ting the bur-den and grief of our race?

21 Would God not search out and un-cov-er this sin?
23 O why are You sleep-ing? A-rouse Your-self, Lord!
25 Our flesh turns to clay and our soul sinks to dust.

For He knows each heart and the se-crets with-in.
A-wake! Do not leave us for-ev-er ig-nored.
26 O help us! Re-deem us! In Your love we trust.

S.A. Sterrett Metheny, 1910

DOMINUS REGIT ME 11.11.11.11

45A

My Heart Is Stirred

Hallelujah! For the Lord God Almighty reigns.
—Revelation 19:6

Psalm 45:1-7

1. ¹ My heart is stirred and o - ver - flows; Up - on a
2. ³ O might - y One, strap on Your sword And clothe Your-
3. ⁶ O God, the throne on which You rule En - dures to

no - ble theme I sing, And, like a skill - ful
self with maj - es - ty! ⁴ For meek - ness, truth and
all e - ter - ni - ty; The scep - ter of Your

writ - er's pen, My tongue will speak a - bout the King.
righ - teous - ness, Go forth and ride to vic - to - ry!
king - dom is A scep - ter of in - teg - ri - ty.

² You are, a - mong the sons of men, By far the
Your right hand teach - es awe - some deeds. ⁵ Be - neath You
⁷ You love the cause of righ - teous - ness, But wick - ed-

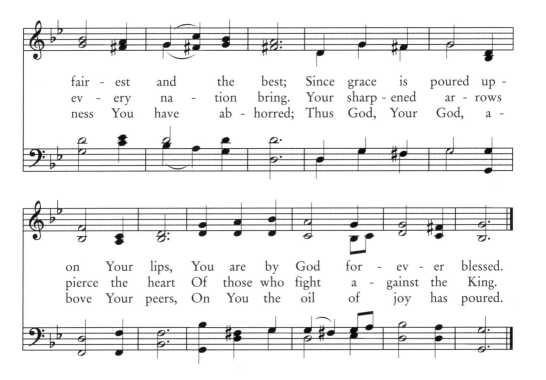

fair - est and the best; Since grace is poured up -
ev - ery na - tion bring. Your sharp - ened ar - rows
ness You have ab - horred; Thus God, Your God, a -

on Your lips, You are by God for - ev - er blessed.
pierce the heart Of those who fight a - gainst the King.
bove Your peers, On You the oil of joy has poured.

Joseph Parry, 1870   MERTHYR TYDFIL LMD

45B   My Heart Is Greatly Stirred

Psalm 45:1-9

Your throne, O God, will last forever and ever.
—Hebrews 1:8

1. [1] My heart is great-ly stirred, I sing a no-ble theme;
2. [3] O War-rior, take Your sword In splen-did maj-es-ty!
3. [6] Your throne, O God, will last For-ev-er, ev-er-more.
4. [8] Your gar-ments are per-fumed With cas-sia, al-oes, myrrh;

My tongue's a skill-ful writ-er's pen To speak a-bout the King.
[4] For meek-ness, truth, and righ-teous-ness— Ride on in vic-to-ry.
The scep-ter of Your king-dom is A scep-ter that is just.
From pal-ac-es of i-vo-ry Stringed mu-sic makes You glad.

[2] Most beau-ti-ful of men, Your lips are full of grace;
Your right hand makes You feared. [5] How sharp Your ar-rows are;
[7] For You loved righ-teous-ness And hat-ed wick-ed-ness;
[9] King's daugh-ters take their place Where no-ble-wo-men stand;

And there-fore God be-stowed on You A bless-ing ev-er-more.
They pierce the King's foes to the heart. Be-neath you na-tions fall.
A-bove all oth-ers, God, Your God, A-noint-ed You with joy.
The queen, ar-rayed in O-phir gold, Is there at Your right hand.

Peter LaTrobe, 1795–1863   FAIRFIELD SMD

Daughter, Incline Your Ear

*Blessed are those who are called to the marriage supper
of the Lamb! —Revelation 19:9*

45C
Psalm 45:10-17

5. ^{10}Daugh-ter, in-cline your ear, Con-si-der well my call:
6. ^{12}Tyre's daugh-ter has ar-rived, A cost-ly gift has brought;
7. ^{14}In her em-broi-dered gown She's tak-en to the King;
8. ^{16}Then in your fa-thers' place Your chil-dren all will stand,

Put out of mind your fa-ther's house, For-get your peo-ple all.
And by the wealth-y of the land Your fa-vor now is sought.
To You her maid-en friends are brought, Com-pan-ions fol-low-ing.
And you will make them princ-es then To rule through-out the land.

^{11}Your beau-ty then the King With great de-light will see;
^{13}The prin-cess now a-waits, Most glo-rious to be-hold,
^{15}With glad-ness they are led, As peo-ple cel-e-brate;
^{17}I'll cause your name to be In ev-ery age re-nowned,

Be-cause He is your Lord, bow down Be-fore Him rev-'rent-ly.
And wo-ven all through-out her gown Are threads of pre-cious gold.
They all ap-proach the King with joy With-in His pal-ace gate.
And so from peo-ples ev-er-more Your prais-es will a-bound.

George J. Elvey, 1868

DIADEMATA SMD

46A
God Is Our Refuge and Our Strength

Psalm 46

*The kingdom of this world has become the kingdom
of our Lord and of His Christ. —Revelation 11:15*

1. ¹God is our ref-uge and our strength, In trials, a prov-en aid.
2. ⁴A riv-er makes God's cit-y glad, The Most High's ho-ly place.
3. ⁸O come! See what the LORD has done: He made earth des-o-late.

²And there-fore, though the earth should change, We will not be a-fraid
⁵God is in her; she won't be moved; God helps at break of day.
⁹He made wars cease, broke bow and spear; He burned the char-i-ot.

Though hills may slide in - to the sea, ³And waves crash down and roar,
⁶ When na-tions rage, then king-doms fall; But when He speaks, earth melts.
¹⁰ "Be still," He says, "Know I am God, Ex - alt - ed o - ver all."

And though the o-cean's rage may shake The moun-tains on the shore.
⁷The LORD of Ar-mies is with us; Our rock is Ja-cob's God.
¹¹The LORD of Ar-mies is with us; Our rock is Ja-cob's God.

William B. Bradbury. 1816–1868

PINNEO CMD

God Is Our Refuge and Our Strength

If God is for us, who is against us?
— Romans 8:31

46B
Psalm 46

1. ¹God is our ref-uge and our strength, In trials, a prov-en aid.
2. ⁴A riv-er makes God's cit-y glad, The Most High's ho-ly place.
3. ⁸O come! See what the LORD has done: He made earth des-o-late.

2 And there-fore, though the earth should change, We will not be a-fraid
5 God is in her; she won't be moved; God helps at break of day.
9 He made wars cease, broke bow and spear; He burned the char-i-ot.

Though hills may slide in-to the sea, 3And waves crash down and roar,
6 When na-tions rage, then king-doms fall; But when He speaks, earth melts.
10 "Be still," He says, "Know I am God, Ex-alt-ed o-ver all."

And though the o-cean's rage may shake The moun-tains on the shore.
7 The LORD of Ar-mies is with us; Our rock is Ja-cob's God.
11 The LORD of Ar-mies is with us; Our rock is Ja-cob's God.

John K. Robb, 1949

SCOTT CMD

46C
Psalm 46

God Is Our Refuge and Our Strength

The angel showed me the river of the water of life...flowing from the throne of God and of the Lamb. —Revelation 22:1

1. [1] God is our ref - uge and our strength,
2. [4] A riv - er brings re - fresh - ing streams
3. [8] O come, see what the LORD has done:

A pres - ent help in our dis - tress.
To cheer the cit - y of our God,
He des - o - la - tions brought on earth;

[2] We will not there - fore be a - fraid
The Most High's ho - ly dwell - ing place.
[9] On earth He puts an end to wars,

Though all the earth should be re - moved,
[5] God is in her; she won't be moved;
Breaks bow and spear, and char - iots burns.

Though moun - tains great be hurled In -
At dawn will great God help her. 6 The
10 Be still! Know I am God. Ex -

to the o - cean's depths, 3 Though seas may
na - tions rage; realms quake; He lifts His
alt - ed o'er all men, Ex - alt - ed

roar and foam And bil - lows shake the shore,
voice; earth melts. 7 The LORD of hosts with us!
o'er all earth. 11 The LORD of hosts with us!

Though moun - tains trem - ble at their pow'r.
Our for - tress strong is Ja - cob's God.
Our for - tress strong is Ja - cob's God.

Martin Luther, 1529   EIN' FESTE BURG 88.88.66.668

47A
Psalm 47

All Nations, Clap Your Hands

He seated Him on the throne in the heavenly realms.
—Ephesians 1:20

1. 1 All na-tions, clap your hands for joy; To God lift shouts and sing!
2. 4 The land of our in-her-i-tance He choos-es out for us,
3. 7 For God is King of all the earth; Sing praise with skill-ful-ness.

2 For awe-some is the LORD Most High, A-bove all earth great King!
And He to us the glo-ry gives Of Ja-cob whom He loves.
8 God rules the na-tions, God sits on His throne of ho-li-ness.

3 He brings the peo-ples un-der us, With mas-ter-y com-plete;
5 God has as-cend-ed with a shout, The LORD with trum-pet-ing.
9 The princ-es of the peo-ples join As men of Abr-'ham's God—

And He it is who na-tions all Sub-dues be-neath our feet.
6 Sing praise to God, sing praise, sing praise, Sing prais-es to our King.
The shields of earth be-long to Him; Ex-alt-ed high is God.

Clement W. Poole, 1875

PETERSHAM CMD

All Nations, Clap Your Hands

47B
Psalm 47

God placed all things under His feet.
—Ephesians 1:22

1. ¹All na - tions, clap your hands and shout;
2. ³He has sub - dued be - neath our feet
3. ⁵God has as - cend - ed with a shout!

To God with joy - ful voic - es sing!
The na - tions who were once our foes.
The LORD a - midst the trum - pet's ring.

²For awe - some is the LORD Most High,
⁴And Ja - cob's glo - ry, whom He loves,
⁶Sing praise! Sing prais - es un - to God!

Who o - ver all the earth is King.
We now in - her - it as He chose.
Sing praise! Sing prais - es to our King!

4. ⁷For God is King of all the earth;
   Sing praises with a skillful tone.
   ⁸God rules the nations from on high;
   God sits upon His holy throne.

5. ⁹Leaders of nations join themselves,
   As those of Abr'ham's God they come,
   Because earth's shields belong to God;
   He is the great exalted One.

Thomas Williams, *Psalmodia Evangelica*, 1789   TRURO LM

48A

The Lord Is Great

Who shall separate us from the love of God?
— Romans 8:35

Psalm 48:1-8

1. ¹The Lord is great, great praise de - serv - ing
2. Mount Zi - on is the great King's cit - y
3. ⁴When kings ad - vanced to fight, ⁵they saw it;

With - in the cit - y of our God;
And heav - en's one true moun - tain height;
Be - hold, it filled them with dis - may;

²His ho - ly hill, raised up in beau - ty,
³With - in her pal - ac - es is safe - ty,
And in their pan - ic and a - maze - ment

Brings joy to all the earth a - broad.
For God pro - tects her by His might.
They turned a - round and ran a - way.

4. ⁶And at that place, like one in labor,
They shook, for they with fear were seized.
⁷You are the One who ships from Tarshish
Destroys by wind sent from the east.

5. ⁸What we had heard of our God's city,
We now have seen and know for sure,
The city of the Lord of Armies,
Which God forever makes secure.

Clement Cotterill Scholefield, 1839–1904

ST. CLEMENT 98.98

The Lord Is Great

He who sits on the throne will spread His tent over them.
—Revelation 7:15

48B

Psalm 48:1-8

1. ¹ The LORD is great, and so His praise Should be pro-claimed a-broad
2. ³ Well known a-mong her pal-ac-es, God is her ref-uge strong.
3. ⁶ With fear and an-guish they were seized, As one whom birth pains take;

With-in His hill of ho-li-ness, The cit-y of our God.
⁴ Be-hold, when kings joined forc-es there, To-geth-er they passed on.
⁷ And You with wind out of the east, The ships of Tar-shish break.

² Mount Zi-on's beau-ty is raised high, Earth joys on her ac-count.
⁵ For what they saw left them a-mazed And filled with deep dis-may;
⁸ As we have heard, we've seen with-in God's cit-y most se-cure;

It is the cit-y of our King, The one true heav'n-ly mount.
So trou-bled were they at the sight They turned and ran a-way.
The cit-y of the LORD of hosts, Our God keeps ev-er-more.

Gottfried W. Fink, 1842; arr. Arthur S. Sullivan

BETHLEHEM CMD

48C
Psalm 48:9-14

Within Your Temple

I saw the Holy City, the new Jerusalem,
coming down out of heaven from God. —Revelation 21:2

4. ⁹With - in Your tem - ple we have thought Up - on Your love, O
5. Your right hand holds all righ - teous - ness. ¹¹Mount Zi - on's joy be
6. ¹²En - cir - cle Zi - on, walk a - bout, And mark her tow - ers
7. Thus you may gen - er - a - tions tell, For what a God is

God. ¹⁰As is Your name, O God, Your praise Is
great! Let Ju - dah's daugh - ters joy - ful - ly Your
well; ¹³Con - sid - er her pro - tec - tive walls, Be -
He! ¹⁴He is our God for ev - er - more, Who

spread through earth a - broad. As is Your name,
judg - ments cel - e - brate. Let Ju - dah's daugh -
hold her cit - a - dels. Con - sid - er her
guides e - ter - nal - ly. He is our God

O God, Your praise Is spread through earth a - broad.
ters joy - ful - ly Your judg - ments cel - e - brate.
pro - tec - tive walls, Be - hold her cit - a - dels.
for ev - er - more, Who guides e - ter - nal - ly.

Lowell Mason, 1837

ZERAH CM

Hear This, All Earth's Nations

Do not store up for yourselves treasures on earth.
—Matthew 6:19

49A
Psalm 49:1-15

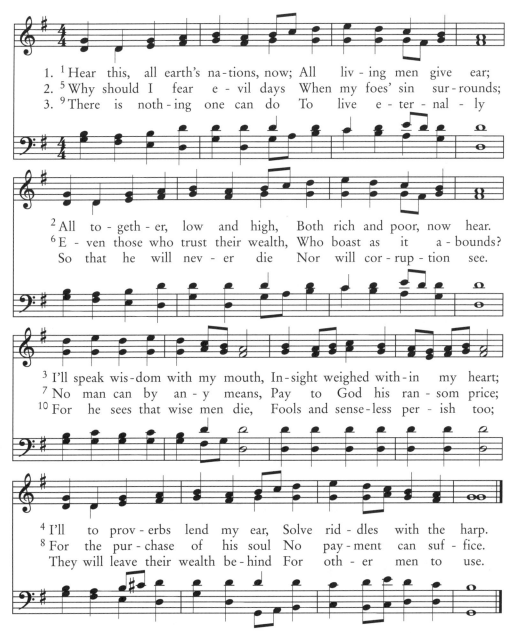

1. ¹Hear this, all earth's na-tions, now; All liv-ing men give ear;
2. ⁵Why should I fear e-vil days When my foes' sin sur-rounds;
3. ⁹There is noth-ing one can do To live e-ter-nal-ly

²All to-geth-er, low and high, Both rich and poor, now hear.
⁶E-ven those who trust their wealth, Who boast as it a-bounds?
So that he will nev-er die Nor will cor-rup-tion see.

³I'll speak wis-dom with my mouth, In-sight weighed with-in my heart;
⁷No man can by an-y means, Pay to God his ran-som price;
¹⁰For he sees that wise men die, Fools and sense-less per-ish too;

⁴I'll to prov-erbs lend my ear, Solve rid-dles with the harp.
⁸For the pur-chase of his soul No pay-ment can suf-fice.
They will leave their wealth be-hind For oth-er men to use.

4. ¹¹Yet they think within themselves
   Their homes will always be;
   By their names they call their lands,
   So every age will see.
   ¹²But man's honor will not last;
   Like the beasts, he too will end.
   ¹³Thus will be the way of fools
   And those who them commend.

5. ¹⁴Just like sheep, their destiny
   Will be within the grave;
   Death's their shepherd, just men rule
   O'er them with each new day.
   And the grave consumes their strength;
   It no habitation leaves.
   ¹⁵Yet will God redeem my soul,
   From death's grip me receives.

Freylinghausen Gesangbüch, 1704; arr. John Wesley, 1742   AMSTERDAM 76.76.77.76

49B
Psalm 49:16-20

Let No Fear Disturb Your Peace

You fool! This night your very life will be demanded of you.
— Luke 12:20

6. ¹⁶Let no fear dis - turb your peace
7. ¹⁸Though through - out the time he lives,
8. ¹⁹To his fa - thers he will go,

When one's house and wealth in - crease;
To him - self he prais - es gives—
Where the eye no light will know.

¹⁷All his glo - ry death will end;
And though men will praise you too,
²⁰Man with hon - or, yet not wise,

With him noth - ing will de - scend.
When good things for self you do—
Like the beasts that per - ish, dies.

Attributed to Martin Herbst, *Nürnbergisches Gesangbüch*, 1676   AUS DER TIEFE (Heinlein) 77.77

God, Most Supreme in Might

The Judge is standing at the door.
—James 5:9

1. ¹ God, Most Su - preme in might, The One who
2. ² From Zi - on, beau - ti - ful, God shines forth
3. ⁴ Fire burns at His ap - proach, And storms a -

is the LORD, As - sem - bles earth from
glo - rious - ly. ³ Our God most sure - ly
round Him rage; He sum - mons heav'n and

east to west By His own spo - ken word.
com - ing is And will not si - lent be.
earth, that He May His own peo - ple judge.

4. ⁵ "My consecrated ones
   Before Me gathered be,
   Those who by sacrifice have made
   A covenant with Me."

5. ⁶ Heaven above proclaims
   His righteousness abroad,
   Because He is Himself the judge;
   There is no judge but God.

Isaac Smith, c. 1770

SILVER STREET SM

50B
Psalm 50:7-15

O You, My People, Hear

Watch your life and doctrine closely.
—1 Timothy 4:16

6. ⁷O you, My peo - ple, hear! I'll
7. ⁸I'm not re - buk - ing you For
8. ⁹I need no bull nor goat Which
9. ¹¹Birds in the moun - tains high Are

speak and tes - ti - fy A - gainst you now, O
lack of sac - ri - fice; Nor for burnt of - f'rings
you in pens con - fine; ¹⁰For cat - tle on a
all to Me well known; The beasts that roam the

Is - ra - el; For God, your God, am I.
which you place Each day be - fore My eyes.
thou - sand hills, And all wild beasts, are Mine.
wilds un - tamed, They, too, are all My own.

10. ¹²If I were hungry now
    I would not speak to you,
    Because the world belongs to Me,
    And all that's in it, too.

11. ¹³Will I eat flesh of bulls?
    Or goats' blood drink will I?
    ¹⁴Make thankfulness your sacrifice;
    Pay vows to God Most High.

12. ¹⁵And always call on Me
    The day you trouble see;
    For I will then deliver you
    That you may honor Me.

Aaron Williams, 1770

ST. THOMAS SM

But to the Wicked One

If I do judge, My decisions are right...
I stand with the Father, who sent Me. —John 8:16

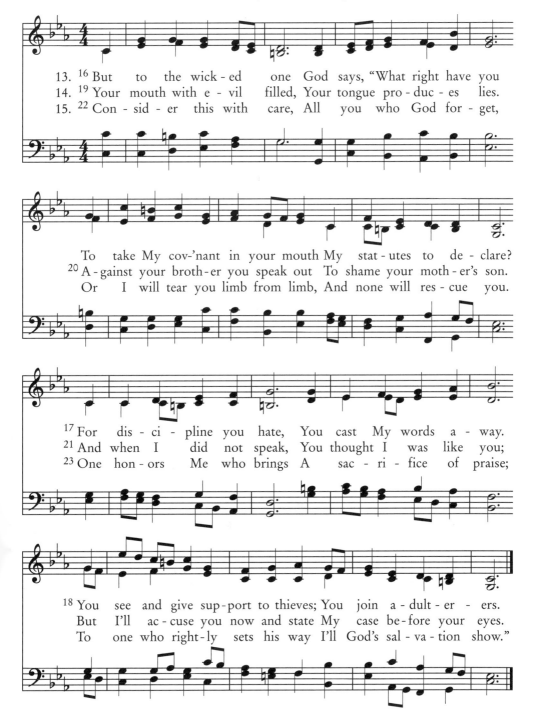

13. 16 But to the wick - ed one God says, "What right have you
14. 19 Your mouth with e - vil filled, Your tongue pro - duc - es lies.
15. 22 Con - sid - er this with care, All you who God for - get,

To take My cov-'nant in your mouth My stat - utes to de - clare?
20 A - gainst your broth-er you speak out To shame your moth - er's son.
Or I will tear you limb from limb, And none will res - cue you.

17 For dis - ci - pline you hate, You cast My words a - way.
21 And when I did not speak, You thought I was like you;
23 One hon - ors Me who brings A sac - ri - fice of praise;

18 You see and give sup-port to thieves; You join a - dult - er - ers.
But I'll ac - cuse you now and state My case be-fore your eyes.
To one who right-ly sets his way I'll God's sal - va - tion show."

Joseph Parry, 1841–1903

DINBYCH SMD

51A
Psalm 51:1-8

God, Be Merciful to Me

*Christ Jesus came into the world to save sinners—
of whom I am the worst. —1 Timothy 1:15*

1. ¹God, be mer-ci-ful to me; On Your love I rest my plea. By Your vast a-bound-ing grace, My trans-gres-sions all e-rase. From the stain of ev-ery sin, ²Wash, and make me clean with-in.

2. ³For my sins be-fore me rise, Al-ways pres-ent to my eyes. ⁴I have sinned 'gainst You a-lone, In Your sight I've e-vil done; So Your words are prov-en true, Righ-teous are Your judg-ments, too.

3. ⁵Tru-ly, I was born in sin, Sin-ful when con-ceived with-in. ⁶Sure-ly You de-sire to find Faith-ful-ness in heart and mind; You will, deep with-in my heart, Wis-dom un-to me im-part.

4. ⁷O with hys-sop sprin-kle me, And from sin I clean will be; Wash me from its stain, and so, I'll be whit-er than the snow. ⁸Make me hear joy's cheer-ing voice, Let the bones You crushed re-joice.

Thomas Hastings, 1830 TOPLADY 77.77.77

O Hide Your Face

I have not come to call the righteous, but sinners, to repentance.
— Matthew 9:13

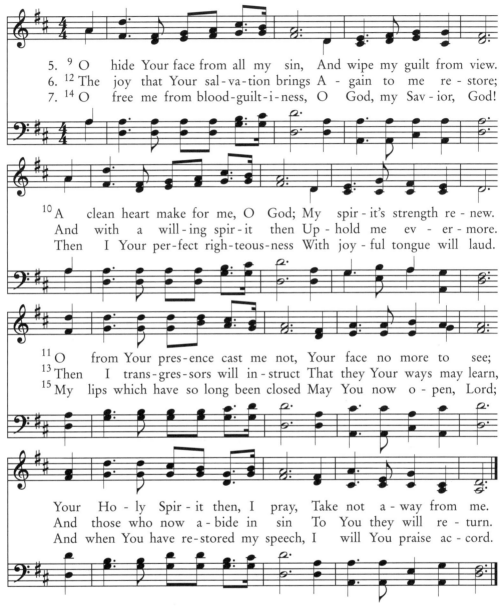

5. 9 O hide Your face from all my sin, And wipe my guilt from view.
6. 12 The joy that Your sal-va-tion brings A - gain to me re - store;
7. 14 O free me from blood-guilt-i-ness, O God, my Sav - ior, God!

10 A clean heart make for me, O God; My spir - it's strength re - new.
And with a will-ing spir-it then Up - hold me ev - er - more.
Then I Your per-fect righ-teous-ness With joy - ful tongue will laud.

11 O from Your pres-ence cast me not, Your face no more to see;
13 Then I trans-gres-sors will in - struct That they Your ways may learn,
15 My lips which have so long been closed May You now o - pen, Lord;

Your Ho - ly Spir - it then, I pray, Take not a - way from me.
And those who now a - bide in sin To You they will re - turn.
And when You have re-stored my speech, I will You praise ac - cord.

8. 16 No sacrifice do you desire,
   Or it I'd surely bring;
   And certainly You are not pleased
   With whole burnt offering.
   17 A broken spirit is to God
   A pleasing sacrifice;
   A broken and a contrite heart,
   O God, You'll not despise.

9. 18 With loving favor that You show
   Make Zion's goodness sure.
   The walls of Your Jerusalem
   Build up to heights secure.
   19 Then You'll delight in sacrifice,
   Burnt off'rings day by day,
   With whole burnt off'rings and young bulls,
   Which on Your altar lay.

Paul D. McCracken, 1948

MYRA CMD

51C
Psalm 51:1-8

God, Be Merciful to Me

God, be merciful to me, a sinner.
—Luke 18:13

1. ¹God, be mer - ci - ful to me; On Your love I
2. ³For my sins be - fore me rise, Al - ways pres - ent
3. ⁵Tru - ly, I was born in sin, Sin - ful when con-
4. ⁷O with hys - sop sprin - kle me, And from sin I

rest my plea. By Your vast a - bound - ing grace,
to my eyes. ⁴I have sinned 'gainst You a - lone,
ceived with - in. ⁶Sure - ly You de - sire to find
clean will be. Wash me from its stain, and so,

My trans - gres - sions all e - rase. From the stain of
In Your sight I've e - vil done; So Your words are
Faith - ful - ness in heart and mind; You will, deep with-
I'll be whit - er than the snow. ⁸Make me hear joy's

ev - ery sin, ²Wash, and make me clean with - in.
prov - en true, Righ - teous are Your judg - ments, too.
in my heart, Wis - dom un - to me im - part.
cheer - ing voice, Let the bones You crushed re - joice.

Johann Crüger, 1653   JESU MEINE ZUVERSICHT 77.77.77

From My Sins, O Hide Your Face

Repent, then, and turn to God, so that your sins may be wiped out.
—Acts 3:19

51D
Psalm 51:9-19

5. [9] From my sins, O hide Your face; My in-iq-ui-ties e-rase.
6. [12] Give sal-va-tion's joy a-gain, And a will-ing mind sus-tain.
7. [14] From blood-guilt-i-ness, O God, Set me free, my Sav-ior, God.

[10] O my God, re-new my heart, And a spir-it right im-part.
[13] Then Your per-fect ways I'll show That trans-gres-sors may them know;
Then my tongue will joy ex-press, [15] Sing-ing of Your righ-teous-ness.

[11] Cast me not from You, I pray; Nor Your Ho-ly Spir-it take.
Sin-ners are con-vert-ed then, Turn-ing back to You a-gain.
O-pen now my lips, O Lord; From my mouth will praise be poured.

8. [16] Sacrifice You will not take,
Or the off'ring I would make.
Off'rings burnt bring no delight,
[17] But a broken heart, contrite,
God's accepted sacrifice,
You, O God, will not despise.

9. [18] Prosper Zion in Your grace;
Build Jerus'lem's walls in place.
[19] Then will sacrifices right,
Off'rings burnt bring You delight;
Then will men, their vows to pay,
Bulls upon Your altar lay.

Richard Redhead, 1853

AJALON 77.77.77

52A

Psalm 52

Why Boast of Wrong?

They have shed the blood of Your saints and prophets, and You
have given them blood to drink, as they deserve. —Revelation 16:6

1. [1] Why boast of wrong, O might-y man? God's
2. [5] For-ev-er God will break you down, Will
3. [8] But I with-in the house of God Am

love en-dures all day. [2] Your tongue plots e-vil;
seize you with His hand, Will tear you from your
like an ol-ive tree; And in the stead-fast

ra-zor sharp, From truth it goes a-stray.
dwell-ing place, Up-root you from the land.
love of God My trust will al-ways be.

[3] You cher-ish e-vil more than good, And
[6] The just will see and laugh and say, [7] "He'd
[9] For-ev-er I will give You thanks, What

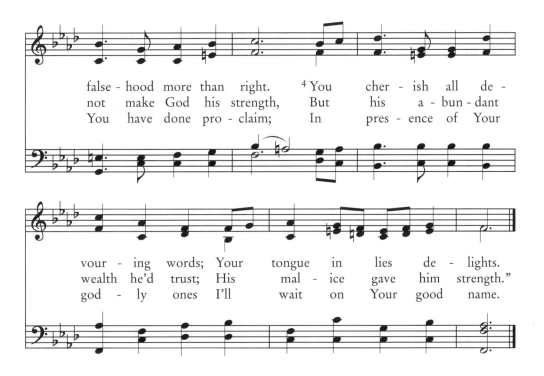

false - hood more than right.   ⁴You   cher - ish all de -
not   make God his strength,   But   his   a - bun - dant
You   have done pro - claim;   In   pres - ence of Your

vour - ing words; Your   tongue in   lies de - lights.
wealth he'd trust; His   mal - ice gave him strength."
god - ly ones I'll   wait on Your good name.

Franki Fuhrman, 2002

ANATEVKA CMD

52B
Psalm 52

Mighty Man, Why Boast in Evil?

Hallelujah!...for true and just are His judgments.
—Revelation 19:1-2

1. [1] Might-y man, why boast in e-vil?
2. [5] God will break you down for-ev-er,
3. [8] But in God's house I am grow-ing

For God's mer-cy is all day long.
Seize and tear you from where you live.
Like a green fruit-ful ol-ive tree.

[2] With your tongue you plot de-struc-tion,
[6] By your roots He then will pull you
With-out ceas-ing I am trust-ing

Like a ra-zor, you work de-ceit.
From the land of all liv-ing men.
In the firm loy-al love of God.

3 You love e - vil more than good - ness,
Just men see with awe, yet laugh - ing,
9 I will give You thanks for - ev - er,

And de - ceit more than truth - ful words.
7 "This man would not make God his trust,
For it's You that has done all this;

4 You love all words with de - struc - tive pow'r
But he trust - ed his a - bun - dant wealth,
In Your good name I will set my hope

O you sharp and de - ceit - ful tongue.
And in mal - ice he gained his strength."
In the midst of Your god - ly ones.

William Owen, 1852   BRYN CALFARIA 88.88.88.98

53A

Psalm 53

The Fool Says in His Heart

All have sinned, and fall short of the glory of God.
—Romans 3:23

1. [1] The fool says in his heart, "There is not any God." They are cor-rupt. Their deeds are vile; There's no one who does good.

2. [2] From heav-en God looks down On sons of men a-broad To see if an-y un-der-stands, If an-y seeks for God.

3. [3] Each one has turned a-side; Cor-rupt have all be-come; There's no one who does what is good, No, not a sin-gle one.

4. [4] Those work-ing wick-ed-ness— Do they not know at all, Who eat My peo-ple as their bread, And on God do not call?

5. [5] Once fearless, now they fear;
   God scatters all their bones;
   And you will put your foes to shame—
   They're God's rejected ones.

6. [6] Let Isr'el's rescue come,
   From Zion help now bring;
   When God restores His captive ones,
   Let Jacob, Isr'el, sing.

William Daman, 1579   SOUTHWELL SM

The Fool Has Spoken in His Heart

53B

*For those who...reject the truth and follow evil,
there will be wrath and anger.* —Romans 2:8

Psalm 53

1. ¹The fool has spo-ken in his heart, "There sure-ly is no God." Un-just, ab-hor-rent works they do, In-tend-ing to cause harm. Not one of them does good.
2. ²God gaz-es down from heav-en high Up-on the hu-man race, To see what their be-hav-ior is. Does an-y un-der-stand? Does an-y seek God's face?
3. ³Each from the right way turned a-side To have his own way done. To-geth-er they be-came cor-rupt, Not one of them does good, No, not a sin-gle one.
4. ⁴But these who work such wick-ed-ness, Do they not know at all? Do they just eat My peo-ple up The way they eat their bread? On God they do not call.

5. ⁵Where once they had no cause to fear,
   There they are terrorized.
   God strewed the bones of these your foes.
   And you have caused them shame,
   Since God has them despised.

6. ⁶From Zion who will come to save,
   And help to Isr'el bring?
   God brings His captive people back!
   Then Jacob will rejoice,
   And Isr'el shout and sing!

Source unknown

LEAF 86.866

54A

Psalm 54

By Your Name, O God

Consider Him who endured such opposition from sinful men,
so that you will not grow weary and lose heart. —Hebrews 12:3

1. ¹By Your name, O God, now save me; Grant me jus-tice
2. ⁴See how God has been my help-er, How my Lord sus-

by Your strength. ²To these words of mine give an-swer;
tains my soul: ⁵To my foes He pays back e-vil—

O my God, now hear my prayer. ³Strang-ers have come
In Your truth de-stroy them all! ⁶I will sac-ri-

up a-gainst me, E-ven men of vi-o-lence.
fice with glad-ness; Your good name I'll praise, O LORD.

And they seek my life's de - struc - tion;
⁷ He has saved me from all trou - ble;

God is not with - in their thoughts.
I have looked on all my foes.

Franz J. Haydn, 1797

AUSTRIA 87.87 D

54B

Psalm 54

By Your Name, O God

It was for this very reason I came to this hour.
Father, glorify Your name! —John 12:27-28

1. ¹By Your name, O God, now save me;
2. ⁴See how God has been my help - er,

Grant me jus - tice by Your strength.
How my Lord sus - tains my soul:

²To these words of mine give an - swer;
⁵To my foes He pays back e - vil—

O my God, now hear my prayer.
In Your truth de - stroy them all!

3 Strang - ers have come up a - gainst me,
6 I will sac - ri - fice with glad - ness;

E - ven men of vi - o - lence.
Your good name I'll praise, O LORD.

And they seek my life's de - struc - tion;
7 He has saved me from all trou - ble;

God is not with - in their thoughts.
I have looked on all my foes.

Traditional Welsh melody; arr. Thomas J. Williams, 1890   EBENEZER (Ton-y-Botel) 87.87 D

55A

Psalm 55:1-8

Give Ear

At daybreak Jesus went out to a solitary place.
— Luke 4:42

1. ¹Give ear to this my prayer, O God, And
2. ³Be - cause I hear the voice of foes, And
3. ⁴Now an - guish is with - in my heart Of

hide not from my cry. ²Give an - swer, for I
wick - ed ones op - press To bring their e - vil
death and ag - o - ny. ⁵I'm touched with trem - bling

can - not rest, But must com - plain and sigh;
down on me— Such ha - tred they ex - press!
and with fear, And hor - ror seiz - es me.

4. ⁶I said, "O make me like a dove,
With wings to fly away,
That I might find another place
To dwell in and to stay.

5. ⁷For then I'd wander far and rest
In some lone desert waste;
⁸From stormy wind and tempest fierce,
I would escape in haste."

William Croft, 1708

ST. ANNE CM

Consume the Wicked

This is to fulfill the Scripture: "He who shares My bread has lifted up his heel against Me". —John 13:18

55B
Psalm 55:9-15

6. ⁹Con-sume the wick-ed, O my Lord: Con-fuse their tongues, di-vide;
7. ¹¹A realm of vast de-struc-tion thrives With-in her ver-y heart;
8. ¹³But it is you, a man, a friend, My col-league all a - long!

For in the cit-y I've seen strife And vi-o-lence a - bide.
And from her streets op-pres-sion, fraud, And graft do not de - part.
¹⁴We shared sweet fel-low-ship and walked To God's house in the throng.

¹⁰For day and night up-on her walls The cit-y they sur-round,
¹²It was no foe re-proach-ing me, For that I could en - dure;
¹⁵Let death now come up-on them all, To She-ol they'll de - part;

While mis-chief and in-iq-ui-ty In-side of her are found.
It was no hat-er ris-ing up, Or I could hide se - cure.
For wick-ed-ness is in their house, And lives with-in their heart.

Georg F. Handel, 1748; harm. Austin C. Lovelace, b. 1919   HALIFAX CMD

55C But as for Me, I'll Call on God

Psalm 55:16-23

Cast all your anxiety on Him, because He cares for you.
—1 Peter 5:7

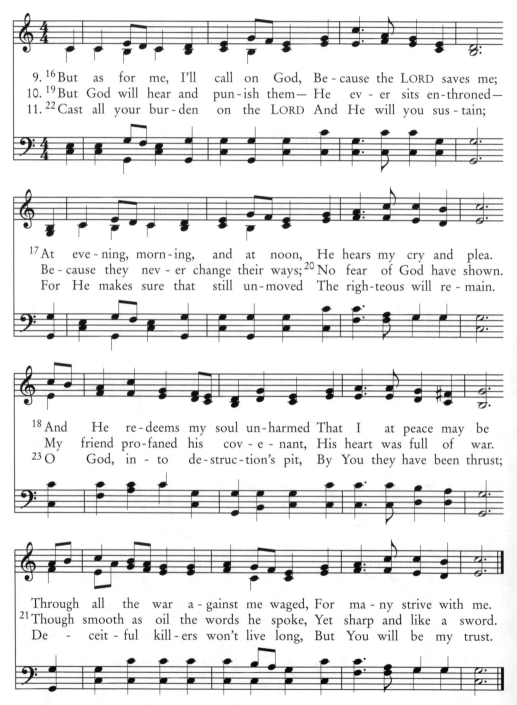

9. ¹⁶But as for me, I'll call on God, Be-cause the LORD saves me;
10. ¹⁹But God will hear and pun-ish them— He ev-er sits en-throned—
11. ²²Cast all your bur-den on the LORD And He will you sus-tain;

¹⁷At eve-ning, morn-ing, and at noon, He hears my cry and plea.
Be-cause they nev-er change their ways; ²⁰No fear of God have shown.
For He makes sure that still un-moved The righ-teous will re-main.

¹⁸And He re-deems my soul un-harmed That I at peace may be
My friend pro-faned his cov-e-nant, His heart was full of war.
²³O God, in-to de-struc-tion's pit, By You they have been thrust;

Through all the war a-gainst me waged, For ma-ny strive with me.
²¹Though smooth as oil the words he spoke, Yet sharp and like a sword.
De-ceit-ful kill-ers won't live long, But You will be my trust.

Laura A. Tate, 1912

BOVINA CMD

Be Merciful to Me, O God

56A
Psalm 56:1-7

Everyone who wants to live a godly life in Christ Jesus
will be persecuted. —2 Timothy 3:12

1. [1] Be mer - ci - ful to me, O God, For
2. [3] When fear - ful, I will trust in God Whose
3. [5] Through - out each day they twist my words; Their

man has hound - ed me; He fights a - gainst me
word I do re - vere. [4] In God I've al - ways
thoughts toward me are hate. [6] They meet, they lurk, they

all day long, To crush me ut - ter - ly. [2] My
put my trust, No ter - ror will come near. What
mark my steps; To take my life, they wait. [7] Can

foes pur - sue me all day long, In pride wage war on me.
can a mor - tal do to me That I could ev - er fear?
wick - ed na - tions flee Your wrath? O God, hu - mil - i - ate!

John Wyeth, *Repository of Sacred Music, II*, 1813   CONSOLATION 86.86.86

56B
Psalm 56:8-13

You Have Recorded All My Ways

Rejoice that you participate in the sufferings of Christ, so that you
may be overjoyed when His glory is revealed to you. —1 Peter 4:13

4. [8] You have re-cord-ed all my ways, All path-ways that I
5. [10] In God whose word I give my praise, The LORD's word I re-
6. [12] Your vows are bind-ing on me, God, I'll ren-der thanks to

took; With-in Your bot-tle placed my tears, Are
vere, [11] In God I now have put my trust, So
You. [13] For You have saved my soul from death, My

they not in Your book? [9] When I cry out then
I will have no fear. In God is where my
feet from stum-bling, too. So I will walk be-

my foes flee; I know God is for me.
trust will be; What can man do to me?
fore God's sight With life and in its light.

Oliver Holden, 1793

CORONATION 86.86.86

Be Merciful to Me, O God

57A

Psalm 57:1-4

His mercy extends to those who fear him.
—Luke 1:50

1. ¹ Be mer - ci - ful to me, O God,
2. I'm safe in shad - ow of Your wings
3. ³ From heav - en He will send and save,
4. ⁴ My soul a - mong the li - ons lies;

Be mer - ci - ful to me,
'Til ru - in pass - es by;
Sham - ing those hound - ing me.
With men who lust for war;

Be - cause my soul has found in You
² I'll cry to God who gives me help,
His lov - ing - kind - ness God will send,
With those whose teeth are spears and darts,

Its true se - cu - ri - ty.
I'll call to God Most High.
And ev - er faith - ful be.
Whose tongues are sharp - ened swords.

E.H. Frost

TABLER CM

57B

Psalm 57:5-11

O Be Exalted High, O God

Love the Lord your God with all your heart,
all your soul, and all your mind. —Matthew 22:37

5. ⁵O be ex - alt - ed high, O God; A -
6. ⁶They spread a net to catch my feet; My
7. ⁷My heart is firm, my heart is firm, O
8. ⁹And I will of - fer thanks to You A -

bove the heav - ens stand; And let Your
soul was bowed with dread. Al - though they
God, I'll praise with song. ⁸My glo - ry
mong the peo - ples, Lord; And I a -

glo - ry be a - bove All earth, both sea and land.
dug a pit for me, They fell in it in - stead.
wake! Wake harp and lyre! My song will wake the dawn.
mong the na - tions will With song my praise sound forth.

9. ¹⁰Because Your cov'nant love is great,
   It reaches heaven high;
   And Your unfailing faithfulness
   Extends up to the sky.

10. ¹¹O be exalted high, O God!
    Above the heavens stand,
    And let Your glory be above
    All earth, both sea and land.

Chester G. Allen, 1869   SUNDERLAND CM

Gods, Do You Really Speak with Righteousness?

58A
Psalm 58

How long, Sovereign Lord, holy and just, until You judge the inhabitants of the earth and avenge our blood? —Revelation 6:10

1. [1] Gods, do you real-ly speak with righ-teous-ness?
2. [3] The wick-ed are es-tranged ev'n from the womb;
3. [6] God, shat-ter all their teeth with-in their mouth;

Do you up-right-ly judge, O sons of men?
These who speak lies have wan-dered since their birth.
Break out the fangs of li-ons young, O LORD.

[2] No! In your heart you work un-righ-teous-ness;
[4] They have the ven-om of a deaf-ened snake,
[7] Like run-ning wa-ter let them flow a-way;

On earth you weigh out vio-lence from your hands.
[5] Which does not e-ven hear its charm-er's spells.
Let ar-rows that they aim be head-less shafts.

4. [8] Let them be as a moving snail that melts;
Like stillborn babes, let them not see the sun.
[9] Before your pots feel heat from burning thorns,
The wicked, green or dry, He blows away.

5. [10] The just is glad when he sees vengeance come;
And in the wicked's blood he'll wash his feet.
[11] Men say, "The righteous surely have reward;
There surely is a God to judge on earth."

Brian E. Coombs, 2002   ADIRONDACK 10.10.10.10

58B
Psalm 58

Do You, O Gods, Speak Righteousness?

Yes, Lord God Almighty, true and just are Your judgments.
—Revelation 16:7

1. ¹ Do you, O gods, speak righ-teous-ness? Do you the peo-ple just-ly judge? ² No! You de-light in do-ing wrong; You vio-lence deal out with your hand. ³ The wick-ed, from the womb es-tranged, Are li-ars stray-ing since their birth.

2. ⁴ They have the ven-om of a snake, And like a ser-pent close their ears. ⁵ They can-not hear the charm-er's song, Though skill-ful-ly he casts a spell. ⁶ O God, now shat-ter all their teeth; De-stroy young li-ons' teeth, O LORD.

3. ⁷ Like wa-ters let them drain a-way; And let their ar-rows blunt-ed be. ⁸ Let them be like a melt-ing slug, Or still-borns nev-er see-ing day. ⁹ Be-fore your pots can feel the fire, He blows the burn-ing thorns a-way.

4. ¹⁰ With joy the just one ven-geance sees, And treads in blood of wick-ed men. ¹¹ Thus peo-ple will be brought to say, "The just will sure-ly have re-ward. It's sure-ly true there is a God Who just-ly judg-es on the earth."

John Bishop, 1711; harm. Harry E. Wooldridge, 1845-1917

LEICESTER 88.88.88

Free Me, My God

God made Him who had no sin to be sin for us.
—2 Corinthians 5:21

1. ¹Free me, my God, from all my en - e - mies;
2. ³See how they lie in am - bush for my life;
3. A - rouse to meet me and be - hold my plight.

From those who rise a - gainst me, keep me safe.
Fierce men have launched at - tacks a - gainst me now;
⁵LORD God of hosts, the God of Is - ra - el,

²Save me from those who work in - iq - ui - ty;
They quick - ly come, op - pos - ing me, O LORD,
A - wake to pun - ish na - tions ev - ery - where;

De - liv - er me from men who thirst for blood.
⁴For no of - fense nor sin— no guilt of mine.
To wick - ed, treach - 'rous men, no fa - vor show.

4. ⁶ They come at evening snarling like a dog;
And they encircle all the city wall.
⁷ See evil things that spew forth from their mouth –
Their lips are swords; they think You will not hear.

5. ⁸ But You, O LORD, will laugh at them in scorn;
You scoff at all the nations in disdain.
⁹ I wait for You, because You are my strength;
Truly a mighty stronghold is my God.

George William Warren, 1892

NATIONAL HYMN 10.10.10.10

59B

Psalm 59:9-17

I Wait For You

Christ redeemed us from the curse of the law
by becoming a curse for us. —Galatians 3:13

6. ⁹ I wait for You, be-cause You are my strength,
7. ¹² Let sin-ful deeds and lies catch up with them,
8. ¹⁶ But as for me, I'll sing a-bout Your strength,

A might-y fort, a strong-hold is my God.
Be-cause of lies and curs-es that they speak.
Each day with joy, sing of Your stead-fast love;

¹⁰ My lov-ing God, my God, will meet with me,
¹³ In wrath con-sume that they may be no more;
For You have been my for-tress, my de-fense,

And let me look in tri-umph on my foes.
Let all earth know that God in Ja-cob rules.
My ref-uge when the times of trou-ble come.

11 Spare them, O Lord, our Shield, lest we for - get;
14 At night like dogs my en - e - mies re - turn;
17 To You I sing my prais - es, O my Strength;

But in Your might dis - perse and bring them down.
15 They prowl for food and growl un - sat - is - fied.
For He is God my Fort, my God of love.

Jean Sibelius, 1899; arr. David Hugh Jones, 1955   FINLANDIA 10.10.10.10.10.10

O God, You Have Rejected Us

We give thanks to You, Lord God Almighty…because You have taken up Your great power and have begun to reign. —Revelation 11:17

1. ¹O God, You have re - ject - ed us, And
2. ²As You have caused the earth to quake, And
3. ³And You have made the peo - ple know The

bro - ken us once more. As You've been an - gry
torn it o - pen wide; O heal its gap - ing
hard - ness of dis - tress; And You have made them

with us all; O once a - gain re - store!
cracks be - cause It rocks from side to side.
drink the wine Of reel - ing drunk - en - ness.

4. ⁴A banner You have given those
   Who look to You with fear;
   Let it before us be unfurled,
   And so let truth appear.

5. ⁵O grant that those You've dearly loved
   May all delivered be;
   O save them with Your strong right hand,
   And answer give to me.

Scottish Psalter, 1615

YORKE TUNE CM

God in His Holiness Declared

I can do everything through Him who gives me strength.
—Philippians 4:13

6. ⁶God in His ho-li-ness de-clared, "I will ex-ult and shout,
7. ⁸"I made My wash-bowl Mo-ab's land, On E-dom threw My shoe;
8. ¹⁰But have not You Your-self, O God, Re-ject-ed us once more?

The land of She-chem I'll di-vide And Suc-coth por-tion out.
So shout a-loud, Phil-is-ti-a, Be-cause of what I do."
And will You not stand up, O God, To go with us to war?

⁷The land of Gil-e-ad is Mine, Man-as-seh, too, I own;
⁹O who is there to bring me to The cit-y for-ti-fied?
¹¹Give help a-gainst the en-e-my, No help does man be-stow.

My head's de-fense is Eph-ra-im, And Ju-dah is My throne."
And who is there to lead me on To E-dom as a guide?
¹²With God we will do val-iant-ly; He tram-ples down our foes.

Henry S. Cutler, 1872

ALL SAINTS NEW CMD

61A

Psalm 61

O God, Hear My Cry

A better hope is introduced, by which we draw near to God.
—Hebrews 7:19

1. ¹O God, hear my cry, give heed to my prayer.
2. ³For You've al - ways been a ref - uge for me,
3. ⁵For, God, You have heard the vows that I made;
4. ⁷Be - fore God he'll sit, en - throned he'll en - dure;

²From earth's far - thest end I call to You there,
A tow - er of strength from each en - e - my.
I'm heir now with all those fear - ing Your name.
Give Your love and truth to make him se - cure.

When my heart grows faint, it is then that I cry;
⁴O let me for - ev - er in Your tent a - bide,
⁶The king's life You'll length - en, pro - long - ing his days;
⁸So I will for - ev - er to Your name sing praise,

Lead me to the rock that is high - er than I.
And un - der Your shel - ter - ing wings let me hide.
His years will be ma - ny from age un - to age.
That I may my vows pay through - out all my days.

Johann M. Hayden; arr. William Gardiner, *Sacred Melodies, II*, 1815

LYONS 10.10.11.11

My Cry and Prayer, O God, Attend

61B

Psalm 61

We have this hope as an anchor of the soul, firm and secure.
—Hebrews 6:19

1. [1] My cry and prayer, O God, at-tend; [2] For from the earth's re-mot-est end To You I raise my cry; I call when trou-bles fill my breast; O lead me to the rock of rest That high-er is than I.

2. [3] A ref-uge You have been for me, You've been a-gainst the en-e-my A tow-er strong and true. [4] With-in Your house I will a-bide, And un-der-neath Your wings will hide, For-ev-er safe in You.

3. [5] For You, O God, my vows have heard, On me the her-i-tage con-ferred Of him Your name that fears. [6] Long life You to the king will give; Through gen-er-a-tions he will live, From age to age his years.

4. [7] Be-fore God's pres-ence, he'll a-bide; So, love and faith-ful-ness pro-vide, Pre-serv-ing him each day. [8] So, to Your name I'll al-ways sing, A song of praise I'll dai-ly bring, That I my vows may pay.

Ernest R. Kroeger, 1862–1934

JOSEPHINE 886.886

62A
Psalm 62:1-8

My Soul Finds Rest in God Alone

If we hope for what we do not yet have, we wait for it patiently.
—Romans 8:25

1. [1]My soul finds rest in God a - lone;
2. [4]They plot to bring his glo - ry down,
3. [7]In God a - lone my glo - ry is,

He my sal - va - tion is.
In lies they take de - light;
And my sal - va - tion sure;

[2]My on - ly Rock, Sal - va - tion's fort;
And while they bless him with their mouths,
My rock of strength is found in God,

I'm safe, for I am His.
Their hearts are filled with spite.
My ref - uge most se - cure.

3 How long will you press your at - tack
5 My soul, find rest in God a - lone;
8 O peo - ple, at all times on Him

To make a per - son fall
He's giv - en hope to me.
Re - ly with con - fi - dence;

As though a - gainst a sag - ging fence,
6 He's my sal - va - tion, strong - hold, rock;
Pour out your hearts in prayer to Him,

A - gainst a lean - ing wall?
Un - shak - en I shall be.
For God is our de - fense.

Andrew K. Schep, 2006

BRUCE CMD

62B

My Soul Finds Rest in God Alone

Psalm 62:1-8

Everyone who calls on the name of the Lord will be saved.
— Romans 10:13

1. ¹My soul finds rest in God a - lone; Sal-va-tion comes from Him.
2. ⁴They plot to bring him top-pling down, In lies they take de - light;
3. ⁷On God a - lone my glo-ry rests, And my sal - va-tion sure.

²He's my sal - va - tion, for-tress, rock; Un - shak-en I'll re - main.
And as they bless him with their mouth, In heart they curse with spite.
God is my might - y rock of strength, My ref-uge most se - cure.

³How long will you at - tack a man, By mur-der make him fall,
⁵Find rest, my soul, in God a - lone, For my hope comes from Him.
⁸In Him, O peo-ple, at all times Re - ly with con - fi - dence;

As though he were a tot-t'ring fence, Or like a lean-ing wall?
⁶He's my sal - va - tion, for-tress, rock; Un - shak-en I'll re - main.
Be - fore Him, now, pour out your heart, For God is our de-fense.

American traditional melody, from William Walker's *Southern Harmony*, 1835

RESIGNATION CMD

They're Lighter Than a Sigh

Command those who are rich…not to put their hope in
wealth, which is uncertain. —1 Timothy 6:17

4. ⁹All low-born men are but a breath,
5. ¹⁰Don't in ex-tor-tion place your hope;
6. ¹¹For God has spo-ken— twice I heard,

All high-ranked men a lie;
For sto-len goods, don't lust.
"All pow'r is God's," You say.

To-geth-er on the bal-anc-es,
And though your rich-es may in-crease,
¹²And mer-cy, Lord, is Yours as well;

They're light-er than a sigh.
On them don't build your trust.
Men's works You will re-pay.

Adapt. from Johann G. Nageli, 1773–1836

MAIN CM

63A

Psalm 63

O God, You are My God

I want men everywhere to lift up holy hands in prayer.
—1 Timothy 2:8

1. [1] O God, You are my God, And ear-ly will I
2. [4] I'll bless You while I live, And I will ev-er
3. [8] My soul clings fast to You; Your right hand holds me

seek for You; My soul is a-thirst for You.
lift my hands To praise and con-fess Your name.
safe-ly up. [9] When men would de-stroy my life,

My flesh cries out for You From out a dry and
[5] My soul will be made full As with all choice and
To depths of earth they go; [10] They are de-liv-ered

thirst-y land, A land where no wa-ter is.
heart-y meats; I'll praise You with joy-ful lips.
to the sword, To jack-als be-come a prey.

Andre Campra; arr. G. Duncan Lowe, 1972

TE DEUM 687.687.10.10.87

63B

Psalm 63:1-5

I'll Seek You Early, God

*Jesus told His disciples a parable to show them
that they should always pray and not give up. —Luke 18:1*

1. [1] I'll seek You ear - ly, God, my God;
2. [2] I've longed for You like this be - fore
3. [3] Be - cause Your love is more than life,
4. [5] My soul, as with the choic - est food,

My soul's a - thirst for You.
With - in Your ho - ly place,
My lips will give You praise.
Is ful - ly sat - is - fied;

In dry, un - wa - tered, wear - y lands,
That there I might be - hold Your strength,
[4] So I will bless You while I live,
With shouts of joy up - on my lips,

My flesh longs af - ter You.
The glo - ry of Your face.
My hands lift in Your name.
My mouth will praise pro - vide.

Samuel S. Wesley, 1872

WETHERBY CM

And When I Turn My Thoughts to You

63C

The Spirit Himself intercedes for us with groans
that words cannot express. —Romans 8:26

Psalm 63:6-11

5. 6 And when I turn my thoughts to You Up -
6. For You're my help; I sing for joy In
7. 9 But they go down to depths of earth Who'd
8. 11 The king will then re - joice in God, And

on my bed at night, 7 As watch - es pass, I
sha - dow of Your wings. 8 And Your right hand has
take my life a - way; 10 They are de - liv - ered
all who by him swear; For stopped will be the

med - i - tate On You with much de - light.
held me up, To You my soul now clings.
to the sword To be the jack - als' prey.
mouths of those Who do a lie de - clare.

Alonzo J. Abbey, 1858

COOLING CM

64A

Psalm 64

God, Hear My Voice

From then on Judas watched for an opportunity to hand Him over.
—Matthew 26:16

1. ¹ God, hear my voice, hear my com - plaint, Pre -
2. ³ Whose tongues are sharp - ened like a sword, With
3. ⁵ They set their minds on e - vil plans, Lay

serve me from my foe. ² Hide me from plots of
bit - ter speech like spears; ⁴ To shoot in se - cret
traps, and say, "Who sees?"; ⁶ With skill de - vise in -

e - vil men, When sin - ners vio - lent grow,
at the just, They shock and do not fear.
jus - tic - es, Man's heart and thoughts are deep.

4. ⁷ But God will shoot a shaft at them
And wound them all with dread.
⁸ So their own tongue will trip them up;
Those seeing shake their head.

5. ⁹ Then all will fear and tell God's work,
Considering His deeds.
¹⁰ The just find refuge in the LORD,
In Him boast joyfully.

Scottish Psalter, 1634

CULROSS CM

God, Hear My Voice

The tongue is a fire, the very world of iniquity.
—James 3:6

64B

Psalm 64

1. ¹ God, hear my voice, hear my com-plaint, Pre-serve me from my foe. ² Hide me from plots of e-vil men, When sin-ners vio-lent grow,

2. ³ Whose tongues are sharp-ened like a sword, With bit-ter speech like spears; ⁴ To shoot in se-cret at the just, They shock and do not fear.

3. ⁵ They set their minds on e-vil plans, Lay traps, and say, "Who sees?"; ⁶ With skill de-vise in-jus-tic-es, Man's heart and thoughts are deep.

4. ⁷ But God will shoot a shaft at them
And wound them all with dread.
⁸ So their own tongue will trip them up;
Those seeing shake their head.

5. ⁹ Then all will fear and tell God's work,
Considering His deeds.
¹⁰ The just find refuge in the LORD,
In Him boast joyfully.

Neil Dougall, 1831

KILMARNOCK CM

65A

Psalm 65:1-4

Awaiting You in Zion

*He who overcomes will inherit all this, and I will
be his God and he will be My son. —Revelation 21:7*

1. ¹A - wait - ing You in Zi - on, Are praise and si - lence, God;
2. ⁴How bless - ed is the per - son Who is Your cho - sen one,

²And prom - is - es com - plet - ed, Which men to You have vowed.
The one You have brought near You And made Your courts his home.

Of prayer You are the hear - er, ³To You will all men come.
With - in Your ho - ly tem - ple We will be sat - is - fied,

Though e - vil words would crush me, You for our sins a - tone.
And filled with all the good - ness Your ho - ly house pro - vides.

George J. Webb, 1837

WEBB 76.76 D

O God of Our Salvation

Now the dwelling of God is with men,
and He will live among them. — Revelation 21:3

3. ⁵O God of our sal - va - tion, You in Your righ - teous - ness,
4. ⁶His strength set firm the moun - tains, Pow'r clothes Him ev - er - more,
5. ⁹You vis - it earth with show - ers, And so en - rich the field;
6. ¹¹You've crowned each year with good - ness, Your paths en - rich the ground.

By awe - some deeds and won - ders Your an - swer will ex - press.
⁷Who stills the peo - ples' clam - or, Makes calm the o - cean's roar.
God's riv - er brims with wa - ter, As You pre - pare earth's yield.
¹²The des - ert pas - tures blos - som, With joy the hills re - sound.

You are the One who's trust - ed To earth's ex - trem - i - ty,
⁸The far and dis - tant peo - ples Be - hold Your signs with fear;
¹⁰You wa - ter its rich fur - rows, Its ridg - es smooth with rain;
¹³The fields with flocks are cov - ered, The val - leys clothed with grain.

By peo - ple who are liv - ing Be - yond the far - thest sea.
You make the dawn and sun - set Shout loud with joy and cheer.
You soft - en earth with show - ers, You bless its sprout - ing grain.
They all re - joice with shout - ing, With songs their joy pro - claim.

Traditional English melody

SHEFFIELD 76.76 D

65C

Praise Awaits You, God

Psalm 65:1-7

They will not need the light of a lamp or the light of the sun,
for the Lord God will give them light. —Revelation 22:5

1. ¹Praise a-waits You, God, in Zi - on; Vows to You will
2. ⁴Bless - ed is the one You've cho - sen, To live near You,
3. You're the trust of all earth's peo - ples To the ends of

be ful - filled. ²You're the One who hears our pray - ing;
in Your courts. We are sat - is - fied with good things
dis - tant seas. ⁶By Your pow'r You placed the moun - tains;

To You all man - kind will come. ³E - vil words have
In Your house, Your ho - ly place. ⁵God, You an - swer
You have clothed Your - self with strength. ⁷You have calmed the

o - ver - whelmed me, But You cov - er all our sins.
us, our Sav - ior, With Your awe - some, righ - teous deeds.
o - cean's roar - ing, Tur - moil of the na - tions stilled.

John Goss, 1869

LAUDA ANIMA 87.87.87

The Far and Distant Peoples Fear

Take your sickle and reap, because the time to reap has come,
for the harvest of the earth is ripe. —Revelation 14:15

4. [8] The   far and dis-tant peo-ples fear   The won-ders You have
5.   God's streams have o-ver-flowed with rain,   Earth is   pre-pared for
6. [11] The   year with good-ness You have crowned, The   pas-tures pros-per

made   ap-pear. From dawn to when the sun goes down, You make their
sprout-ing grain. [10] You   wa-ter fur-rows thor-ough-ly, And smooth its
and   a-bound. [12] The hills are clothed with joy-ful-ness, [13] The   mea-dow-

songs   of   joy re-sound. [9] You   vis-it earth, its   wa-ters flow; Great
ridg-es   ten-der-ly.   Your show-ers have the earth ca-ressed; In
lands with flocks are dressed. The   val-leys' fields a-bound with grain, They

rich-es on it You be-stow. Great rich-es on it   You be-stow.
all   of this, its growth You blessed. In   all of this, its growth You blessed.
shout and sing, their joy pro-claim. They shout and sing, their joy pro-claim.

William B. Bradbury, 1863, alt.   SOLID ROCK 88.88.888

66A

O All the Earth

Psalm 66:1-7

Our forefathers were all under the cloud and...
they all passed through the sea. —1 Corinthians 10:1

1. ¹O all the earth, in joy-ful shouts, To God, your voic-es raise. ²And sing the glo-ry of His name, And glo-rious make His praise, And glo-rious make His praise.

2. ³To God de-clare, "How awe-some are The won-drous works You do!" So great Your strength! Your en-e-mies In haste sub-mit to You, In haste sub-mit to You.

3. ⁴Yes, all the earth will wor-ship You, They praise to You will sing; And to Your name most glo-ri-ous Their songs of praise will bring, Their songs of praise will bring.

4. ⁵O come, be-hold the works of God, His might-y do-ings see; In won-drous works on man's be-half How tru-ly great is He, How tru-ly great is He!

5. ⁶ He turned the sea into dry land,
Their feet a pathway had
Where they then through the river walked
Let us in Him be glad!

6. ⁷ He rules forever by His might,
On nations keeps His eye.
Let not the proud, rebellious ones
Exalt themselves on high!

William Shrubsole, 1779

MILES LANE CM

O All You Peoples, Bless Our God

66B

Psalm 66:8-20

Your faith…may be proved genuine and may result in praise,
glory, and honor when Jesus Christ is revealed. —1 Peter 1:7

7. [8] O all you peo-ples, bless our God, A-broad pro-claim His praise;
8. [12] You let men tram-ple on our heads; We passed through fire and flood.
9. [15] Burnt of-fer-ings of fat-tened beasts With smoke of rams I'll take;
10. [18] If in my heart I cher-ished sin, The Lord then would not hear.

[9] The One who keeps our souls a-live, Our feet from stum-bling stays.
But then at last you brought us to A place of boun-teous good.
And from the cat-tle and the goats I will an of-f'ring make.
[19] But sure-ly God has heard my voice, He to my prayer gave ear.

[10] For You, O God, have test-ed us As sil-ver is re-fined.
[13] And so I'll come in-to Your house; Burnt of-fer-ings I'll pay
[16] All you that fear God, come and hear What God did for my soul.
[20] For-ev-er bless-ed be our God! My prayer He has not spurned;

[11] You caught us in a net, and on Our backs a load You bind.
[14] To keep the vows my lips had made When trou-bles filled my way.
[17] For with my mouth I cried to Him, My tongue did Him ex-tol.
And He has not a-way from me His lov-ing-kind-ness turned.

Traditional English melody, Ralph Vaughan-Williams, 1906   FOREST GREEN CMD

66C
Psalm 66

All Earth to God Raise Joyful Song

Christ, our Passover lamb, has been sacrificed.
Therefore let us keep the festival. —1 Corinthians 5:7-8

1. ¹All earth to God raise joy-ful song; Sing forth the
2. ⁵O come and see the works of God, He's awe-some
3. ⁸Bless God, O peo-ples, sound His praise; ⁹He who ap-

glo-ry of His name. ²To Him give prais-es glo - rious.
in the things He does Be - fore the eyes of man - kind.
points our soul to live, And keeps our feet from slip - ping.

³Tell God, "How awe-some are Your deeds; Your great strength
⁶He turned the sea in - to dry land; They through the
¹⁰As sil - ver, God, You test-ed us, ¹¹De - liv - ered

leads Your foes in haste To show You their sub-mis - sion.
riv - er passed on foot; We'll there re-joice be-fore Him.
us in - to the net, Op-pressed us with a bur - den.

All earth worships; To You bow - ing,
He rules ev - er In His might; He
Men rode o'er us; We have gone through

to You prais - ing, To You sing - ing.
sees the na - tions, His eyes watch - ing;
fire and wa - ter By Your do - ing.

To Your name they sing their prais - es."
Let none rise up in re - bel - lion.
Yet You brought us forth to free - dom.

4. ¹³ I'll enter, then, into Your house,
I'll bring burnt offerings with me;
To You I'll make my pledges.
¹⁴ I made these with my lips and mouth;
I promised many offerings
When I was in great trouble.
¹⁵ I will offer
Burning sacrifice of fatlings,
With ram's incense;
I'll make bulls and goats an off'ring.

5. ¹⁶ Come listen, all who rev'rence God;
I'll tell what He has done for me:
¹⁷ I cried to Him and praised Him.
¹⁸ If in my heart I cherished sin,
The Lord would not have heeded me;
¹⁹ But truly God has listened;
He has heard me.
²⁰ God be blessed because He has not
Scorned my praying,
Nor His faithful love turned from me.

Philipp Nicolai, 1599

WIE SCHÖN LEUCHTET 887.887.48.48

67A

Psalm 67

O God, Give Us Your Blessing

They were all filled with awe and praised God.
—Luke 7:16

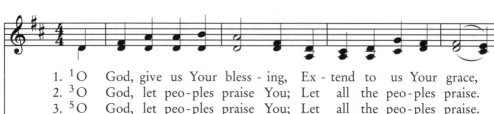

1. ¹O God, give us Your bless - ing, Ex - tend to us Your grace,
2. ³O God, let peo - ples praise You; Let all the peo - ples praise.
3. ⁵O God, let peo - ples praise You; Let all the peo - ples praise.

And cause to shine up - on us The ra - diance of Your face;
⁴Let na - tions come re - joic - ing, And songs of glad - ness raise;
⁶The earth has brought its boun - ty Through-out its har - vest days;

²In or - der that Your path-ways Would through the earth be known,
For You will judge the peo - ples With per - fect eq - ui - ty;
⁷Since God, our God, will bless us; Yes, God will bless - ing send,

That You to ev - ery na - tion Would Your sal - va - tion show.
You will for all earth's na - tions Their guide and lead - er be.
That all the earth may fear Him To its re - mot - est end.

Lowell Mason, 1824

MISSIONARY HYMN 76.76 D

O God, Give Us Your Blessing

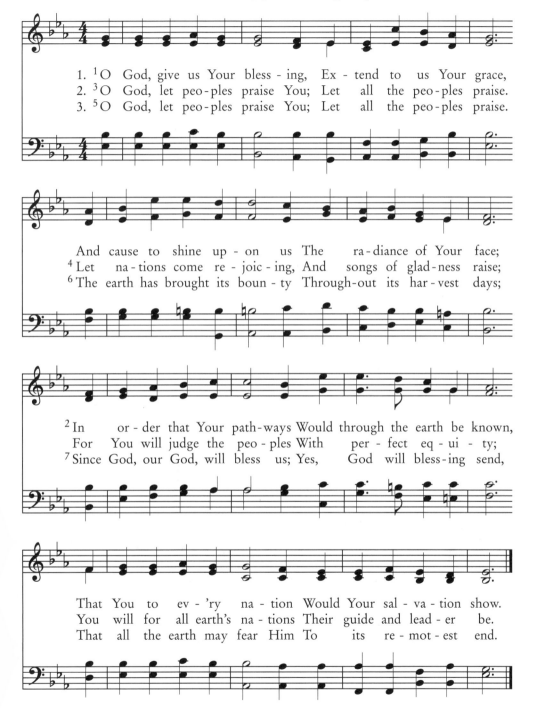

67B
Psalm 67

Blessed be the God and Father of our Lord Jesus Christ, who has blessed us in Christ with every spiritual blessing. —Ephesians 1:3

1. [1]O God, give us Your bless-ing, Ex-tend to us Your grace,
2. [3]O God, let peo-ples praise You; Let all the peo-ples praise.
3. [5]O God, let peo-ples praise You; Let all the peo-ples praise.

And cause to shine up-on us The ra-diance of Your face;
[4]Let na-tions come re-joic-ing, And songs of glad-ness raise;
[6]The earth has brought its boun-ty Through-out its har-vest days;

[2]In or-der that Your path-ways Would through the earth be known,
For You will judge the peo-ples With per-fect eq-ui-ty;
[7]Since God, our God, will bless us; Yes, God will bless-ing send,

That You to ev-'ry na-tion Would Your sal-va-tion show.
You will for all earth's na-tions Their guide and lead-er be.
That all the earth may fear Him To its re-mot-est end.

Samuel S. Wesley, 1825   AURELIA 76.76 D

67C

Psalm 67

O God, Show Mercy to Us

God's salvation has been sent to the Gentiles,
and they will listen. —Acts 28:28

1. [1]O God, show mer-cy to us, And bless us with Your grace; And cause to shine up-on us The bright-ness of Your face; [2]So that the whole world o-ver May tru-ly know Your way, And

2. For You will judge the peo-ples With per-fect eq-ui-ty; To na-tions of the whole earth A gov-er-nor You'll be. [5]O God, let peo-ples praise You; Let all the peo-ples praise. [6]The

so that Your sal - va - tion All na - tions see dis -
earth has brought its boun - ty Through - out its har - vest

played. ³O God, let peo - ples praise You; Let
days Since God, our God, will bless us. ⁷Yes,

all the peo - ples praise. ⁴Let na - tions come re -
God will bless - ing send, That all the earth may

joic - ing And songs of glad - ness raise.
fear Him To its re - mot - est end.

Gustav Holst, 1918; arr. Brian E. Coombs, 2003

THAXTED 76.76 T

68A

Psalm 68:1-6

Let God Arise

He is not here; He is risen, just as He said.
—Matthew 28:6

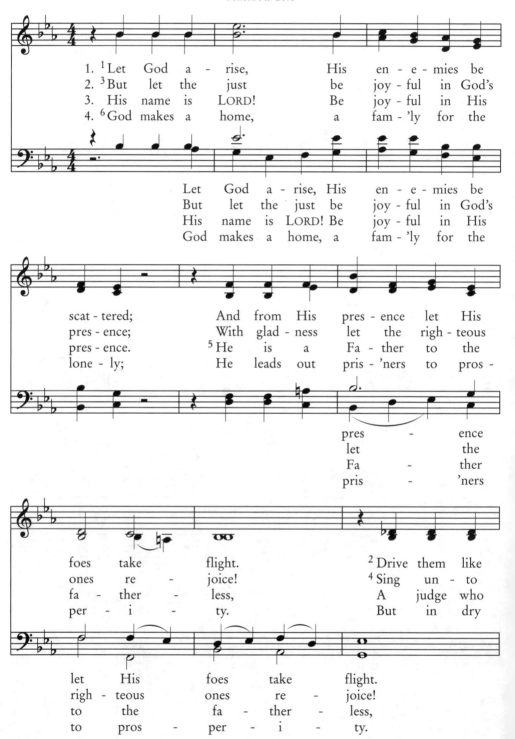

1. ¹Let God a - rise, His en - e - mies be
2. ³But let the just be joy - ful in God's
3. His name is LORD! Be joy - ful in His
4. ⁶God makes a home, a fam - 'ly for the

Let God a - rise, His en - e - mies be
But let the just be joy - ful in God's
His name is LORD! Be joy - ful in His
God makes a home, a fam - 'ly for the

scat - tered; And from His pres - ence let His
pres - ence; With glad - ness let the righ - teous
pres - ence. ⁵He is a Fa - ther to the
lone - ly; He leads out pris - 'ners to pros -

pres - ence
let the
Fa - ther
pris - 'ners

foes take flight. ²Drive them like
ones re - joice! ⁴Sing un - to
fa - ther - less, A judge who
per - i - ty. But in dry

let His foes take flight.
righ - teous ones re - joice!
to the fa - ther - less,
to pros - per - i - ty.

Andrew K. Schep, 2007

EXSURGAT DEUS 11.10.4.4.10

68B

Psalm 68:1-6

Let God Arise

*The Son of Man must be delivered into the hands of sinful men,
be crucified, and on the third day be raised again.* — Luke 24:7

1. ¹Let God a - rise, and scat - tered far Be all His en - e - mies. And let all those who hate Him flee; Let none be - fore Him stay. ²Like smoke drive them a - way!

2. As melt - ing wax be - fore a fire, Be - fore God let them die. ³But let the righ - teous all ex - ult; In God let them have joy; Let them shout loud for joy!

3. ⁴O sing to God! O praise His name! A high - way make for Him, The Rid - er through the des - ert wastes! The LORD— this is His name— Be - fore Him joy pro - claim!

4. ⁵The or - phans' fa - ther, wid - ows' help, God's in His ho - ly house. ⁶God leads the pris - 'ners out to peace, Gives need - y ones a home; But reb - els des - erts roam.

Thomas Hastings, 1784–1872

LAIGHT STREET 86.866

When With Your People You Went Forth

68C

Psalm 68:7-14

It was Mary Magdalene, Joanna, Mary the mother of James, and the others with them who told this to the apostles. — Luke 24:10

5. [7] When with Your peo - ple You went forth, And marched through
6. [9] O God, You sent a - bun - dant rain, Your wear - y
7. [11] The Lord an - nounc - es this His word, Great hosts of
8. [13] Though you a - mong the camp - fires sleep, You're like a

des - ert lands, O God, [8] Earth shook; skies fell be -
her - i - tage re - freshed. [10] Your con - gre - ga - tion
wom - en spread the news: [12] "The kings of ar - mies
dove with sil - ver wings, Whose feath - ers are a

fore God's face; Be - fore God's pres - ence Si - nai
set - tled there, And in Your good - ness You, O
flee! They flee! And she who stays be - hind at
glis - t'ning gold. [14] When the Al - might - y scat - tered

quaked, Be - fore the God of Is - ra - el.
God, Made rich pro - vi - sion for the poor.
home Will be there to di - vide the spoil!"
kings, It looked like snow on Zal - mon's hill.

Frederic M.A. Venua; arr. William Gardiner, *Sacred Melodies, I,* 1812

PARK STREET 88.888

68D

Psalm 68:15-23

Bashan's Mountains

To each one of us grace has been given as Christ has apportioned it.
—Ephesians 4:7

9. ¹⁵Bash - an's   moun - tains   are   ma   -   jes - tic,
10. ¹⁷Ma   - ny   thou - sands   are   God's   char - iots
11. ¹⁹Praise the   Lord   our   God   and   Sav - ior;
12. ²²"I   will   bring them   back   from   Bash - an,"

Bash - an's   peaks   are   strong   and   fair.
More than   thou - sands,   num - ber   - less;
Dai - ly   bur - dens   He   re   - lieves.
So   the   Lord   said   for - mer - ly.

¹⁶Why   do   you,   O   rug - ged   moun - tains,
With   them   comes   the   Lord   from   Si - nai
²⁰Our   God   is   a   God   who   saves us,
"Sure - ly   I   will   yet   re   - trieve them

With   deep   en - vy   gape   and   stare
To   His   place   of   ho - li   - ness.
God   the   LORD   from   death   sets   free.
From   the   bot - tom   of   the   sea

At the hill which God has cho - sen
[18] You've as - cend - ed to the high - est,
[21] Sure - ly God will crush in piec - es
[23] So that you may strike and crush them,

To es - tab - lish as His own?
Lead - ing cap - tives as Your own;
Heads of ev - ery en - e - my,
In their blood im - merse your feet;

There the LORD has made His dwell - ing,
Gain - ing gifts from men and reb - els,
And the heads of those per - sist - ing,
Then your dogs may have their por - tion,

And it shall re - main His home.
There the LORD God makes His home.
Work - ing their in - iq - ui - ty.
Feed up - on your en - e - mies."

Traditional Dutch melody; arr. Julius Roentgen, 1906   IN BABILONE 87.87 D

68E God, Your Procession Now Comes into View

Psalm 68:24-31

To him who overcomes...I will give authority over the nations.
— Revelation 2:26

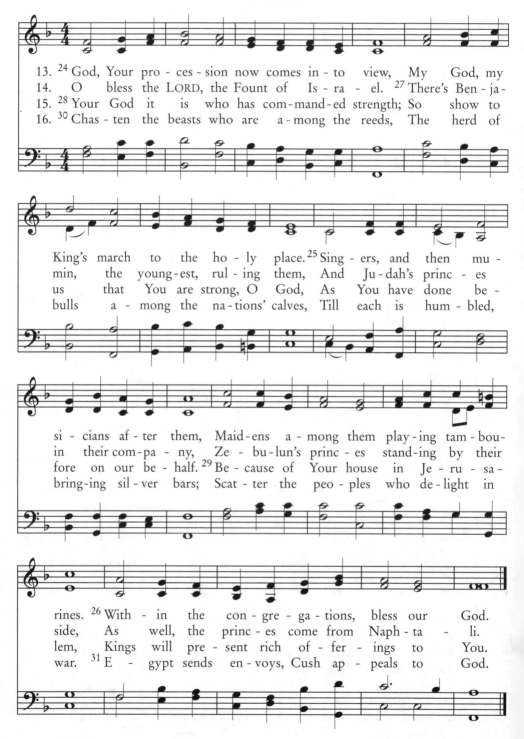

13. ²⁴ God, Your pro - ces - sion now comes in - to view, My God, my
14. O bless the LORD, the Fount of Is - ra - el. ²⁷ There's Ben - ja-
15. ²⁸ Your God it is who has com - mand - ed strength; So show to
16. ³⁰ Chas - ten the beasts who are a - mong the reeds, The herd of

King's march to the ho - ly place. ²⁵ Sing - ers, and then mu -
min, the young - est, rul - ing them, And Ju - dah's princ - es
us that You are strong, O God, As You have done be -
bulls a - mong the na - tions' calves, Till each is hum - bled,

si - cians af - ter them, Maid - ens a - mong them play - ing tam - bou -
in their com - pa - ny, Ze - bu - lun's princ - es stand - ing by their
fore on our be - half. ²⁹ Be - cause of Your house in Je - ru - sa -
bring - ing sil - ver bars; Scat - ter the peo - ples who de - light in

rines. ²⁶ With - in the con - gre - ga - tions, bless our God.
side, As well, the princ - es come from Naph - ta - li.
lem, Kings will pre - sent rich of - fer - ings to You.
war. ³¹ E - gypt sends en - voys, Cush ap - peals to God.

Louis Bourgeois, 1551

OLD 124TH 10.10.10.10.10

Sing Out Your Praises

68F
Psalm 68:32-35

*The twenty-four elders fall down before Him who sits on the throne,
and worship Him who lives for ever and ever. —Revelation 4:10*

17. ³²Sing out your prais - es un - to God, O
18. ³³Praise Him who rides from an - cient times In

king - doms of the earth; And sing un - to the
heav - en's high - est height. Be - hold, He speaks out

Lord of all In praise of His great worth,
with His voice, A voice of pow'r and might,

In praise of His
A voice of pow'r

In praise of His great worth.
A voice of pow'r and might.

great worth, In praise of His great worth.
and might, A voice of pow'r and might.

In praise of His great worth.
A voice of pow'r and might.

19. ³⁴Declare that God possesses strength;
His majesty is high,
Exalted over Israel,
His strength is in the skies.

20. ³⁵O God, You're awesome from Your throne,
Isr'el's own God is He,
Who gives His people strength and power;
O let God blessed be!

Ludwig van Beethoven, 1770–1827, alt.

CROYDON CM

69A

Save Me, O God

Psalm 69:1-13

The Gentiles...will mock Him, insult Him, spit upon Him,
flog Him, and kill Him. —Luke 18:32

1. ¹Save me, O God, be-cause the might-y wa - ters
2. My wrong-ful, might-y foes seek to de - stroy me.
3. ⁷For Your own sake I have en-dured de - ri - sion;
4. ¹¹When in my grief I clothed my-self in sack-cloth,

Have come up - on my soul on ev - ery side.
I must re - store the things I did not steal.
My face is cov-ered with con - tempt and shame.
A laugh-ing-stock I then be-came to them.

²I sink in mir - y depths. There is no foot - hold;
⁵But as for You, O God, You know my fol - ly;
⁸I am a for - eign - er to my own broth - ers;
¹²Those sit-ting in the gate now talk a - bout me,

I am en - gulfed be - neath the wa - ter's tide.
From You my guilt - i - ness I can't con - ceal.
And from my moth-er's sons I am es - tranged.
I am the theme of songs by drunk-en men.

3 My throat is parched and dry. I'm worn out cry - ing;
6 My Lord, O LORD of hosts, may those who trust You
9 Since for Your house I am con-sumed with fer - vor
13 But as for me, I lift my prayer to You, LORD;

My eyes fail while I wait on God for aid.
Not ev - er be a - shamed be - cause of me.
Those who in - sult You turn their taunts on me.
Ac - cept it in the time that pleas - es You.

4 Those peo - ple hat - ing me with - out a rea - son
May those who seek for You, O God of Is - r'el,
10 And though with - in my soul I wept with fast - ing,
In the a - bun-dance of Your lov - ing - kind - ness,

Are more than all the hairs up - on my head.
Not ev - er be dis - graced be - cause of me.
Yet ev - en this be - came re - proach to me.
Re - spond, O God, with Your sal - va - tion true.

Andre Campra; arr. G. Duncan Lowe, 1972   SALVUM FAC 11.10.11.10 D

69B

Psalm 69:14-21

Save Me from Sinking

One man ran, filled a sponge with vinegar, put it on a stick, and offered it to Him to drink. —Mark 15:36

5. [14] Save me from sink - ing down in mir - y wa - ters;
6. [17] O do not hide Your face from me, Your ser - vant.
7. [20] Scorn cut my heart, and sick - ness came up - on me;

De - liv - er me from hat - ers and deep floods.
I am dis - tressed; O quick - ly an - swer me.
For sym - pa - thy I looked, but there was none.

[15] Let not the flood of wa - ters ov - er - whelm me,
[18] Draw near to me and grant my soul re - demp - tion;
And though I looked for com - fort - ers to help me;

Let not the pit en - close and swal - low me.
Be - cause of all my foes, O ran - som me.
Yet e - ven then I found not one of them.

16 LORD, an-swer me, for good is Your love;
19 You know my shame, dis - hon - or, dis - grace;
21 But they have giv - en gall in my food;

And in Your great com-pas-sion turn un-to me.
My per - se - cu-tors are well known un-to You.
They gave me vin-e-gar to drink for my thirst.

Henry Smart, 1868

PILGRIMS 11.10.11.10.9.11

69C

O Let Their Table Be a Snare

Psalm 69:22-29

*The Holy Spirit spoke long ago through the mouth of David
concerning Judas. —Acts 1:16*

8. ²²O let their ta - ble be a snare be - fore them;
9. ²⁴Your in - dig - na - tion be poured out up - on them,
10. ²⁶For they have hound - ed him that You have smit - ten,
11. ²⁸Out of the book of life let them be blot - ted,

When they're at peace, let it be - come a trap.
Your burn - ing an - ger catch them in their flight.
Talk - ing a - bout the grief of those You pierced.
And let them not be list - ed with the just.

²³O let their eyes be dark - ened in their see - ing,
²⁵O let their camp be brought to de - so - la - tion;
²⁷Add to their guilt more guilt - i - ness up - on them,
²⁹But as for me, I am in pain, af - flict - ed;

And make their bod - ies shake with - out con - trol.
Let not one dwell - ing in their tents re - main.
May they not come in - to Your righ - teous - ness.
O God, may Your sal - va - tion raise me up.

Louis Bourgeois, 1551; arr. Lois Schaefer, 1972

OLD 110ᵀᴴ 11.10.11.10

The Name of God

He was heard because of His reverent submission.
—Hebrews 5:7

12. ³⁰ The name of God I with a song Most
13. ³¹ For this will please the LORD far more Than
14. ³² The meek will see and then be glad; Those

cheer-ful-ly will praise; And I in giv-ing
will the of-fer-ing Of an-y bull with
seek-ing God re-vive! ³³ Be-cause the LORD will

thanks to Him His name will high-ly raise.
horns or hoofs Or ox that I may bring.
hear the poor; He'll pris-'ners not de-spise.

15. ³⁴ Let heav'n and earth praise Him, the seas,
And all with which they're filled.
³⁵ For God will Zion surely save,
And Judah's cities build.

16. They and their children there will live,
Their own possession claim.
³⁶ The ones inheriting the land,
Are those who love His name.

Thomas E. Perkins, 1831–1912

SABBATH EVENING CM

70A

Psalm 70

Hasten, God, My Rescue

My God, My God, why have You forsaken Me?
— Mark 15:34

1. [1] Has-ten, God, my res-cue; help me quick-ly, LORD;
2. [4] Let all seek-ing You, with joy in You a-bide;

[2] Frus-trate those who hunt me; shame be their re-ward.
Say-ing for Your res-cue, "God be mag-ni-fied."

Turn back, con-fuse those who in my hurt de-light;
[5] God, I am need-y; O come to me, I pray;

[3] Pay them back with shame who jeer "A-ha" with spite.
You're my Help, my Sav-ior; LORD, do not de-lay.

Traditional French carol

NOEL NOUVELET 11.11.11.11 (Trochaic)

Hasten, O God

If we hope for what we do not yet have, we wait for it patiently.
—Romans 8:25

70B
Psalm 70

1. ¹Has - ten, O God, to my res - cue; Has - ten to
2. Turned back be they and dis - hon - ored Who in my
3. ⁴Let those who seek You be joy - ful, Let them be
4. ⁵But I am poor and af - flict - ed; Has - ten to

help, O LORD. ²Let there be shame and con -
hurt de - light. ³By their dis - grace be they
glad in You; Let those who love Your sal -
me, O God! You are my help and my

fu - sion On those who seek my life.
cov - ered Who jeer, "A - ha! A - ha!"
va - tion Say, "God be mag - ni - fied!"
Sav - ior; O LORD, do not de - lay.

Franki Fuhrman, 2003

JACKI'S 1ST LAMENT 86.86

71A
Psalm 71:1-8

In You, O Lord, I Put My Trust

Take this cup from Me; yet not what I will, but what You will.
— Mark 14:36

1. ¹In You, O Lord, I put my trust; A-
2. ³O be my rock, my dwell-ing place, My
3. ⁴Save me, my God, from wick-ed hands, Hands

shamed let me not be. ²O save me in Your
con-stant safe re-sort; For my sal-va-tion
cru-el and un-just; ⁵For Lord, my Lord, You

righ-teous-ness; Give ear, and res-cue me.
You've or-dained; You are my rock and fort.
are my hope, From youth You are my trust.

4. ⁶For I have been sustained by You
   Through birth and early days.
   You brought me from my mother's womb;
   I'll give You constant praise.

5. ⁷To many I'm a wondrous sign,
   You are my refuge strong.
   ⁸My mouth is brimming with Your praise
   And honor all day long.

Frederick A.G. Ouseley, 1825–1889

CONTEMPLATION CM

Do Not Forsake Me in Old Age

He would not see death before he had seen the Lord's Christ.
— Luke 2:26

71B
Psalm 71:9-15

6. ⁹Do not for - sake me in old age; When
7. ¹¹They say, "God has for - sak - en him; Come
8. ¹³Let all my foes be swal - lowed up, And
9. ¹⁴But as for me, I'll al - ways hope, And

strength fails, leave me not. ¹⁰For en - e - mies a -
seize him, none will save." ¹²O God, do not be
put them all to shame; Clothe them with scorn who
add to all Your praise. ¹⁵All day I'll tell Your

gainst me speak; To take my life, they plot.
far from me; God, hur - ry to my aid.
seek my hurt, Re - proach bring on their name.
sav - ing acts, Your count - less righ - teous ways.

Alexander R. Reinagle, c. 1836

ST. PETER CM

71C
I'll Come to Tell the Mighty Deeds

Psalm 71:16-24

We have testified about God that He raised Christ from the dead.
—1 Corinthians 15:15

10. 16 I'll come to tell the might-y deeds That God the LORD has done;
11. 18 And e-ven when I'm old and gray, O God, for-sake me not,
12. 20 Though in the past You made me see Much trou-ble and dis-tress,
13. O Ho-ly One of Is-ra-el, The harp I will em-ploy;

And I'll de-clare Your righ-teous-ness, I'll speak of Yours a-lone.
Un-til Your strength and pow'r I have Each gen-er-a-tion taught.
You will re-vive and raise me up From earth's en-clos-ing depths.
23 Re-deemed by You, I'll sing Your praise, Will shout Your praise with joy.

17 O God, I have been taught by You From ear-ly days of youth;
19 For God, Your righ-teous-ness ex-tends Be-yond the heights we view;
21 In-crease my hon-or, turn a-gain To give me peace and rest.
24 My tongue will al-so speak a-bout Your jus-tice all day long;

And all the won-ders You have done I still de-clare as truth.
And You have done such won-drous things, O God, who is like You?
22 My God, with harps I'll praise and sing A-bout Your faith-ful-ness.
For they are hum-bled and a-shamed Who seek to do me wrong.

Horatio R. Palmer, 1834–1907

POLITZ CMD

God, Give Your Judgments to the King

72A
Psalm 72:1-8

Isaiah says, "The Root of Jesse…will arise to rule over the nations; the Gentiles will hope in Him." —Romans 15:12

1. ¹ God, give Your judg - ments to the king, And give his son Your righ - teous - ness. ² He to Your peo - ple right will bring, With jus - tice will Your poor re - dress.
2. ³ Moun - tains will bring pros - per - i - ty, The hills bring peace by righ - teous - ness. ⁴ He'll judge the poor, their young set free, And crush the ones who have op - pressed.
3. ⁵ Long as the sun and moon are known They'll fear You through the ag - es all. ⁶ He'll come as rain on mead - ows mown, Like show - ers on the earth that fall.
4. ⁷ The just will flour - ish in his days, While lasts the moon will peace ex - tend. ⁸ From sea to sea will be his reign, And from the Riv - er to earth's end.

Thomas Williams, *Psalmodia Evangelica*, 1789

TRURO LM

72B

Nomads Will Bow

Psalm 72:9-15

The Lion of the tribe of Judah, the Root of David, has triumphed.
—Revelation 5:5

5. [9]No - mads will bow to him as king;
6. [11]So shall all kings be - fore him fall,
7. [13]He'll show the poor his sym - pa - thy,
8. [15]So he will live, and She - ba's gold

Lick - ing the dust, his foes will bend.
All na - tions his com - mands o - bey.
And he will save the need - y's life.
They'll as a gift be - fore him lay;

[10]Is - lands and Tar - shish gifts will bring,
[12]He'll save the need - y when they call,
[14]From fraud and force he'll set them free;
In con - stant prayer they'll him up - hold,

She - ba and Se - ba trib - ute send.
Those who are poor and have no aid.
Their blood is pre - cious in his sight.
And they will bless him all the day.

John Hatton, 1710–1793

DUKE STREET LM

May Waving Grain on Hilltops Thrive

72C

*Praise be to the Lord, the God of Israel, because He has come
and has redeemed His people. —Luke 1:68*

Psalm 72:16-19

9. ^{16}May wav - ing grain on hill - tops thrive; Like
10. ^{17}O may his name for - ev - er live; Yes,
11. ^{18}May God be blessed— the LORD a - lone— Blessed
12. ^{19}And may His name of glo - rious worth Re -

Leb - a - non, its har - vest yield. May
like the sun, may his fame last. By
be the God of Is - ra - el. For
ceive its praise e - ter - nal - ly; And

peo - ple flour - ish, towns re - vive, Like grass - es grow - ing
him may peo - ple bless - ings give, May all the na - tions
on - ly He has won - ders done; His works all oth - er
may His glo - ry fill the earth. A - men, A - men; so

in the field, Like grass - es grow - ing in the field.
call him blessed, May all the na - tions call him blessed.
deeds ex - cel, His works all oth - er deeds ex - cel.
may it be. A - men, A - men; so may it be.

William Bradbury, 1816–1868

ANDRE LM

72D

O God, Bestow Your Judgments on the King

The Lord God will give Him the throne of His Father David....
His kingdom will never end. —Luke 1:32-33

Psalm 72:1-11

1. ¹O God, be-stow Your judg-ments on the king,
2. ⁴The poor a-mong the peo-ple he will judge,
3. ⁶He will come down like rain up-on the grass,
4. ⁹The des-ert dwell-ers then will bow to him,

Your righ-teous-ness up-on the roy-al son.
And save the chil-dren of the in-di-gent.
As show-ers wa-ter-ing the thirst-y ground.
Be-fore him all his foes will lick the dust.

² With righ-teous-ness Your peo-ple he will judge,
The strong op-pres-sor he will break a-part.
⁷ Through-out his reign the righ-teous ones will thrive,
¹⁰ The kings of Tar-shish and the coast-al lands

Your poor af-flict-ed ones with eq-ui-ty.
⁵And they will look to You with god-ly fear
And peace will flour-ish while the moon en-dures.
Will come to him and bring an of-fer-ing;

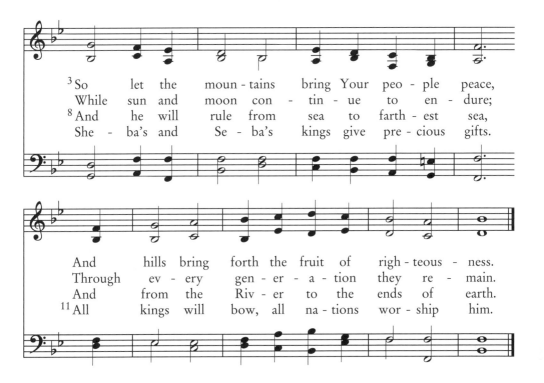

3 So let the moun-tains bring Your peo-ple peace,
While sun and moon con - tin - ue to en - dure;
8 And he will rule from sea to farth-est sea,
She - ba's and Se - ba's kings give pre-cious gifts.

And hills bring forth the fruit of righ - teous - ness.
Through ev - ery gen - er - a - tion they re - main.
And from the Riv - er to the ends of earth.
11 All kings will bow, all na - tions wor - ship him.

John Wainwright, 1750   YORKSHIRE 10.10.10.10.10.10

72E
Psalm 72:12-19

He Will Save the Needy

*Amen! Praise, glory, wisdom, thanks, honor and strength be
to our God forever and ever. Amen! —Revelation 7:12*

5. ¹² He will save the need-y when they call, Save the
6. ¹⁵ May he live, and gold from She-ba's realm Then be
7. ¹⁷ May his name en-dure for-ev-er-more; May it

poor, and those who have no help. ¹³ He has pit - y on the
giv-en as a gift to him. May the peo - ple al-ways
grow as un-der shin-ing sun. And may peo - ple then be

poor and weak, And he saves the lives of those in need.
pray for him, May they bless his name through-out the day.
blessed in him, And may all the na-tions call him blessed.

¹⁴ From op-pres-sion—   O
¹⁶ In all re-gions—   O
¹⁸ May the LORD God—   O

and from ev-ery vio-lence—
and up-on the hill-tops—
who a-lone does won-ders—

He re-deems their life and buys them back!
may there be a-bun-dant crops of grain!
may the God of Is-ra-el be blessed!

And how pre-cious—
Be-ing fruit-ful—
19 Blessed be His name—

O
O
O

pre-cious is their life-blood—
Leb-a-non with ce-dars—
glo-ri-ous for-ev-er—

how their life is pre-cious in his sight!
may the cit-y thrive like grass-y fields!
may His glo-ry fill the earth! A-men.

Traditional South African melody; arr. Brian E. Coombs, 2002   SIYAHAMBA 9.9.9.9.10.9.10.10

72F

Psalm 72:18-19

Book Two Doxology

*To Him who sits on the throne and to the Lamb be praise and
honor and glory and power forever and ever. —Revelation 5:13*

1. ¹⁸Now bless - ed be the LORD our God, The
2. ¹⁹And bless - ed be His glo - rious name, To

God of Is - ra - el; For He a - lone does
all e - ter - ni - ty. The whole earth let His

won - drous works, In glo - ry that ex - cel.
glo - ry fill; A - men, so let it be.

George Wittwe, *Musikalisches Handbüch*, 1690

EFFINGHAM CM

Book Two Doxology

To Him who sits on the throne and to the Lamb be praise
and honor and glory and power forever and ever. —Revelation 5:13

72G
Psalm 72:18-19

18 Bless - ed be the LORD, the God of Is - ra -
el, Who a - lone does won - drous things.

19 Bless - ed be His glo - rious name for - ev - er. Let His
glo - ry fill the whole earth. A - men, and A - men.

Eleanor Hutcheson, 1972

BETA (Irr.)

Yes, God is Good to Israel

Be content with what you have.
—Hebrews 13:5

1. ¹ Yes, God is good to Is - ra - el, To ev - ery one whose heart is pure. ² But as for me, I near - ly fell; My foot - steps were no long - er sure. ³ For I was en - vious of the proud And wick - ed ones with wealth en - dowed.

2. ⁴ For in their death no pains they know; Their strength is firm from day to day. ⁵ They share no part in oth - ers' woe, Nor plagued as oth - er men are they. ⁶ They make their neck - lace ar - ro - gance, And clothe them - selves with vi - o - lence.

3. ⁷ Their eyes are bulg - ing with ex - cess; Their hearts are full of things they seek. ⁸ They scoff; they threat - en to op - press. Dis - dain - ful words they proud - ly speak. ⁹ Their mouth the heights of heav - en raids; Their tongue a - round the world pa - rades.

4. ¹⁰ Their peo - ple there - fore with them turn To drink from streams that o - ver - flow. ¹¹ "For how," they say, "can God dis - cern?" And, "Does the Most High real - ly know?" ¹² Be - hold, un - god - ly men are these, Who gain in wealth and live at ease.

Henri F. Hemy, 1864; arr. James G. Walton, 1870   ST. CATHERINE 88.88.88

Then Surely I Have Toiled in Vain

God is not unjust so as to forget your work.
—Hebrews 6:10

73B

Psalm 73:13-22

5. [13]Then sure-ly I have toiled in vain To cleanse my heart from
6. [15]If I would let my thoughts so lead To speak with doubt-ing
7. [17]I en-tered then God's dwell-ing place And there I un-der-
8. [20]As from a dream You, Lord, a-wake; Then You their im-age

all of-fense, And vain-ly from each guilt-y stain Have
words this way, Be-hold, I then would cer-tain-ly The
stood their end; [18]You set them in a slip-pery place, And
will de-spise. [21]When pierced, with heart a-bout to break, When

washed my hands in in-no-cence. [14]Still griev-ous plagues all
chil-dren You have called be-tray. [16]But though the facts I
to de-struc-tion them You send. [19]How rap-id-ly de-
bit-ter thoughts with-in me rise, [22]I sense-less was and

day I've borne, And I was chas-tened ev-ery morn.
tried to see, The prob-lem deep-ly trou-bled me.
stroyed are they, By sud-den ter-rors swept a-way!
blind with-in; A beast be-fore You I have been.

Valentin Schumann, *Geistliche Lieder*, 1539

VATER UNSER 88.88.88

73C
Yet Constantly I Am with You

Psalm 73:23-27

I will never desert you, nor will I ever forsake you.
—Hebrews 13:5

9. ²³ Yet con-stant-ly I am with You; You've tak-en
10. ²⁵ Are You not all I have in heav'n? None else on
11. ²⁷ Those far from You will sure-ly die, Who dealt with

hold of my right hand. ²⁴ Your coun-sel shows me what to do,
earth do I de-sire. ²⁶ Though hu-man strength come to an end—
You un-faith-ful-ly. But as for me, I will draw nigh.

And guides me in the things I plan; And af-ter-
My flesh may fail, my heart ex-pire— My heart's strength
²⁸ How good that God is near to me! I ref-uge

ward, so shall it be, You will with hon-or wel-come me.
God Him-self will be, My por-tion through e-ter-ni-ty.
take in God the LORD, That all Your works I may re-cord.

D. Bruce Martin, 1920

TRUST 88.88.88

God, Why Forever Cast Us Off?

74A

Destroy this temple, and in three days I will raise it up.
—John 2:19

Psalm 74:1-11

1. [1] God, why for - ev - er cast us off? Why does Your an - ger
2. [2] Re - mem - ber them that You re - deemed Your tribe and her - i -
3. [4] Your foes laid waste the ho - ly place; They shout - ed in Your
4. [6] Their ax - es broke its fine-carved wood; [7] The ho - ly place they

burn A - gainst the flock of Your own field? Re -
tage, And Zi - on's moun - tain where You live. [3] O
halls, They set their for - eign em - blems up. [5] It
burned. The place You made Your name to dwell, Now

call Your gath - ered ones You pur - chased long a - go.
turn Your steps to walk Where ru - in is com - plete.
seemed as if an axe Had cut down for - est trees.
e - ven to the ground They have pro - faned and razed.

5. [8] "O let us crush them utterly!"
   So did their hearts declare.
   [9] They burned each God-appointed place.
   No prophet now, no signs,
   And none who knows how long!

6. [10] How long, O God, will foes insult
   And always scorn Your name?
   [11] O why do You hold back Your hand?
   Reach forth with Your right hand
   To end and to destroy!

Brian E. Coombs, 2001

HOLOCAUST 86.866

74B Yet God My King Brings Forth

Psalm 74:12-23

How long, O Lord, holy and true, will You refrain from judging?
—Revelation 6:10

7. ¹² Yet God my King brings forth of old Sal-va-tion
8. ¹⁵ You o-pened springs; You dried the streams. ¹⁶ Both day and
9. ¹⁸ O LORD, re-count how foes in-sult; How fools have

in the earth. ¹³ The sea You part-ed by Your strength;
night are Yours; You have or-dained both light and sun.
scorned Your name. ¹⁹ Your tur-tle-dove give not to beasts;

¹⁴ You smote Le-vi-a-than, And fed him to the beasts.
¹⁷ You gave the earth its bounds, And made the heat and cold.
Your meek ones' lives re-gard And not al-ways for-get.

10. ²⁰ O bring to mind the covenant;
See how the land grows dark,
²¹ Filled with the dens of violence.
Let not the meek be shamed,
But let them praise Your name.

11. ²² Arise, O God! Take up Your cause!
Recall the scorn of fools!
²³ Recall Your adversaries' cries,
The raging noise of foes
Which rises endlessly!

Thomas Williams, *Psalmodia Evangelica*, 1789

BROOMSGROVE 86.866

To You, O God, We Render Thanks

75A
Psalm 75

He will judge the world in righteousness
through a Man whom He has appointed. —Acts 17:31

1. ¹ To You, O God, we ren-der thanks, To You give thanks sin-cere,
2. ⁴ "'Boast not!' I said to boast-ful men, To vile men, 'Lift no horn!
3. ⁸ The LORD's hand holds a foam-ing cup Which po-tent wine con-tains;

Be-cause Your won-drous works de-clare That Your great name is near.
⁵ Do not lift up your horn on high, Nor speak with haugh-ty scorn!'"
He pours and makes the wick-ed drink Un - til the dregs he drains.

² "When My ap-point-ed time is come, I'll judge with e - ven hand.
⁶ From east or west or wil-der-ness None comes to glo - ri - fy.
⁹ But I for-ev - er will de-clare, To Ja-cob's God sing praise;

³ Though earth and all its dwell-ers melt, I make its pil - lars stand."
⁷ But God is Judge, de - bas - ing one, An - oth - er rais - ing high.
¹⁰ All horns of sin - ners He'll cut off, The righ-teous' horns are raised.

Benjamin C. Unseld, 1901

ANCYRA CMD

75B

Psalm 75

To You, O God, We Render Thanks

They will be tormented day and night forever and ever.
—Revelation 20:10

1. ¹To You, O God, we ren-der thanks, To You give thanks sin-cere,
2. ⁴ "'Boast not!' I said to boast-ful men, To vile men, 'Lift no horn!
3. ⁸ The LORD's hand holds a foam-ing cup Which po-tent wine con-tains;

Be-cause Your won-drous works de-clare That Your great name is near.
⁵Do not lift up your horn on high, Nor speak with haugh-ty scorn!'"
He pours and makes the wick-ed drink Un - til the dregs he drains.

² "When My ap-point-ed time is come, I'll judge with e - ven hand.
⁶ From east or west or wil-der-ness None comes to glo - ri - fy.
⁹ But I for-ev - er will de-clare, To Ja-cob's God sing praise;

³ Though earth and all its dwell-ers melt, I make its pil-lars stand."
⁷ But God is Judge, de - bas-ing one, An - oth - er rais-ing high.
¹⁰ All horns of sin-ners He'll cut off, The righ-teous' horns are raised.

William B. Bradbury, 1816-1868

PINNEO CMD

God Is Truly Known in Judah

He has a name written: King of kings and Lord of lords.
—Revelation 19:16

76A
Psalm 76

1. ¹God is tru-ly known in Ju-dah; Great His name in
Is-ra-el. ²He has pitched His tent in Sa-lem;
His house stands on Zi-on's hill. ³There He broke the
flam-ing ar-rows, There war's shield and sword made still.

2. ⁴You're more glo-rious and ma-jes-tic Than the moun-tains
filled with prey. ⁵Brave and val-iant ones You plun-dered,
Now they slum-ber in the grave; Though they once were
might-y war-riors, None can lift his hands to save.

3. ⁶Horse and rid-er both lie sleep-ing, Cast down in-to
death's dark night. You re-buked them, God of Ja-cob—
⁷Awe-in-spir-ing in Your might! Once Your an-ger
has been kin-dled, Who can stand be-fore Your sight?

4. ⁸You from heaven spoke Your verdict,
And the earth in fear was still.
⁹Saving all the earth's afflicted,
God arose to do His will.
¹⁰With what's left from wrath You're girded;
Human wrath will praise You still.

5. ¹¹Give the LORD your God your promise,
And fulfill your vows sincere.
Let all those around bring tribute
To the One to be revered.
¹²He brings low the pride of princes,
And by kings of earth is feared.

Henry Smart, 1867   REGENT SQUARE 87.87.87

76B
Psalm 76

God Is Truly Known in Judah

We know Him who said, "Vengeance is Mine; I will repay."
—Hebrews 10:30

Descant

5. [11]Give the LORD your God your prom - ise, And ful -

1. [1]God is tru - ly known in Ju - dah; Great His
2. [4]You're more glo - rious and ma - jes - tic Than the
3. [6]Horse and rid - er both lie sleep - ing, Cast down

fill your vows sin - cere. Let all those a -

name in Is - ra - el. [2]He has pitched His
moun - tains filled with prey. [5]Brave and val - iant
in - to death's dark night. You re - buked them,

round bring trib - ute To the One to be re -

tent in Sa - lem; His house stands on Zi - on's
ones You plun - dered, Now they slum - ber in the
God of Ja - cob— [7]Awe - in - spir - ing in Your

vered. He brings low the pride of princ - es,

hill. ³There He broke the flam - ing ar - rows,
grave; Though they once were might - y war - riors,
might! Once Your an - ger has been kin - dled,

And by kings of earth is feared.

There war's shield and sword made still.
None can lift his hands to save.
Who can stand be - fore Your sight?

4. ⁸ You from heaven spoke Your verdict,
    And the earth in fear was still.
    ⁹ Saving all the earth's afflicted,
    God arose to do His will.
    ¹⁰ With what's left from wrath You're girded;
    Human wrath will praise You still.

5. ¹¹ Give the LORD your God your promise,
    And fulfill your vows sincere.
    Let all those around bring tribute
    To the One to be revered.
    ¹² He brings low the pride of princes,
    And by kings of earth is feared.

Henry Purcell, 1659–1695   WESTMINSTER ABBEY 87.87.87

77A

Psalm 77:1-10

My Voice to God, Aloud I Plead

My soul is deeply grieved to the point of death.
—Mark 14:34

1. ¹My voice to God, aloud I plead!
2. ⁴You do not let my eye-lids close;
3. ⁸For - ev - er has His kind-ness ceased?

My voice to God, He will me heed!
I am made speech-less by my woes.
And is He from His word re - leased?

²I sought the Lord, I was dis - tressed,
⁵The days of old I think up - on,
⁹Did God for - get to show His grace?

I gave my out - stretched hands no rest.
The years that long a - go have gone.
Does wrath His mer - cy now re - place?

My   rest - less   soul   all   through   the   night
⁶ I   pon - der   songs   I   sang   at   night;
¹⁰ Then   I   re - plied, "Such   ques - tions   show

No   com - fort   found   in   com - ing   light.
My   heart   and   spir - it   search   for   light.
That   I   my   weak - ness   need   to   know.

³ With   thoughts   of   God   my   fears   a -   rise;
⁷ For - ev - er   will   the   Lord   re -   ject?
The   Most   High   has   a   firm   right   hand

My   fail - ing   spir - it   faints   with   sighs.
Can   I   His   fa - vor   not   ex - pect?
That   through   the   years   will   change - less   stand."

William Bradbury, 1864

HE LEADETH ME   LMD

77B

Psalm 77:11-20

The Lord's Deeds I Remember

He rescued us from the domain of darkness and
transferred us to the kingdom of His beloved Son. —Colossians 1:13

4. ¹¹The Lord's deeds I re-mem-ber all, Your won-drous
5. ¹³O God, Your ways most ho-ly are. What god can
6. ¹⁵You by Your arm Your peo-ple freed, The sons of

works of old re-call. ¹²I'll pon-der all that
with our God com-pare? ¹⁴You are the God by
Ja-cob, Jo-seph's seed. ¹⁶O God, the wa-ters

You have done And weigh Your might-y acts, each one.
won-ders known; A-mong the peo-ples, strength You've shown.
sight-ed You, Deep seas shook when You came in view.

7. ¹⁷⁻¹⁸From clouds the rain in torrents poured,
Across the sky tornadoes roared.
The world was lit when lightning flashed,
Earth trembled when the thunder crashed.

8. ¹⁹Great waters formed a path for You,
Your footprints hidden from our view.
²⁰Your people like a flock were fed,
By Moses and by Aaron led.

William Knapp, 1738

WAREHAM LM

O Come, My People

He spoke many things to them in parables.
— Matthew 13:3

1. ¹ O come, my peo-ple, to my law At-ten-tive-ly give ear;
2. ⁴ We'll from their chil-dren hide them not, But tell the age to come
3. That chil-dren yet un-born might know, And their de-scen-dants lead,

The words that from my mouth pro-ceed In-cline your-selves to hear.
The prais-es of the LORD, His strength, The won-ders He has done.
⁷ To trust in God, re-call God's works, And His com-mand-ments heed;

² My mouth will speak a par-a-ble, The say-ings dark of old,
⁵ His word He un-to Ja-cob gave, His law to Is-ra-el,
⁸ And not be what their fa-thers were— Re-bel-lious through and through,

³ Which we have lis-tened to and known As by our fa-thers told.
Which He our fa-thers did com-mand ⁶ To teach their chil-dren well,
For they would not cor-rect their hearts, Nor un-to God stay true.

Ludwig Spohr, 1784–1859

ILLA CMD

78B
O Come, My People

Psalm 78:1-8

He did not speak to them without a parable.
— Mark 4:34

1. ¹O come, my peo-ple, to my law At-ten-tive-ly give ear;
2. ⁴We'll from their chil-dren hide them not, But tell the age to come
3. That chil-dren yet un-born might know, And their de-scen-dants lead,

The words that from my mouth pro-ceed In-cline your-selves to hear.
The prais-es of the LORD, His strength, The won-ders He has done.
⁷To trust in God, re-call God's works, And His com-mand-ments heed;

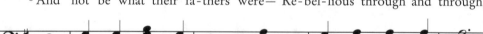

²My mouth will speak a par-a-ble, The say-ings dark of old,
⁵His word He un-to Ja-cob gave, His law to Is-ra-el,
⁸And not be what their fa-thers were— Re-bel-lious through and through,

³Which we have lis-tened to and known As by our fa-thers told.
Which He our fa-thers did com-mand ⁶To teach their chil-dren well,
For they would not cor-rect their hearts, Nor un-to God stay true.

Traditional French melody

CHAMPS ELYSEES CMD

Ephraim's Sons

If anyone is thirsty, let him come to Me and drink.
—John 7:37

78C
Psalm 78:9-16

4. ⁹Eph - ra - im's sons, though armed with bows, In
5. ¹¹All of His deeds they soon for - got, His
6. ¹³He split the sea to let them pass, The
7. ¹⁵He split the rocks and gave them drink, As

bat - tle did re - treat. ¹⁰They in God's law re -
mir - a - cles of might, ¹²In E - gypt's land, in
wa - ters stood a - side; ¹⁴By day He led them
from great deeps be - low; ¹⁶He from the rock brought

fused to walk, His cov - 'nant would not keep.
Zo - an's field, Be - fore their fa - thers' sight.
with a cloud, And fire at night to guide.
run - ning streams; Like riv - ers, wa - ters flowed.

Johann G. Nageli; arr. Lowell Mason, 1836

NAOMI CM

78D

Yet in the Desert Still They Sinned

I am the bread of life.
—John 6:48

Psalm 78:17-25

8. [17] Yet in the des - ert still they sinned, And
9. [20] "Be - hold, He struck the rock, and out Gushed
10. [22] For they did not be - lieve in God Nor

from the Most High turned. [18] They test - ed God, de -
streams of wa - ter sweet; But can He give His
trust His sav - ing love. [23] But still He o - pened

mand - ing food And all for which they yearned.
peo - ple bread And fur - nish them with meat?"
heav - en's doors, Com - mand - ed skies a - bove,

[19] They spoke a - gainst their God and said, "Can
[21] Be - cause the LORD heard this, His wrath Was
[24] And rained His man - na down on them; From

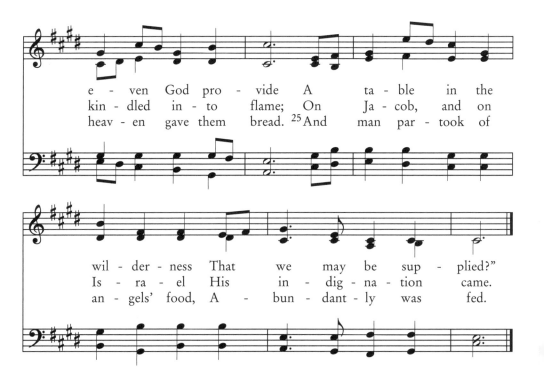

even God pro - vide A ta - ble in the
kin - dled in - to flame; On Ja - cob, and on
heav - en gave them bread. [25]And man par - took of

wil - der - ness That we may be sup - plied?"
Is - ra - el His in - dig - na - tion came.
an - gels' food, A - bun - dant - ly was fed.

Franki Fuhrman, 2002

DONNELLY CMD

78E

In Heav'n He Made the East Wind Blow

Psalm 78:26-33

Now these things happened to them as an example.
—1 Corinthians 10:11

11. 26 In heav'n He made the east wind blow, The
12. 28 He let them fall in - side their camp By
13. 30 But while their mouths were crammed with food 31 God's
14. 32 And yet de - spite His mir - a - cles, They

south wind did com - mand; 27 He rained down meat on
tents on ev - ery side. 29 And so they ate till
wrath up - on them fell; He killed their strong young
sinned in un - be - lief; 33 So He cut off their

them like dust, And birds like o - cean sand.
they were filled; Their greed He sat - is - fied.
men, cut down The best of Is - ra - el.
fu - tile lives, Their years with sud - den grief.

William Robert Broomfield, 1826–1888   ST. KILDA CM

They'd Turn and Seek God Eagerly

The rock was Christ.
—*1 Corinthians 10:4*

78F

Psalm 78:34-39

15. [34] They'd turn and seek God ea - ger - ly When
16. [36] But Him they served with emp - ty words, And
17. [38] Yet He, in - stead of kill - ing them, For -
18. His an - ger He does not stir up. [39] That

He had made some die; [35] Then they re - mem - bered
with their tongue they lied; [37] Their heart was not sin -
gave in - iq - ui - ty, And in com - pas - sion
they are flesh He knows— A wind that nev - er

God, their Rock, Their Sav - ior, God Most High.
cere toward Him, His cov - 'nant they de - nied.
He re - strained His wrath re - peat - ed - ly.
does re - turn When once it comes and goes.

Thomas Est, *The Whole Book of Psalmes*, 1592; arr. George Kirbye

WINCHESTER OLD CM

78G

These Rebels in the Wilderness

Psalm 78:40-50

Do not grieve the Holy Spirit of God.
—Ephesians 4:30

19. ⁴⁰These reb-els in the wil-der-ness Kept griev-ing Him a-gain, ⁴¹Kept test-ing Is-r'el's Ho-ly One, And so to God brought pain! ⁴²His pow'r in free-ing them from foes They

20. ⁴⁴He turned their riv-ers in-to blood, Which could not quench their thirst. ⁴⁵He sent de-vour-ing swarms of flies, With frogs their land He cursed. ⁴⁶Their crops by in-sects were de-stroyed, To

21. ⁴⁸He struck their flocks with light-ning bolts, With hail their herds de-stroyed. ⁴⁹In an-ger, wrath, and hos-tile rage, Death's an-gels He de-ployed. ⁵⁰He for His an-ger smoothed a path, They

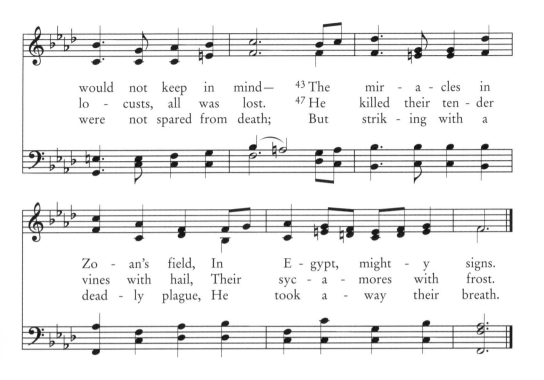

would not keep in mind— 43 The mir - a - cles in
lo - custs, all was lost. 47 He killed their ten - der
were not spared from death; But strik - ing with a

Zo - an's field, In E - gypt, might - y signs.
vines with hail, Their syc - a - mores with frost.
dead - ly plague, He took a - way their breath.

Franki Fuhrman, 2002

ANATEVKA CMD

78H

Psalm 78:51-55

Then He Struck Down

...The great Shepherd of the sheep through the blood of the eternal covenant, even Jesus our Lord. —*Hebrews 13:20*

22. [51] Then He struck down in E-gypt's land Their
23. [53] He led them safe - ly, un - a - fraid; The

first-born sons, their pride, Un - til in all the
sea en - gulfed their foes. [54] He brought them to His

tents of Ham Their heirs of strength had died. [52] But
ho - ly land, The hills His right hand chose. [55] Be -

His own peo - ple forth like sheep He brought with guid - ing
fore them He drove na - tions out, From lands and from their

hand,   And led His peo - ple   like a   flock
tents;   Al - lot - ted these   to   Is - r'el's tribes

A - cross the des - ert   land.
For   their in - her - i - tance.

Robert Lowry, 1860   ENDLESS SONG CMD

781

Psalm 78:56-64

Yet They Rebelled

Behold, your house is being left to you desolate!
— Matthew 23:38

24. [56] Yet they re-belled and test-ed God; The Most High's law they spurned. [57] As faith-less as their fa-thers were, Like treach-'rous bow, they turned.

25. [58] Their shrines and i-dols an-gered Him, Pro-voked His jeal-ou-sy. [59] God heard and turned from Is-ra-el, He spurned them an-gri-ly.

26. [60] His place in Shi-loh He has left, The tent He made with men. [61] To ex-ile He gave up His strength, To foes His glo-ry then.

27. [62] He gave His people to the sword,
    Allowed them to be killed.
    Against His own inheritance
    With anger He was filled.

28. [63] Their young men were devoured by fire,
    Their maidens left unwed;
    [64] And when their priests fell by the sword,
    No tears their widows shed.

William Bradbury, 1816–1868   AGAWAM CM

As When Wine Makes the Soldier Bold

Do not be afraid, little flock, for your Father
has chosen gladly to give you the kingdom. —Luke 12:32

78J

Psalm 78:65-72

29. [65] As when wine makes the sol - dier bold, As
30. [67] Then He re - ject - ed Jo - seph's tent, The
31. [69] Like heights He built His ho - ly place, For -

one wakes with a start; [66] The Lord drove back His
tribe of E - phra - im. [68] But He the tribe of
ev - er firm to keep. [70] He for His ser - vant

en - e - mies, Whose shame shall not de - part.
Ju - dah chose, Mount Zi - on, loved by Him.
Da - vid chose, Took him from guard - ing sheep.

32. [71] From tending ewes He brought him out
To shepherd Jacob well,
To care for His inheritance,
His chosen Israel.

33. [72] So with integrity of heart
Them faithfully he fed;
And with his understanding hands,
He guided as he led.

Charles Steggall, 1849   ST. AMBROSE CM

79A

Psalm 79:1-7

O God, To Your Inheritance

You will be hated by all because of My name.
—Matthew 10:22

1. ¹O God, to Your in-her-i-tance
2. ²Flesh of Your ser-vants they have cast
3. ³Their blood a-bout Je-ru-sa-lem
4. ⁴To all our neigh-bors we've be-come

The na-tions en-tered in, Your house de-
To heav-en's birds for meat; They gave the
Like wa-ter has been shed; There was no
Ob-jects of their re-proach, A laugh-ing-

filed, in ru-ins laid Je-ru-sa-lem.
bod-ies of Your saints For beasts to eat.
one to bur-y them When they were dead.
stock to all who now On us en-croach.

5. ⁵How long, O LORD? Your wrath toward us
   Will You forever turn?
   And will Your jealousy, like fire,
   Forever burn?

6. ⁶On heathen nations pour Your wrath,
   Who call not on Your name;
   ⁷For Jacob they devour, and waste
   His fields in flame.

Arthur H. Brown, 1830–1926

HOLY CROSS 86.84

O Charge Us Not with Former Sins

79B

Your sins have been forgiven you for His name's sake.
—1 John 2:12

Psalm 79:8-13

7. ⁸O charge us not with for - mer sins, But
8. ⁹O God of our sal - va - tion, help! To
9. ¹⁰Do na - tions say, "Where is their God?" Let
10. ¹¹O let the pris - 'ner's sigh - ing groans As -

Your com - pas - sion show. Come quick - ly,
Your name glo - ry take! De - liv - er
na - tions know in - stead Your ven - geance
cend to You on high; Pre - serve them

meet us in our need; We are brought low.
us; for - give our sins For Your name's sake.
for Your ser - vants' blood Which has been shed.
by Your might - y arm, Those doomed to die.

11. ¹²And back upon our neighbors turn,
In sevenfold reward,
Reproachful words which they have cast
On You, O Lord.

12. ¹³So we Your people, Your own flock
Forever thank Your name;
We will to generations all
Your praise proclaim.

D. Bruce Martin, 1920

FAIR HAVEN 86.84

80

Hear, O Hear Us

I am the good Shepherd.
—John 10:14

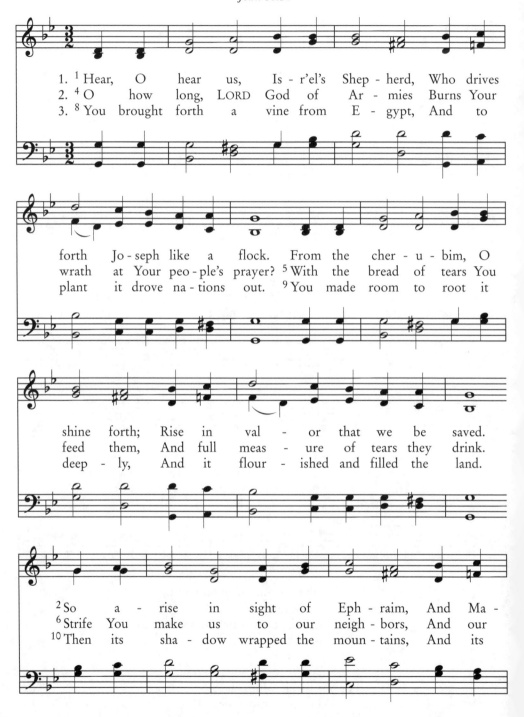

1. [1] Hear, O hear us, Is-r'el's Shep-herd, Who drives
2. [4] O how long, LORD God of Ar-mies Burns Your
3. [8] You brought forth a vine from E-gypt, And to

forth Jo-seph like a flock. From the cher-u-bim, O
wrath at Your peo-ple's prayer? [5] With the bread of tears You
plant it drove na-tions out. [9] You made room to root it

shine forth; Rise in val - or that we be saved.
feed them, And full meas - ure of tears they drink.
deep - ly, And it flour - ished and filled the land.

[2] So a - rise in sight of Eph - raim, And Ma -
[6] Strife You make us to our neigh - bors, And our
[10] Then its sha - dow wrapped the moun - tains, And its

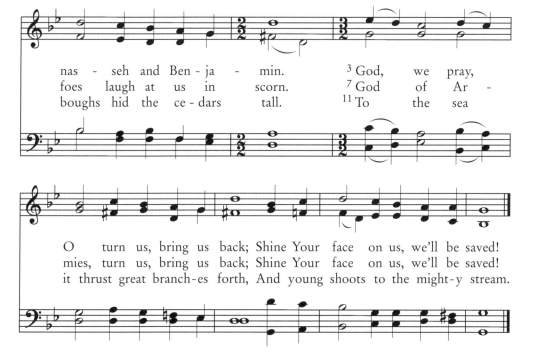

nas - seh and Ben - ja - min. [3] God, we pray,
foes laugh at us in scorn. [7] God of Ar -
boughs hid the ce - dars tall. [11] To the sea

O turn us, bring us back; Shine Your face on us, we'll be saved!
mies, turn us, bring us back; Shine Your face on us, we'll be saved!
it thrust great branch-es forth, And young shoots to the might-y stream.

4. [12] Why have You torn down its fences?
   It is plucked by each passing hand.
   [13] Forest boars have gnawed upon it,
   And wild creatures have pastured there.
   [14] Turn again, O God of Armies,
   Look from heav'n, visit this Your vine.
   [15] So uphold what Your right hand did plant,
   And the son You raised up in strength.

5. [16] It is burned and hewn in pieces;
   By Your frown will they be destroyed.
   [17] Lay Your hand on him You favored,
   Son of man that You raised in strength.
   [18] Then from You we will not wander;
   Make us live; we will call Your name.
   [19] O LORD God of Armies, turn us back;
   Shine Your face on us, we'll be saved!

William Owen, 1852   BRYN CALFARIA 88.88.88.98

81A

Psalm 81:1-7

To God Our Strength

Come to Me, all who are weary and heavy-laden,
and I will give you rest. —Matthew 11:28

1. ¹To God our Strength, to Ja-cob's God, A song and shout now raise! ²With psalm and tim-brel, harp and lute, A-wake to joy-ous praise! ³At each new moon the trum-pet blow For sol-emn fes-tal days.

2. ⁴This is the law of Ja-cob's God, For Is-r'el His com-mand. ⁵This wit-ness He in Jo-seph set, When he ruled E-gypt's land. I heard a tongue I did not know And could not un-der-stand.

3. ⁶"I from his shoul-ders took the load, His bur-dened hands found rest. ⁷You called in trou-ble; My re-sponse In thun-der I ex-pressed. And by the streams of Mer-i-bah, I put you to the test."

J.L. Macbeth Bain, c.1840–1925; arr. Brian E. Coombs, 2004

BROTHER JAMES' AIR 86.86.86

Hear, O My People

Long for the pure milk of the word.
—1 Peter 2:2

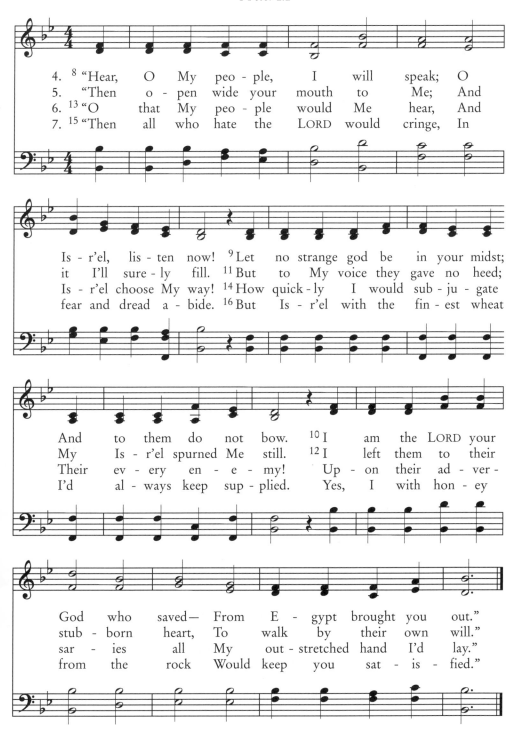

4. [8] "Hear, O My peo-ple, I will speak; O
5. "Then o-pen wide your mouth to Me; And
6. [13] "O that My peo-ple would Me hear, And
7. [15] "Then all who hate the LORD would cringe, In

Is - r'el, lis - ten now! [9] Let no strange god be in your midst;
it I'll sure - ly fill. [11] But to My voice they gave no heed;
Is - r'el choose My way! [14] How quick - ly I would sub - ju - gate
fear and dread a - bide. [16] But Is - r'el with the fin - est wheat

And to them do not bow. [10] I am the LORD your
My Is - r'el spurned Me still. [12] I left them to their
Their ev - ery en - e - my! Up - on their ad - ver -
I'd al - ways keep sup - plied. Yes, I with hon - ey

God who saved— From E - gypt brought you out."
stub - born heart, To walk by their own will."
sar - ies all My out - stretched hand I'd lay."
from the rock Would keep you sat - is - fied."

William Bradbury, 1816–1868

KEOKUK 86.86.86

82A

God Is in His Congregation

Psalm 82

He called them "gods"...I am the Son of God.
—John 10:34-36

1. ¹God is in His con-gre-ga-tion; Judge a-
2. ³Judge the need-y and the or-phan, And the
3. ⁵These are they who have no knowl-edge, To per-

mong the gods He stands. ²How long will you judge un-
poor, dis-tressed de-fend; ⁴Free the des-ti-tute and
ceive no ef-fort make; They walk on in ut-ter

just-ly, Fa-vor-ing the wick-ed hands?
need-y; Save them from the wick-ed's hand.
dark-ness; All of earth's foun-da-tions shake.

4. ⁶Gods you are, I have declared it,
   You are sons of Him Most High;
   ⁷Yet you'll fall like other princes,
   And as common men you'll die.

5. ⁸Now, O God, arise, we pray You,
   And the earth to judgment call;
   For You, as Your own possession,
   Shall inherit nations all.

Latvian folk song

LATVIA 87.87

God Is in His Congregation

82B
Psalm 82

The Scripture cannot be broken.
—John 10:35

1. [1] God is in His con - gre - ga - tion;
2. [3] Judge the need - y and the or - phan,
3. [5] These are they who have no knowl - edge,

Judge a - mong the gods He stands. [2] How long will you
And the poor, dis - tressed de - fend; [4] Free the des - ti -
To per - ceive no ef - fort make; They walk on in

judge un - just - ly, Fa - vor - ing the wick - ed hands?
tute and need - y; Save them from the wick - ed's hand.
ut - ter dark - ness; All of earth's foun - da - tions shake.

4. [6] Gods you are, I have declared it,
   You are sons of Him Most High;
   [7] Yet you'll fall like other princes,
   And as common men you'll die.

5. [8] Now, O God, arise, we pray You,
   And the earth to judgment call;
   For You, as Your own possession,
   Shall inherit nations all.

Christian F. Witt, *Psalmodia Sacra*, 1715   STUTTGART 87.87

Do Not Be Silent, God

There were gathered together against Your holy servant,
Jesus...the Gentiles and the peoples of Israel. —Acts 4:27

1. ¹ Do not be si - lent, God, or un - re - spond - ing!
2. ⁵ To - geth - er they con - spire in dead - ly ear - nest;
3. ⁹ Treat them like Mid - i - an, like Ja - bin's ar - my.
4. ¹⁴ Like fire that burns the woods, like flames of light - ning,

Do not re - main at rest, O Might - y One!
A - gainst You they have made a cov - e - nant.
Treat them like Sis - e - ra at Ki - shon's brook.
¹⁵Pur - sue them with Your storms and strike with fear.

² For now Your foes a - rouse and make a clam - or;
⁶ The Ish - mael - ites are there, the tents of E - dom,
¹⁰ At En - dor they were all an - ni - hi - lat - ed,
¹⁶ Fill up their fac - es with hu - mil - i - a - tion,

Your bit - ter en - e - mies lift up the head.
The men of Mo - ab with the Hag - a - renes.
And they be - came like dung up - on the ground.
And let them come, O LORD, to seek Your name.

3 A - gainst Your peo - ple now they plot in se - cret;
7 See Ge - bal, Am - a - lek, with men of Am - mon;
11 Like Ze - bah, Zal - mun - na, O - reb, and Ze - eb,
17 Let them be ter - ri - fied and shamed for - ev - er,

They meet to work a - gainst Your hid - den ones.
Be - hold Phi - lis - ti - a and them of Tyre.
12 Those chiefs who tried to seize the land of God.
And let them be dis - mayed and be de - stroyed.

4 They say, "Let us go up and end their na - tion.
8 For As - shur too has come and joins their forc - es;
13 My God, O make them be like whirl - ing dust clouds;
18 Let them know You a - lone— whose name is Yah - weh—

The name of Is - ra - el shall be no more!"
They are the pow - er of the sons of Lot.
Make them like bits of chaff be - fore the wind.
You are the One Most High o'er all the earth.

Andre Campra; arr. G. Duncan Lowe, 1972   SALVUM FAC 11.10.11.10 D

84A
Psalm 84:1-6

How Lovely, LORD

Did you not know that I had to be in My Father's house?
— Luke 2:49

1. ¹How love-ly, LORD of hosts, to me The tab-er-na-cles
2. ³The spar-row has her place of rest; The swal-low through Your
3. ⁴Blessed they who in Your house a-bide; To You they ev-er

of Your grace! ²O how I long, yes, faint to see The
kind-ly care Has found where she may build her nest And
ren-der praise. ⁵Blessed they who in Your strength con-fide, And

LORD's own courts, His dwell-ing place! My heart and flesh with
brood her young in safe-ty there. Your al-tars as my
in whose heart are pil-grims' ways. ⁶They make the vale of

joy draw nigh; As to the liv-ing God I cry.
rest I sing, O LORD of hosts, my God, my King.
tears a spring, With showers of bless-ing cov-er-ing.

Traditional English melody, 19th century

STELLA 88.88.88

Advancing Still

You have come to Mount Zion and to the city of the living God.
—Hebrews 12:22

84B
Psalm 84:7-12

4. [7] Ad - vanc-ing still from strength to strength They go where oth - er
5. [9] And look, O God, up - on our Shield; The face of Your A -
6. [11] For God the LORD is shield and sun; The LORD will grace and

pil - grims trod, Till each to Zi - on comes at length And
noint - ed view; [10] One day with - in Your courts will yield More
glo - ry give. No good will He with - hold from one Who

stands be - fore the face of God. [8] LORD God of hosts, my
good than thou - sands with - out You. I'd rath - er stand near
does up - right - ly walk and live. [12] O LORD of hosts, that

plead - ing hear; O Ja - cob's God, to me give ear.
my God's house Than dwell in tents of wick - ed - ness.
one is blessed, Who makes his trust up - on You rest.

John B. Dykes, 1861

MELITA 88.88.88

84C

84C
Psalm 84:1-7

Your Dwelling Places, Lord

You also, as living stones, are being built up as a spiritual house.
— 1 Peter 2:5

1. ¹ Your dwell-ing plac-es, LORD of hosts, How beau-ti-ful they
2. ³ My God, my King, with-in Your house The spar-row has a
3. ⁵ Those find-ing strength in You are blessed, With pil-grims' hearts they

are to me. ² The LORD's courts are my soul's de-sire, I'm
dwell-ing there. O LORD of hosts, Your al-tars are Where
on-ward reach, ⁶ The val-ley's tears they turn to springs, While

yearn-ing for them ea-ger-ly. I to the liv-ing God cry
swal-lows choose their young to bear. ⁴ Blessed all who in Your house do
rain with bless-ings cov-ers each. ⁷ They, gain-ing strength, toward Zi-on

out, With joy my heart and bod-y shout!
live, To You their praise they ev-er give.
run; Be-fore God then ap-pears each one.

Traditional English carol; arr. Ralph Vaughan-Williams, 1919   SUSSEX CAROL 88.88.88

O Hear My Prayer

The Lord God, the Almighty, and the Lamb are its temple.
— Revelation 21:22

84D
Psalm 84:8-12

4. 8 O hear my prayer, LORD God of hosts;
5. 10 Much bet-ter one day in Your courts
6. 11 A sun and shield is God the LORD;

O Ja-cob's God, give ear to me.
Com-pared to thou-sands spent out-side!
The LORD gives grace and glo-ry too;

9 With fa-vor, God, look on our shield,
I'd rath-er as God's door-man stand
From blame-less ones, no good with-holds.

The face of Your a-noint-ed see.
Than in the wick-ed's tents re-side.
12 Blessed, LORD of hosts, those trust-ing You.

William Bradbury, 1849

WOODWORTH LM

85A

Psalm 85:1-7

O Lord, Unto Your Land

He has given help to Israel His servant,
in remembrance of His mercy. —Luke 1:54

1. ¹O LORD, un - to Your land You showed
2. ²For - giv - en have Your peo - ple been,
3. ⁴So now, O God our Sav - ior, turn!
4. ⁶Will You not give us life once more,

Your fa - vor gra - cious - ly be - stowed;
And You have cov - ered all their sin.
Let in - dig - na - tion cease to burn!
Your peo - ple's joy in You re - store?

The cap - tive Ja - cob You set free,
³From us You've tak - en all Your wrath,
⁵Will You for - ev - er an - gry stay?
⁷O LORD, Your lov - ing - kind - ness show,

Re - stored his wealth and lib - er - ty.
And turned from Your fierce an - ger's path.
From age to age Your wrath dis - play?
And Your sal - va - tion now be - stow.

John E. Gould, 1849

BERA LM

I'll Hear What God the LORD Will Say

Grace and truth were realized through Jesus Christ.
—John 1:17

85B

Psalm 85:8-13

5. ⁸I'll hear what God the LORD will say:
6. ⁹His sav - ing help is sure - ly near
7. ¹⁰To - geth - er met are truth and grace,
8. ¹²The LORD will give us what is good;

Peace to His peo - ple He'll con - vey;
To those who wor - ship Him in fear,
While righ - teous - ness and peace em - brace;
Our land will yield a - bun - dant food.

To god - ly ones He's prom - ised this,
That glo - ry great may ev - er dwell
¹¹True faith - ful - ness springs from the ground,
¹³Be - fore Him righ - teous - ness shall go,

If they re - frain from fool - ish - ness.
With - in the land of Is - ra - el.
From heav - en righ - teous - ness looks down.
Which for His feet a path will show.

William Bradbury, 1843

BRADBURY LM

86A

Lord, Listen and Answer

Psalm 86:1-10

In the days of His flesh, He offered up
both prayers and supplications. —Hebrews 5:7

1. ¹ LORD, lis-ten and an-swer; O hear me, I pray.
2. ³ Since all the day long I am cry-ing to You,
3. ⁵ You tru-ly, O Lord, are for-giv-ing and good,

I, need-y and poor, cry to You.
Toward me, Lord, Your mer-cy re-new.
A-bound-ing in kind-ness and love

² Watch o-ver my soul; save Your ser-vant, O God;
⁴ Bring joy to the soul of Your ser-vant, O Lord;
⁶ To all those who call to You. LORD, hear my prayer;

De-vot-ed, I'm trust-ing in You.
I lift up my soul un-to You.
My plead-ing at-tend from a-bove.

4. ⁷ In day of my trouble upon You I'll call;
   An answer for me You'll prepare.
   ⁸ Among all the gods, LORD, there's no one like You,
   And no works with Yours can compare.

5. ⁹ All nations created by You, Lord, will come,
   And bowing, Your name they will laud.
   ¹⁰ Because You are great and great wonders have done;
   For You, and You only, are God.

John K. Robb, 1949

CONWELL 11.8.11.8

Your Way Teach Me, Lord

86B

This Jesus God raised up again.
—Acts 2:32

Psalm 86:11-17

6. ¹¹Your way teach me, LORD; I will walk in Your truth;
7. ¹³For great are Your love and Your kind-ness to me;
8. ¹⁵Lord, mer-ci-ful God, full of grace, slow to wrath,
9. The son of Your hand-maid de-liv-er and save;

U - nite my heart Your name to fear.
My soul You have freed from the grave.
A - bound - ing in truth and in love,
¹⁷A sign of Your good - ness re - new,

¹²My Lord and my God, with my whole heart I'll praise,
¹⁴O God, vio - lent men and the proud seek my life,
¹⁶Re - turn un - to me; Your rich grace now be - stow;
That all those who hate me may see and be shamed.

And ev - er Your name will re - vere.
For - get - ful of You and Your praise.
Your ser - vant make strong from a - bove.
My help, LORD, and strength are in You.

Hart P. Danks, 1834–1903

DELPHINE 11.8.11.8

87A

Psalm 87

The Lord's Foundation

*Behold, a great multitude...from every nation and all tribes
and peoples and tongues. —Revelation 7:9*

1. ¹ The LORD's foun - da - tion has been set Up-
2. ³ A - bout you glo - rious things are said, O
3. "Phi - lis - tia, E - gypt, Bab - y - lon, And

on the ho - ly hills; ² He loves the gates of
cit - y of our God: ⁴ "I will make men - tion
Tyre to - geth - er share A - long with E - thi -

Zi - on more Than homes where Ja - cob dwells.
of the lands Where I am known a - broad."
o - pi - a: 'That this is one born there!'"

4. ⁵ Of Zion it will be declared:
   "Each one was born in her."
   Behold, the Most High will Himself
   Establish her secure.

5. ⁶ The LORD, in listing citizens,
   Notes, "He was born there, too."
   ⁷ The choristers and minstrels sing,
   "My springs are found in you."

Henry Smart, 1867

ST. LEONARD CM

The Lord's Foundation

No one can lay a foundation other than that which is laid,
which is Jesus Christ. —1 Corinthians 3:11

1. ¹The Lord's foun-da-tion has been set Up-
2. ³A-bout you glo-rious things are said, O
3. "Phil-is-tia, E-gypt, Bab-y-lon, And

on the ho-ly hills; ²He loves the gates of
cit-y of our God: ⁴"I will make men-tion
Tyre to-geth-er share A-long with E-thi-

Zi-on more Than homes where Ja-cob dwells.
of the lands Where I am known a-broad."
o-pi-a: 'That this is one born there!'"

4. ⁵Of Zion it will be declared:
   "Each one was born in her."
   Behold, the Most High will Himself
   Establish her secure.

5. ⁶The Lord, in listing citizens,
   Notes, "He was born there, too."
   ⁷The choristers and minstrels sing,
   "My springs are found in you."

George Wittwe, *Musikalisches Handbüch*, 1690

EFFINGHAM CM

88A

Psalm 88:1-9a

LORD, My Salvation

Christ redeemed us from the curse of the Law,
having become a curse for us. — Galatians 3:13

1. ¹ LORD, my sal - va - tion You, O God, sup - plied;
2. ³ My soul is full of anx - ious cares and gloom;
3. ⁵ As one cast off a - mong the dead am I;

All day and night be - fore You I have cried.
My wear - y life draws near the si - lent tomb.
I'm like the slain ones in the grave that lie,

² O let my prayer be - fore Your pres - ence rise,
⁴ I count as those that to the pit de - scend;
Whom You do not re - mem - ber an - y - more,

Your ear in - cline to hear my plead - ing cries.
I'm like the man whose strength is at an end.
Those cut off from Your hand where none re - store.

4. ⁶ By You within the lowest pit I'm laid,
In deeps and in the place of darkest shade.
⁷ On me Your anger pressed down heavily,
And all Your breaking waves afflicted me.

5. ⁸ My former friends You have estranged from me;
Yes, their abhorrence You have made me be.
Shut up am I, imprisoned here must stay;
⁹ Through deep distress my eyes both waste away.

Brian E. Coombs, 2002

ADIRONDACK 10.10.10.10

O Lord, I've Daily Called

"My God, My God, why have You forsaken Me?"
— Matthew 27:46

88B
Psalm 88:9b-18

6. 9 O Lord, I've dai - ly called up - on Your name,
7. 11 Shall Your great love be in the grave ex - tolled?
8. 13 But un - to You, O Lord, for help I've cried;

Spread forth my hands Your gra - cious help to claim.
Your faith - ful - ness be in de - struc - tion told?
My prayer shall rise to You with morn - ing light.

10 Will You Your won - ders make the dead to know?
12 In dark - ness will Your won - ders be con - fessed?
14 O Lord, why cast my soul a - way from You?

And shall the dead a - rise Your praise to show?
Where mem - 'ries fade who knows Your righ - teous - ness?
Why do You keep Your face hid from my view?

9. 15 From youth I've been distressed, about to die;
Your terrors I have borne, distraught was I.
16 Your burning anger over me has passed,
Your terrors all have cut me off at last.

10. 17 All day like floods Your terrors 'round me surged.
They cover me; by them I've been submerged.
18 By You I am of all my friends bereft,
And those who loved me are in darkness left.

Edward J. Hopkins, 1869

ELLERS 10.10.10.10

89A
Psalm 89:1-6

The Lovingkindness of the Lord

The Lord God will give Him the throne of His father David.
—Luke 1:32

1. ¹ The lov-ing-kind-ness of the LORD For-ev-er I will sing. Your faith-ful-ness to ev-ery age My mouth in song shall bring.
2. ² I will pro-claim, "Your stead-fast love For-ev-er will en-dure. Your faith-ful-ness in heav-en high You will es-tab-lish sure."
3. ³ "I've made a cov-e-nant with him Who is My cho-sen one; To Da-vid, who My ser-vant is, What I have sworn be done."
4. ⁴ "Your seed I will es-tab-lish firm, For-ev-er to en-dure; And I through ev-ery com-ing age Will make your throne se-cure."

5. ⁵ The praises of Your wonders, LORD,
   The heavens shall express,
   In council of the holy ones
   Your faithfulness confess.

6. ⁶ For who in heaven with the LORD
   Could ever be compared?
   Among the ranks of angels great,
   Who has His likeness shared?

R.S. Taylor

NEW JERUSALEM CM

God Is Revered

Who then is this, that even the wind and the sea obey Him?
— Mark 4:41

7. ⁷God   is re-vered by   ho-ly ones, More feared than all a-round—
8. ¹¹The heav-ens and the earth are Yours; You found-ed ev-ery-thing—

⁸LORD God of hosts, the LORD of might, For   faith-ful-ness re-nowned.
¹²The   north and south: and to Your name Mount Ta-bor, Her-mon sing.

⁹You   rule the wa-ter's surg-ing waves; You   still the storm-y   seas.
¹³Your arm and hand are full of strength; Your right hand's lift-ed high.

¹⁰You with a strong arm slew the beast, And scat-tered en-e-mies.
¹⁴On right and jus-tice rests Your throne; Your love and truth draw nigh.

English melody; arr. Arthur S. Sullivan, 1871

NOEL CMD

89C

Psalm 89:15-18

Behold How Blessed the People Are

Christ Jesus...who became to us righteousness
and wisdom and sanctification. —1 Corinthians 1:30

9. ¹⁵Be - hold how blessed the peo - ple are Who
10. ¹⁶Yes, they re - joice in Your great name With
11. ¹⁷You are the beau - ty of their strength For
12. ¹⁸Be - cause our shield be - longs to Him, The

know the joy - ful sound; For in Your light and
glad - ness all the day; And in Your per - fect
them You glo - ri - fy; And by Your fa - vor,
LORD will safe - ty bring; The Ho - ly One of

pres - ence, LORD, Their foot - steps will be found.
righ - teous - ness Ex - alt - ed high are they.
Your good will, Our horn is lift - ed high.
Is - ra - el, He on - ly is our King.

Jeremiah Clark, 1707

ST. MAGNUS CM

In Visions Once You Spoke

He has raised up a horn of salvation for us in the house
of David His servant. —Luke 1:69

89D
Psalm 89:19-29

13. ¹⁹ In vi-sions once You spoke this word Un-to Your god-ly ones:
14. ²² "No foe shall trib-ute take from him, Nor wick-ed cast him down.
15. ²⁶ "'You are my Fa-ther and my God, My Rock of Help,' he'll cry;

"I've helped and raised a might-y one, One from the peo-ple drawn.
²³ His ad-ver-sar-ies I will crush; Strike hat-ers to the ground.
²⁷ I'll al-so make him My first-born, A-bove all kings most high.

²⁰ My ser-vant Da-vid I have found, Poured ho-ly oil on him.
²⁴ My faith-ful love will be with him, In My name his horn raised.
²⁸ My love for him I'll ev-er keep, My cov-e-nant se-cure.

²¹ With him My hand es-tab-lished is; My arm will strength-en him."
²⁵ I'll set his right hand on the sea And o-ver riv-ers' waves."
²⁹ His line and throne I will set up To last while heav'ns en-dure."

Georg F. Handel, 1748; harm. Austin C. Lovelace, b. 1919   HALIFAX CMD

89E

Psalm 89:30-37

And If His Sons Forsake My Law

The eternal covenant.
—Hebrews 13:20

16. ³⁰ "And if his sons for - sake My law, Walk
17. ³² "I'll pun - ish their trans - gres - sions then, On
18. ³³ "Yet I'll not take My love from him, Nor

not as I or - dain, ³¹ If My com - mands they
them My rod will lay. And I will their in -
break My faith - ful - ness. ³⁴ I'll not pro - fane My

do not keep, If they My laws pro - fane,
iq - ui - ty With heav - y stripes re - pay."
cov - e - nant, Nor change My prom - is - es."

19. ³⁵ "I've sworn this by My holiness,
   To David I'll not lie:
   ³⁶ His line and throne with Me endure
   Just as the sun on high."

20. ³⁷ "It like the moon shall ever be
   Established firm and sure;
   A faithful witness in the sky,
   It steadfast shall endure."

Kenneth G. Finlay, 1936   AYRSHIRE CM

Now Your Anointed You Have Spurned

Those passing by were hurling abuse at Him, wagging their heads.
— Matthew 27:39

89F
Psalm 89:38-45

21. ³⁸ Now Your a - noint - ed You have spurned, In
22. ⁴⁰ And You have bro - ken all his walls, And
23. ⁴² You have raised up his foes' right hand, And
24. ⁴⁴ His glo - ry You have made to cease, His

an - ger cast him down; ³⁹ Your ser - vant's cov - e -
down his strong - holds torn; ⁴¹ The pass - ers - by all
giv - en them de - light. ⁴³ His sword's keen edge You
throne to earth cast down. ⁴⁵ You have cut short his

nant ab - horred, In dust de - filed his crown.
plun - der him, He is his neigh - bor's scorn.
have turned back, No long - er helped him fight.
days of youth, To shame brought his re - nown.

Thomas Ravenscroft, *The Whole Book of Psalms*, 1621

NORWICH CM

89G

Psalm 89:46-52

How Long, LORD?

He raised Him from the dead...
"I will give You the holy and sure blessings of David." —Acts 13:34

25. [46] How long, LORD, will You hide Yourself, Your wrath still burning be? [47] Recall my life span! Why have You Made men mere vanity?

26. [48] Who is the man that's now alive Who death will never see? Or from the power of death's realm Who can his soul set free?

27. [49] Where are Your lovingkindnesses Which once, O Lord, were there When in Your lasting faithfulness You did to David swear?

28. [50] They mock Your servants, Lord, recall How in my heart I bear The taunts that from the nations come, From peoples everywhere.

29. [51] For such insulting things, O LORD,
    Your enemies have done;
    Each step of Your anointed one
    They cast their scorn upon.

30. [52] Now to the LORD all blessings be
    Ascribed forever then;
    Forevermore, so let it be!
    Amen, and yes, Amen!

Scottish Psalter, 1615

YORKE TUNE CM

Book Three Doxology

To Him be honor and eternal dominion!
—1 Timothy 6:16

52 Now to the LORD all bless - ings be As -
cribed for - ev - er then; For - ev - er - more, so
let it be! A - men, and yes, A - men!

Ludwig van Beethoven, 1770–1827

EMMANUEL CM

Lord, You Have Been Our Dwelling Place

For as in Adam, all die...
—1 Corinthians 15:22

1. 1 Lord, You have been our dwell-ing place Through all the a - ges of our race. 2 E - ven be - fore the moun-tains' birth, Be - fore the time You formed the earth, From years which no be - gin - ning had To years un - end - ing, You are God.

2. 3 You turn man back to dust a - gain, You say, "Re - turn, O sons of men." 4 To You a thou-sand years will last Like yes - ter - day when it has passed; A thou-sand years are in Your sight Brief like the watch - es of the night.

3. 5 You like a flood swept men a - way, Till in the sleep of death they lay; They are like grass that sprouts a - new With blades of green in morn - ing dew. 6 At morn it sprouts to grow and rise, When eve - ning comes it fades and dies.

4. 7 For by Your anger we're consumed,
And by Your wrath to terror doomed.
8 You place our sins before Your sight,
Our secret sins You bring to light.
9 For in Your wrath our days decrease,
And with a sigh our years then cease.

5. 10 For our life's years are seventy,
Or eighty years the strong may see.
Our years at best are toil and woe,
How soon they end, and then we go.
11 Who has Your anger understood?
Who fears Your fury as he should?

Joseph Barnby, 1872

ST. CHRYSOSTOM 88.88.88

O Teach Us How to Count Our Days

90B

…Even so, in Christ shall all be made alive.
—1 Corinthians 15:22

Psalm 90:12-17

6. ¹²O teach us how to count our days And set our hearts on
7. ¹⁵As ma - ny days as we have spent Un - der af - flic - tion
8. ¹⁷On us may there be shed a - broad Good fa - vor from the

wis - dom's ways. ¹³How long, O LORD? O now re - turn
You have sent, For all the years we e - vil knew,
Lord our God. What our hands made, es - tab - lish sure,

And for Your ser - vants show con - cern. ¹⁴Each morn - ing fill us
Now make us glad; our joy re - new. ¹⁶Your work to all Your
So that our la - bors may en - dure; Yes, may the la - bor

with Your grace; We'll sing for joy through all our days.
ser - vants show; Your glo - ry let their chil - dren know.
of our hands Be made by You to ev - er stand.

Henri F. Hemy, 1864; arr. James G. Walton, 1870

ST. CATHERINE 88.88.88

91A

Psalm 91

Who With God Most High Finds Shelter

My prayer is...that You protect them from the evil one.
—John 17:15

1. ¹Who with God Most High finds shelter;
2. God's truth is your shield and buck - ler.
3. ⁹Since you made my LORD your ref - uge,
4. ¹³You will tram - ple snakes and li - ons,

In th'Al - might - y's shad - ow hides.
⁵You'll no ter - ror fear at night,
God Most High your dwell - ing place,
Tread on all your dead - ly foes.

²To the LORD I'll say, "My Ref - uge."
Nor by day the ar - row fly - ing,
¹⁰Noth - ing e - vil will be - fall you;
¹⁴For his love to Me I'll save him,

In my God my trust a - bides.
⁶Nor dis - ease that stalks at night,
In your tent no scourge you'll face.
Keep him, for My name he knows.

Rowland Hugh Pritchard, c. 1855

HYFRYDOL 87.87 D

91B

The One Who Has a Refuge Safe

Psalm 91:1-4

Take heart! I have overcome the world.
—John 16:33

1. ¹The one who has a refuge safe,
2. ²I there-fore of the LORD will say,
3. ³For He will with His watch-ful care
4. ⁴He'll hide you with His out-spread wing,

The Most High as his dwell-ing place,
"He is my ref-uge and my stay;
Pre-serve you from the trap-per's snare;
Be-neath His pin-ions safe-ty bring;

Will with Al-might-y God a-bide,
My cit-a-del of strength is He,
Yes, He will be your sure de-fense
His faith-ful-ness, for-ev-er true,

And in His shad-ow safe-ly hide.
My God, in whom my trust will be."
A-gainst the dead-ly pes-ti-lence.
Pro-vides a shield and fort for you.

William B. Bradbury, 1849

WOODWORTH LM

Night's Terrors Will Not Cause Alarm

91C

We are more than conquerors through Him who loved us.
—Romans 8:37

Psalm 91:5-12

5. ⁵Night's ter - rors will not cause a - larm;
6. ⁷Though at your side ten thou - sand fall,
7. ⁹You've made the LORD, my ref - uge safe,
8. ¹¹Be - cause His an - gels He com - mands

Nor in the day will ar - rows harm;
No harm will come to you at all.
The One Most High, your dwell - ing place.
To bear you safe - ly in their hands;

⁶Nor sick - ness stalk - ing in the night,
⁸You on - ly with your eyes will see
¹⁰On you no e - vil will be sent,
¹²To guard your ways lest, left a - lone,

Nor plagues de - stroy - ing in day's light.
What wick - ed men's re - ward will be.
Nor an - y plague come near your tent
You strike your foot a - gainst a stone.

Thomas Hastings, 1842

RETREAT LM

91D
Psalm 91:13-16

The Lion Will Become Your Prey

The God of peace will soon crush Satan under your feet.
—Romans 16:20

9. ¹³ The li - on will be - come your prey,
10. ¹⁴ From dan - ger I will set him free,
11. ¹⁵ As of - ten as he calls on Me,
12. To him I will sal - va - tion show;

You'll crush the co - bra in your way;
Be - cause he's shown his love for Me;
I'll an - swer him with cer - tain - ty;
On him great hon - or I'll be - stow.

The li - on and the ser - pent too
On high I'll set him as My own,
I will be with him in dis - tress,
¹⁶ I'll give to him a - bun - dant life;

You'll crush and ut - ter - ly sub - due.
Be - cause to him My name is known.
When he is trou - bled and op - pressed.
He'll see My res - cue with de - light.

William Gardiner, *Sacred Melodies II*, 1815

WALTON LM

It's Good to Thank the Lord

92
Psalm 92

Give thanks in all circumstances,
for this is God's will for you in Christ Jesus. —1 Thessalonians 5:18

1. [1] It's good to thank the LORD, To praise Your name, Most High; [2] To tell Your love at dawn, Your faithfulness by night [3] With ten-stringed lyre, Resounding music played upon the harp and lyre.

2. [4] Your deeds, LORD, made me glad; I'll sing of what You've done. How great Your works, O LORD, [5] How deep Your thoughts each one. [6] A senseless man Devoid of knowledge, this truth will not understand:

3. [7] All sinners grow like grass, The wicked multiply; And yet they'll be destroyed. [8] But, LORD, You stay on high. [9] Your foes, LORD, fall; Your foes will perish, evildoers scattered all.

4. [10] You've poured oil on my head,
Like oxen I'm made strong.
[11] I've seen and heard the fate
Of those who've done me wrong.
[12] Like thriving palm
The righteous grows,
like cedars tall in Lebanon.

5. [13] Those planted by the LORD
Will in God's courts be seen;
[14] When old they'll still bear fruit
And flourish fresh and green,
[15] And this proclaim—
How upright is the LORD,
my Rock, no wrong in Him!

John Darwall, 1770

DARWALL 66.66.4.12

93A

The LORD Is Crowned as King

You of little faith, why are you so afraid?
— Matthew 8:26

1. ¹The LORD is crowned as King, He's clothed with
2. The world is firm - ly set, And nev - er
3. ³The floods lift up, O LORD; The floods lift

maj - es - ty. The LORD has clothed Him - self with
moved can be. ²And long es - tab - lished is Your
up their voice. The floods are lift - ing up their

might And great au - thor - i - ty.
throne, You're from e - ter - ni - ty.
waves; They make a might - y noise.

4. ⁴But yet the LORD on high—
   Of greater strength is He
   Than is the thunder of the waves,
   Or breakers of the sea.

5. ⁵Your testimonies all
   Have been confirmed, O LORD;
   Your house adorned with holiness,
   Shall be forevermore.

George F. Root, 1859   RIALTO SM

The Lord Is Crowned as King

What kind of man is this?
Even the winds and the waves obey Him? — Matthew 8:27

1. [1] The LORD is crowned as King; He's clothed with great-ness.
2. [3] The floods have lift - ed, LORD, The floods lift their voice.

The LORD has clothed Him - self, He's dressed with pow - er.
The floods lift up their waves, They make a great noise.

The world is firm-ly set, And it will not be moved.
[4] The LORD on high is strong, More than the o-cean's waves.

[2] Your throne is set of old; You are e - ter - nal.
[5] Your word is true; O LORD, Your house is ho - ly.

Traditional English melody; arr. Ralph Vaughan-Williams, 1872–1958

MONKS GATE 65.65.66.65

94A

God, the LORD, from Whom Is Vengeance

Psalm 94:1-15

Do not take revenge, my friends, but leave room for God's wrath.
— Romans 12:19

1. ¹ God, the LORD, from whom is ven-geance, God, A - veng - er,
2. ⁵ They, O LORD, beat down Your peo - ple, And Your her - i -
3. ⁹ Who the ear made, can He hear not? Who formed eyes, can
4. ¹³ Give him rest from days of trou - ble Till the wick - ed

O shine forth! ² Judge of all the earth, O rise up!
tage op - press. ⁶ They kill for - eign - er and wid - ow;
He not see? ¹⁰ Who warns na - tions, will He strike not?
are brought down. ¹⁴ For the LORD stays with His peo - ple,

Pay the proud what they are worth. ³ O LORD, how long
They have slain the fa - ther - less. ⁷ They have said, "The
Who men teach - es, knows not He? ¹¹ All the thoughts of
He will not for - sake His own. ¹⁵ Righ - teous judg - ments

will the wick - ed, How long will the wick - ed gloat?
LORD does not see, Ja - cob's God has closed His eyes."
men the LORD knows; Knows that but a breath are they.
will be ren - dered, Jus - tice will re - turn a - gain;

4 From their mouths they pour out vio - lence,
8 Un - der - stand, you sense - less peo - ple;
12 Blessed the man whom You re - prove, LORD;
Those of up - right heart will fol - low

Of them - selves all wick - ed boast.
When, O fools, will you be wise?
Through Your law You point his way.
In the way of jus - tice then.

Franz Joseph Haydn, 1797

AUSTRIA 87.87 D

94B

Who For Me Withstands the Wicked?

Psalm 94:16-23

When He suffered...
He entrusted Himself to Him who judges justly. —1 Peter 2:23

5. [16] Who for me with - stands the wick - ed?
6. [20] Can de - struc - tive rul - ers join You,

Who a - gainst wrong pleads for me?
And by law dis - or - der build?

[17] If the LORD were not my help - er,
[21] They con - spire a - gainst the righ - teous,

Soon my soul would si - lent be.
Sen - tence just ones to be killed.

18 If I say, "My foot is slip - ping!"
22 But the LORD is still my strong - hold;

LORD, Your mer - cy will up - hold.
God, my ref - uge, will re - pay.

19 When my anx - ious thoughts are ma - ny,
23 He'll for sin wipe out the wick - ed;

How Your com - forts cheer my soul!
Them the LORD our God will slay.

Thomas John Williams, 1890   EBENEZER (Ton-y-Botel) 87.87 D

95A
Psalm 95:1-7a

Come to the LORD and Sing for Joy

He is before all things, and in Him all things hold together.
— Colossians 1:17

1. ¹Come to the LORD, and sing for joy; Let
2. ²In - to His pres - ence let us come With
3. ³The LORD's a might - y God and King; A -
4. ⁵To Him the spa - cious sea be - longs, Made

us our voic - es raise. In joy - ful shouts, let
praise and thank - ful voice. Let us then sing to
bove all gods He is. ⁴The depths of earth are
by His own com - mand; And by the work - ing

us the Rock Of our sal - va - tion praise.
Him with psalms; With shouts let us re - joice.
in His hand; The moun - tain peaks are His.
of His hands He formed the earth's dry land.

5. ⁶O come and let us worship Him;
   Let us with one accord
   In presence of our Maker kneel,
   And bow before the LORD;

6. ⁷Because He truly is our God,
   And we His chosen sheep,
   The people of His pasture land,
   Whom His own hand will keep.

William Arnold, 1768–1832

ALEXANDRIA CM

O Come and Let Us Worship Him

He is the head of the body, the church.
—Colossians 1:18

95B

Psalm 95:6-7a

5. ⁶O come and let us wor-ship Him; Let us with
6. ⁷Be-cause He tru-ly is our God, And we His

one ac-cord In pres-ence of our Mak-er
cho-sen sheep, The peo-ple of His pas-ture

kneel, In pres-ence of our Mak-er
land, The peo-ple of His pas-ture

kneel, And bow be-fore the LORD;
land, Whom His own hand will keep.

John Campbell, *The Sacred Psaltery*, 1854

ORLINGTON CM

95C

Psalm 95:7b-11

Today If You Will Hear His Voice

Come to Me...and I will give you rest.
—Matthew 11:28

7. [7]To - day if you will hear His voice, [8]Then
8. [9]Your fa - thers tried and tempt - ed Me, Though
9. I said, "They have a wand - 'ring heart, And

hard - en not your heart. Strive not as those at
they My work per - ceived; [10]And with that gen - er -
they My ways de - test." [11]In wrath I swore they

Mer - i - bah, Nor Mas - sah's test - ing start.
a - tion I For for - ty years was grieved.
should not come In - to My prom - ised rest.

Thomas Ravenscroft, *The Whole Booke of Psalms*, 1621

NORWICH CM

O Come to the LORD

You have returned to the Shepherd and Overseer of your souls.
—1 Peter 2:25

1. ¹O come to the LORD, joy-ful songs let us sing;
2. ³The LORD, King of all gods, the God who is great,
3. ⁶Come give the LORD wor-ship, for He made us too;

Loud praise to our Rock of sal-va-tion we'll bring!
Pos-sess-ing all things that His hands did cre-ate:
Let's bow down and of-fer the praise He is due.

²With thanks-giv-ing let us be-fore Him ap-pear;
⁴Earth's val-leys and moun-tains He holds in His hand;
⁷For He is our God, we're the flock of His land,

Come sing joy-ful psalms, let us praise Him with cheer.
⁵He made them, He owns them— the sea and the land.
His peo-ple, His sheep nur-tured by His own hand.

Michael Tabon, 2002

COME JOYFULLY 11.11.11.11

96A

Psalm 96:1-8

O Sing a New Song

Woe to me if I do not preach the gospel!
—1 Corinthians 9:16

1. [1] O sing a new song to the LORD; All earth sing to the LORD. [2] Sing to the LORD, and bless His name; "He saves!" each day proclaim. [3] His glory to all nations show; His deeds let peoples know.

2. [4] The LORD is great, great praise He's due. He's feared above all gods. [5] For peoples' gods mere idols are; The LORD the heavens made. [6] Before Him honor, majesty, And strength and splendor dwell.

3. [7] O families of earth, ascribe All glory to the LORD. All strength ascribe unto the LORD; [8] Give glory due His name. Come to the LORD, into His courts, And bring an offering.

Oliver Holden, 1793

CORONATION 86.86.86

In Radiant Robes

96B
Psalm 96:9-13

I am the Alpha and Omega… who is, and who was,
and who is to come, the Almighty. —Revelation 1:8

4. ⁹In ra - diant robes of ho - li - ness Bring wor - ship
5. The world stands firm and will not move; With jus - tice
6. ¹²Let ev - ery thing in ev - ery field In ju - bi -
7. ¹³For He will come to judge the earth, Yes, He will

to the LORD. All earth, be - fore Him stand in
He'll judge all. ¹¹Let heav'ns be glad, let earth re -
la - tion join. Then woods and trees will shout for
sure - ly come; He'll judge the world in righ - teous -

awe, All earth, be - fore Him stand in
joice Let heav'ns be glad, let earth re -
joy, Then woods and trees will shout for
ness, He'll judge the world in righ - teous -

awe, ¹⁰Pro - claim, "The LORD is King!"
joice With seas and all they hold.
joy, And sing be - fore the LORD.
ness, And peo - ples with His truth.

John Campbell, *The Sacred Psaltery*, 1854

ORLINGTON CM

96C

O Sing a New Song to the LORD

Psalm 96:1-6

He alone is immortal and lives in unapproachable light.
—1 Timothy 6:16

1. ¹O sing a new song to the LORD, Let
2. Pro-claim this good news con-stant-ly, ³His
3. ⁴Be-hold the great-ness of the LORD! So
4. Not so the LORD! He heav-en made, ⁶And

all the earth sing to the LORD. ²Sing to the LORD and
glo-ry and His maj-es-ty; His mir-a-cles to
great-ly should He be a-dored, And feared a-bove all
there be-fore Him is dis-played All splen-dor, maj-es-

bless His name, And His sal-va-tion loud pro-claim!
all de-clare Through-out the na-tions ev-ery-where.
else by far, ⁵For Gen-tile gods mere i-dols are.
ty and grace; All strength dwells in His ho-ly place.

Musikalisches Handbüch, Hamburg, 1690

WINCHESTER NEW LM

Ascribe Unto the LORD

"Yes, I am coming soon." Amen. Come, Lord Jesus.
—*Revelation 22:20*

96D

Psalm 96:7-13

5. [7]As-cribe un-to the LORD, All fam-i-lies of earth,
6. [9]In ho-ly splen-dor robed, Bow down be-fore the LORD;
7. [11]O let the skies be glad, And let the earth re-joice.
8. [13]They'll sing be-fore the LORD, For He is draw-ing near

As-cribe un-to the LORD His strength And His most glo-rious worth.
Be-fore Him trem-ble all the earth. [10]To na-tions speak this word:
Let seas and all that they con-tain Lift up their roar-ing voice.
To be the judge of all the earth; He sure-ly will ap-pear.

[8]As-cribe un-to the LORD The glo-ry of His name;
"The LORD reigns o-ver all!" The world un-moved will be,
[12]Let ev-ery beast ex-ult, Let fields with glad-ness sing;
Then He will rule the world In per-fect righ-teous-ness,

Come, make your way in-to His courts, And bring an of-fer-ing.
It firm re-mains; He'll na-tions rule And judge with eq-ui-ty.
The joy-ful sing-ing of the trees Shall make the for-ests ring.
And gov-ern all the na-tions in His truth and faith-ful-ness.

Franklin L. Sheppard, 1915; arr. Edward Shippen Barnes, 1926

TERRA BEATA SMD

97A The LORD Reigns (Let Earth Rejoice)

Psalm 97:1-9

Remember Jesus Christ, raised from the dead,
descended from David. This is my Gospel. —2 Timothy 2:8

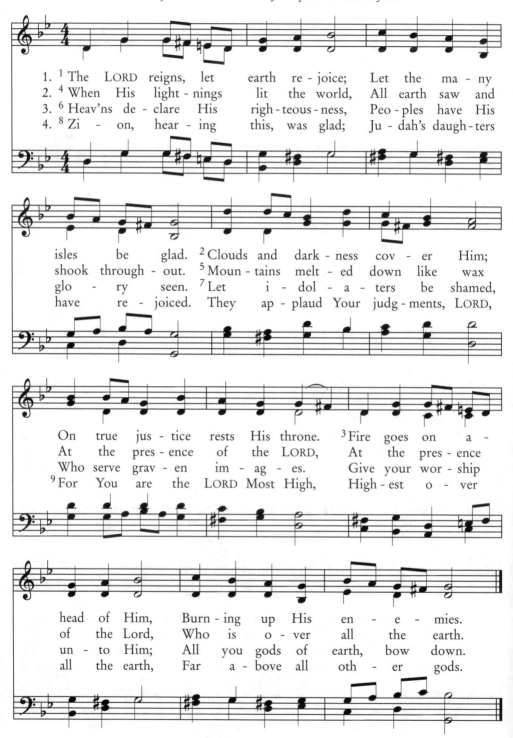

1. ¹The LORD reigns, let earth re-joice; Let the ma-ny
2. ⁴When His light-nings lit the world, All earth saw and
3. ⁶Heav'ns de-clare His righ-teous-ness, Peo-ples have His
4. ⁸Zi-on, hear-ing this, was glad; Ju-dah's daugh-ters

isles be glad. ²Clouds and dark-ness cov-er Him;
shook through-out. ⁵Moun-tains melt-ed down like wax
glo-ry seen. ⁷Let i-dol-a-ters be shamed,
have re-joiced. They ap-plaud Your judg-ments, LORD,

On true jus-tice rests His throne. ³Fire goes on a-
At the pres-ence of the LORD, At the pres-ence
Who serve grav-en im-ag-es. Give your wor-ship
⁹For You are the LORD Most High, High-est o-ver

head of Him, Burn-ing up His en-e-mies.
of the Lord, Who is o-ver all the earth.
un-to Him; All you gods of earth, bow down.
all the earth, Far a-bove all oth-er gods.

Traditional Welsh melody

ARFON 77.77.77

Since You Love the LORD

97B

If you love Me, you will obey what I command.
—John 14:15

Psalm 97:10-12

5. [10] Since you love the LORD, hate e - vil;
6. [11] Light is sown for all the righ - teous,

God - ly ones He keeps se - cure. From the grip of
Joy for up - right hearts to claim. [12] In the LORD re -

e - vil - do - ers He will bring de - liv - 'rance sure.
joice, you righ - teous; Thanks give to His ho - ly name.

Sicilian melody, 18th century

SICILIAN MARINERS 87.87

97C
Psalm 97

The LORD Is King!

God appointed Him to be head over everything for the church.
—Ephesians 1:22

1. ¹The LORD is King! Let all the earth be joy-ful,
2. ⁶His righ-teous-ness the heav-ens are pro-claim-ing;
3. ¹⁰Let all of you who love the LORD hate e-vil.

And let the ma-ny is-lands all be glad.
His glo-ry all who live on earth be-hold.
He guards the lives of all His faith-ful ones.

²Bil-low-ing clouds and dark-ness swirl a-
⁷Let them be shamed who serve and boast of
And from the hand of ev-ery e-vil-

round Him; On jus-tice rests His throne.
i-dols; Let gods bow down to Him.
do-er He sure-ly res-cues them.

3 Be - fore Him burns a fire, His foes con - sum - ing.
8 Your judg-ments Zi - on hears with much re - joic - ing,
11 For light is cast like seed up - on the righ-teous,

4 His light-nings lit the world; earth trem - bling saw.
And they, O LORD, make Ju - dah's daugh - ters glad.
And glad-ness for the firm and true in heart.

5 Moun - tains, like wax, be - fore the LORD are
9 For o - ver earth You are the LORD, the
12 Now in the LORD be joy - ful all you

melt - ing— Lord o - ver all the earth.
High - est, And far a - bove all gods.
righ - teous, And thank His ho - ly name.

Charles McBurney and Eleanor Hutcheson, 1969   THRONE 11.10.11.6 D

98A

O Sing a New Song to the Lord

He gives us the victory through our Lord Jesus Christ.
—1 Corinthians 15:57

Psalm 98

1. [1]O sing a new song to the LORD For won-ders He has done; For won - ders He has done; By His right hand and ho - ly arm

He He vic - to - ry has

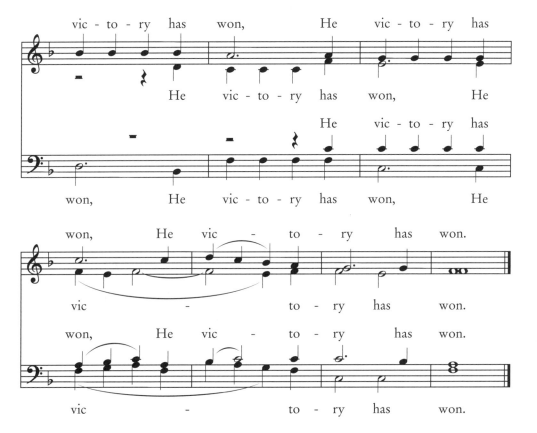

2. [2] The LORD's salvation is revealed
For He has made it known;
He to the nations of the world
His righteousness has shown.

3. [3] He called to mind His faithfulness,
His love to Isr'el's house;
The great salvation of our God
Is seen the earth throughout.

4. [4] O all the earth, shout to the LORD,
And make a joyful sound.
Lift up your voice aloud to Him;
Sing praise, let joy resound.

5. [5] Make music to the LORD with harps;
With harps your praises sing.
[6] With horn and trumpets shout with joy
Before the LORD, the King.

6. [7] Let sea and land and all they hold
Resound with one accord.
[8] Let rivers clap, let mountains sing
For joy before the LORD.

7. [9] For He shall come, He surely comes
The judge of earth to be;
He'll judge the world with righteousness,
And all with equity.

Thomas Jarman, c. 1803   DESERT (Lyngham) CM

98B

Psalm 98

To the Lord O Sing a New Song

"You have taken Your great power and have begun to reign."
—Revelation 11:17

1. ¹To the LORD O sing a new song
2. He re-called His love for Is-r'el,
3. ⁶With the blast of horn and trum-pet

For the won-ders He has done;
And to them has faith-ful been;
Shout be-fore the LORD, the King.

His right hand and arm most ho-ly
When our God sent His sal-va-tion
⁷Let the sea re-sound with prais-es,

Have for Him the vic-t'ry won.
It a-round the earth was seen.
Earth with all its peo-ple, sing.

Ludwig van Beethoven, 1824; arr. Edward Hodges, 1796–1867

ODE TO JOY 87.87 D

99A

Psalm 99

Let the Nations Tremble

Christ entered heaven itself, now to appear for us in God's presence.
—Hebrews 9:24

1. ¹Let the na-tions trem — ble, For the LORD is
2. ⁴King of might and pow — er, He whose strength loves
3. ⁶Mos - es was with Aar - on Num-bered in His
4. ⁸LORD, our God, You an - swered; You, O God, for-

reign - ing From His throne a - bove the an - gels.
jus - tice, Eq - ui - ty You have es - tab - lished.
priest - hood, So too, Sam - u - el in-voked Him.
gave them, Though You chas-tened them for e - vil.

Let the earth be shak - en! ²High a - bove all
In the midst of Ja - cob You have ex - e-
They called on the LORD's name; He gave them His
⁹High - est ex - al - ta - tion Un - to Him be

na - tions Is the LORD, great King in Zi - on.
cut - ed Per - fect righ - teous-ness and jus - tice.
an - swer, ⁷Speak-ing from the cloud - y pil - lar.
giv - en, For the LORD our God is ho - ly.

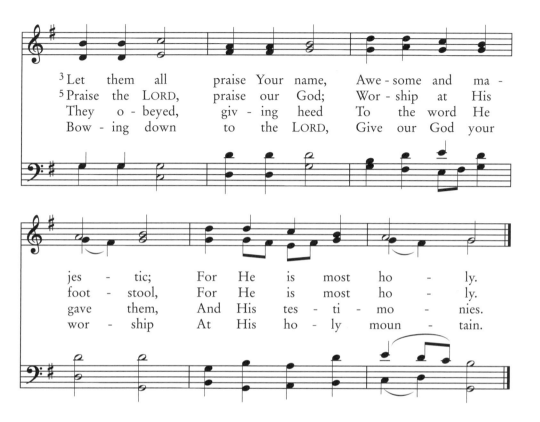

Joachim Neander, 1680

ARNSBERG 668.668.666

99B

Psalm 99

The LORD Is King Indeed

We have confidence to enter the Most Holy Place by the blood of Jesus.
—Hebrews 10:19

1. [1] The LORD is King in-deed; Let na-tions shake with fear.
2. [4] The pow-er of the King De-lights in eq-ui-ty;
3. [6] For Mo-ses was His priest, And Aar-on, too, did serve,
4. [8] O LORD our God, You heard, Your an-swer gave to them.

He sits a-bove the cher-u-bim; Let earth be moved.
In Ja-cob You es-tab-lished law And righ-teous-ness.
And Sam-u-el with them who called Up-on His name.
You were a God for-giv-ing, yet A-veng-ing wrongs.

[2] The LORD in Zi-on rules And o-ver all is high.
[5] Ex-alt and cel-e-brate The LORD who is our God,
They called the LORD; He heard. [7] He spoke from out the cloud.
[9] Ex-alt the LORD our God; Bow to His ho-ly hill.

[3] O praise His great and awe-some name, The Ho-ly One.
And at His foot-stool wor-ship Him, The Ho-ly One.
His tes-ti-mo-nies they o-beyed, They kept His laws.
Be-hold, He is the Ho-ly One, The LORD our God.

Jewish melody; arr. Meyer Lyon, 1777

LEONI 66.84 D

All People That on Earth Do Dwell

Jesus said, "I tell you the truth, I am the gate for the sheep."
—John 10:7

1. ¹All peo-ple that on earth do dwell,
2. ³Know that the LORD is God in-deed;
3. ⁴O en-ter then His gates with praise;
4. ⁵Be-cause the LORD our God is good,

Sing to the LORD with cheer-ful voice.
With-out our aid He did us make.
With-in His courts your thanks pro-claim;
His mer-cy is for-ev-er sure;

²HIM serve with mirth; His praise forth tell;
We are His folk; He doth us feed,
With grate-ful hearts your voic-es raise
His truth at all times firm-ly stood

Come ye be-fore Him and re-joice.
And for His sheep He doth us take.
To bless and mag-ni-fy His name.
And shall from age to age en-dure.

Louis Bourgeois, 1551

OLD 100TH LM

100B

Psalm 100

O Shout for Joy unto the Lord

"I am the gate; whoever enters through Me will be saved."
—John 10:9

1. ¹O shout for joy unto the LORD
2. ³Know well the LORD is God in - deed;
3. ⁴O en - ter through His gates with thanks,
4. ⁵Be - cause the LORD is good in - deed,

Earth's peo - ple far and near;
He made us; we are His.
His courts ap - proach with praise;
His mer - cy nev - er ends;

² With glad - ness come and serve the LORD,
We are His peo - ple, and the sheep
Give thanks to Him with joy - ful - ness,
And un - to ev - ery com - ing age

And bring Him songs of cheer.
Kept where His pas - ture is.
And bless His name al - ways.
His faith - ful - ness ex - tends.

Thomas Moore, 1756

GLASGOW CM

All Earth, With Joy

I am the good Shepherd; I know My sheep and
My sheep know Me. —John 10:14

1. 1 All earth, with joy, to the LORD come with loud voic - es
2. 4 En - ter His gates with thanks - giv - ing, to His courts come

ring - ing. 2 With glad - ness serve the LORD; come to Him
prais - ing. To Him be thank - ful, and bless His name,

joy - ful - ly sing - ing. 3 The LORD is God. Know that He
your voic - es rais - ing. 5 The LORD is good; His lov - ing-

made us His own. We are the sheep of His pas - ture.
kind - ness en - dures, His faith - ful - ness lasts for - ev - er.

Stralsund Gesangbüch, 1665

LOBE DEN HERREN 14.14.4.7.8

100D

Psalm 100

Make a Joyful Noise

The good Shepherd lays down His life for the sheep.
—John 10:11

1. ¹Make a joy-ful noise, shout to the LORD all the earth.

²Serve the LORD with glad-ness. Come in-to His pres-ence with

sing - ing. ³Know that the LORD, He is God; It is

He who has made us and not we our-selves. We are His

peo - ple, the sheep of His pas - ture. ⁴En - ter in - to His

gates with thanks - giv - ing, And in - to His courts with

praise. Show thank - ful - ness to Him and bless His name.

⁵For the LORD is good; His love is ev - er - last - ing. His

truth en - dures to ev - ery gen - er - a - tion.

Eleanor Hutcheson, 1970

ENTER (Irr.)

100E

Psalm 100

In All the Land Rejoice

There shall be one flock and one Shepherd.
—John 10:16

1. ¹In all the land re - joice And
2. ³Know that the LORD is God. He
3. ⁴With thanks come through His gates, Praise
4. ⁵Be - cause the LORD is good, His

to the LORD cry out. ²In wor - ship glad - ly
made us, we are His, His peo - ple and the
in His courts pro - claim; De - clare the glo - ry
love will yet en - dure; To gen - er - a - tions,

serve the LORD, For joy be - fore Him shout.
cho - sen flock Set where His pas - ture is.
He de - serves, Give bless - ings to His name.
on and on, His faith - ful - ness is sure.

William H. Walter, 1894

FESTAL SONG SM

Of Loyalty and Justice

I am He who searches hearts and minds.
—Revelation 2:23

1. [1] Of loy-al-ty and jus - tice, I raise my voice in song;
2. [3] I do not let my eyes dwell On an - y worth-less thing;
3. [5] I'll up-root him who sly - ly His neigh-bor vil - i - fies.
4. [7] The one who is de-cep - tive Will not a - bide with me;

To You, O LORD, I lift up These words with mu-sic strong.
The deeds of an a-pos-tate Will nev - er to me cling.
I'll not en-dure the proud heart, Or him with loft-y eyes.
He'll not keep his po-si - tion Who speaks de-ceit-ful - ly.

[2] The per-fect way I pon-der; When will You come to me?
[4] May think-ing that is twist-ed Be kept a-way from me;
[6] My eyes are on the faith-ful, That they may dwell with me;
[8] Each morn-ing on the wick-ed De - struc-tion I will pour;

I'll live with-in my pa - lace With true in-teg-ri-ty.
I'll not con-sent to e - vil Or do wrong know-ing-ly.
The one whose walk is blame - less Will serve and wait on me.
To free from e-vil-do - ers The cit-y of the LORD.

Traditional Welsh melody, 19th century

LLANGLOFFAN 76.76 D

101B
Psalm 101

Of Loyalty and Justice

Did I Myself not choose you....Yet one of you is a devil?
—John 6:70

1. ¹Of loy-al-ty and jus-tice, I raise my voice in song;
2. ³I do not let my eyes dwell On an-y worth-less thing;
3. ⁵I'll up-root him who sly-ly His neigh-bor vil-i-fies.
4. ⁷The one who is de-cep-tive Will not a-bide with me;

To You, O LORD, I lift up These words with mu-sic strong.
The deeds of an a-pos-tate Will nev-er to me cling.
I'll not en-dure the proud heart, Or him with loft-y eyes.
He'll not keep his po-si-tion Who speaks de-ceit-ful-ly.

²The per-fect way I pon-der; When will You come to me?
⁴May think-ing that is twist-ed Be kept a-way from me;
⁶My eyes are on the faith-ful, That they may dwell with me;
⁸Each morn-ing on the wick-ed De-struc-tion I will pour;

I'll live with-in my pal-ace With true in-teg-ri-ty.
I'll not con-sent to e-vil Or do wrong know-ing-ly.
The one whose walk is blame-less Will serve and wait on me.
To free from e-vil-do-ers The cit-y of the LORD.

Samuel S. Wesley, 1810–1876

AURELIA 76.76 D

To This My Prayer

Cast all your anxiety on Him because He cares for you.
—1 Peter 5:7

1. [1] To this my prayer, O lis-ten, LORD; And let my
2. [3] For all my days go up in smoke, As in a
3. [6] Now am I like the pel-i-can That dwells in

cry for help reach You. [2] In time of grief,
hearth, my bones are burned. [4] My heart is crushed
emp-ty wil-der-ness, The owl that roams

hide not Your face, In-cline to me Your lis-t'ning
like with-ered grass, I food for-get; [5] and by loud
a bar-ren land. [7] I'm like a bird, a-wake at

ear; And an-swer quick-ly when You hear.
groans I am re-duced to skin and bones.
night, Perched high up on a lone-ly height.

4. [8] My foes reproach me all day long
Subjecting me to ridicule,
And as a curse they use my name.
[9] For ashes I consume as bread,
And mix my drink with tears I've shed.

5. [10] By this Your anger was expressed,
Your indignation was displayed;
You picked me up and cast me off.
[11] My days, like length'ning shadows pass,
And soon I wither like the grass.

William B. Bradbury, c. 1858   BACA 88.888

102B
Psalm 102:11-17

My Days Like Evening's Shade

Whoever believes in Him shall not perish but have eternal life.
—John 3:16

6. ¹¹My days like eve-ning's shade ex-tend, Like grass I
7. ¹³Roused with com-pas-sion, You will stand; Kind-ness to
8. ¹⁴Your ser-vants cher-ish Zi-on's stones, E-ven her
9. ¹⁶Zi-on the LORD will ed-i-fy; He in His

die and wilt a-way. ¹²But LORD, Your days will
Zi-on You will show. The time has come which
dust to them is dear. ¹⁵So for-eign lands and
glo-ry will a-rise. ¹⁷And when to Him the

nev-er end, Your name through ev-ery age will
You have planned; Your gra-cious fa-vor she will
Gen-tile thrones Will the LORD's name and glo-ry
need-y cry, Their plead-ing He will not de-

stay Your name through ev-ery age will stay.
know, Your gra-cious fa-vor she will know.
fear, Will the LORD's name and glo-ry fear.
spise, Their plead-ing He will not de-spise.

Frederic M.A. Venua, c. 1810; arr. William Gardiner, 1812

PARK STREET LM

Let This Be Written

When the time had fully come, God sent His Son.
— Galatians 4:4

10. ¹⁸Let this be writ - ten for the sake
11. ¹⁹From ho - ly heights the LORD looked down,
12. ²¹That Zi - on may the LORD's name tell,

Of those a - live in fu - ture days,
To view the earth from heav - en high,
Je - ru - sa - lem His praise re - cord,

So peo - ple He has yet to make
²⁰That He might hear the pris - 'ner's groan,
²²When gath - ered are the peo - ples all,

Will to the LORD lift up their praise.
And free them who are doomed to die;
And king - doms join to serve the LORD.

Traditional Gaelic melody

TEANN A NALL LM

102D

Psalm 102:23-28

My Strength He Weakened

Whoever believes in the Son has eternal life.
—John 3:36

13. ²³My strength He weak-ened in the way; My
14. ²⁵The earth You found-ed long a - go; Your
15. These will be changed and pass a - way. ²⁷But

days He short-ened. Then I pled, ²⁴"In mid-life
might-y hands the heav-ens made. ²⁶Yet they will
You are ev-er-more the same Be-cause Your

take me not a - way, O God, whose years will
die while You en - dure; Like worn out clothes whose
years will nev-er end. ²⁸Your ser-vants' chil-dren

nev-er end, But will through-out all time ex - tend."
use is done, So You will change them, ev-ery one.
will en - dure; Their seed be - fore You is se - cure.

Brian E. Coombs, 2003

SANDBANKS 88.888

O Bless the LORD, My Soul

How great is the love the Father has lavished on us!
— 1 John 3:1

1. ¹ O bless the LORD, my soul His
2. ² O bless the LORD my soul, His
3. ³ He par - dons and for - gives All

bless - ed - ness pro - claim; Let all that is with -
mer - cies bear in mind; For - get not all the
your in - iq - ui - ties; He from each sick - ness

in me join To bless His ho - ly name.
ways in which He has to you been kind.
makes you well And heals you from dis - ease.

4. ⁴ He purchases your life
To raise you from the dead;
A crown of mercy and of love
He places on your head.

5. ⁵ With good things, your desires
He fully satisfies;
And therefore, like an eagle, you
With youth renewed, arise.

Mason and Webb, *Cantica Laudis*, 1850

SCHUMANN SM

103B

Psalm 103:1-13

Bless the LORD, My Soul

Where sin increased, grace increased all the more.
—Romans 5:20

1. ¹Bless the LORD, my soul. My whole heart,
2. ⁵He with love and mer - cy crowns you,
3. ⁷He re - vealed His deeds to Is - r'el,
4. ¹¹For as high as are the heav - ens

Ev - er bless His ho - ly name.
Sat - is - fies your years with good;
And made Mo - ses know His path.
Far a - bove the earth be - low,

²Bless the LORD, my soul. For - get not
So that you will, like the ea - gle,
⁸LORD of grace and full of pit - y,
Just as great to those who fear Him

All His bless - ings to pro - claim.
With youth's vi - gor be re - newed.
Rich in love and slow to wrath!
Is the stead - fast love He'll show.

John Zundel, 1870

BEECHER 87.87 D

103C

For Our Frame He Well Remembers

Psalm 103:14-18

The body that is sown is perishable, it is raised imperishable.
—1 Corinthians 15:42

5. ¹⁴ For our frame He well re - mem - bers; That we're mere - ly dust He knows. ¹⁵ As for man, like grass, his days are; As the mea - dow's flower, he grows.

6. ¹⁶ When the wind has blown up - on it, In a mo - ment it is gone; In the place where once it flour - ished, It will nev - er - more be known.

7. ¹⁷ But the LORD's great lov - ing - kind - ness On all those who fear His name, From e - ter - ni - ty con - tin - ues To e - ter - ni - ty the same.

8. ¹⁸ And His righ - teous - ness con - tin - ues To their chil - dren and their seed, To all those who keep His cov - 'nant And His laws re - call and heed.

George C. Stebbins, 1878

EVENING PRAYER 87.87

In the Heavens

At the name of Jesus, every knee shall bow.
—Philippians 2:10

103D

Psalm 103:19-22

9. ¹⁹In the heav - ens by the LORD's hand
10. ²⁰Bless the LORD, you might - y an - gels,
11. Bless the LORD, all you His ar - mies,

He es - tab - lished there His throne. O - ver all is
You that hear and do His will. ²¹Bless the LORD, all
²²You His works, with one ac - cord In all parts of

His do - min - ion; He is King and He a - lone.
you His ser - vants Who His pleas - ure do ful - fill.
His do - min - ion; O my soul, O bless the LORD.

Traditional Sicilian melody, 18ᵗʰ century

SICILIAN MARINERS 87.87

104A

Psalm 104:1-8

My Soul, Bless the Lord!

The Son sustains all things by His powerful word.
—Hebrews 1:3

1. ¹ My soul, bless the LORD! LORD God, You are great,
2. ³ The beams of Your courts in wa - ters You laid;
3. ⁵ You set up the earth on foun - da - tions sure,
4. ⁷ But at Your re - buke the high wa - ters fled;

With hon - or ar - rayed, ma - jes - tic in state!
On wings of the wind Your path - way You made.
That al - ways it should un - shak - en en - dure.
Your thun - der they heard and from there they sped.

² You cov - er Your - self with a gar - ment of light
The clouds are Your char - iot; the winds do Your will;
⁶ Deep seas like a gar - ment a - bout it You cast;
⁸ The moun - tains a - rose, and the val - leys sank low,

And stretch out the sky as a cur - tain by night.
⁴ The flames and the light - nings Your pleas - ure ful - fill.
The wa - ters stood high; o - ver moun - tains they passed.
And went to the place You or - dained them to go.

Johann Michael Haydn; arr. William Gardiner, 1815

LYONS 10.10.11.11

By Limits You Set

104B

My God will meet all your needs according to His glorious
riches in Christ Jesus. —Philippians 4:19

Psalm 104:9-15

5. [9] By lim - its You set, the wa - ters are bound,
6. [11] The beasts of the field the streams sat - is - fy,
7. [13] You wa - ter the hills with rain from Your sky,
8. So man brings forth food by work - ing the ground,

Lest they should re - turn and cov - er the ground.
The wild don - key's need they ful - ly sup - ply.
With fruit of Your works the earth sat - is - fy.
[15] And wine makes his heart with glad - ness a - bound.

10 You make springs gush forth in the val - leys be - low,
12 The birds make their nests in the trees by the spring;
14 To nour - ish the cat - tle You cause grass to grow;
To make his face shine he ex - tracts fra - grant oil,

And cause rush - ing streams through the moun-tains to flow.
And there in the branch - es they joy - ful - ly sing.
For man's dai - ly la - bor, the plants You be - stow.
And finds bread that strength-ens his heart for his toil.

John K. Robb, 1949

EMSWORTH 10.10.11.11

104C
Psalm 104:16-26

The Trees of the LORD

What may be known about God is plain...being understood
from what has been made. —Romans 1:19-20

9. ⁱ⁶ The trees of the LORD are pro - vid - ed with wa - ter,
10. ²⁰ When You bring the dark - ness, and night fol - lows day - time,
11. ²⁴ Your works, LORD, are ma - ny, cre - at - ed in wis - dom;

The ce - dars of Leb - a - non plant - ed by Him.
The beasts of the for - est all come out to prowl.
The whole earth is filled with the things You have made.

¹⁷ The birds build their nests there, the storks choose the fir trees.
²¹ The young li - ons roar as for prey they go search - ing,
²⁵ Con - sid - er the o - cean, so vast, filled with crea - tures:

¹⁸ Wild goats climb high moun - tains where rock bad - gers hide.
De - pend - ing on God to pro - vide them with food.
The large and the ti - ny— too ma - ny to count.

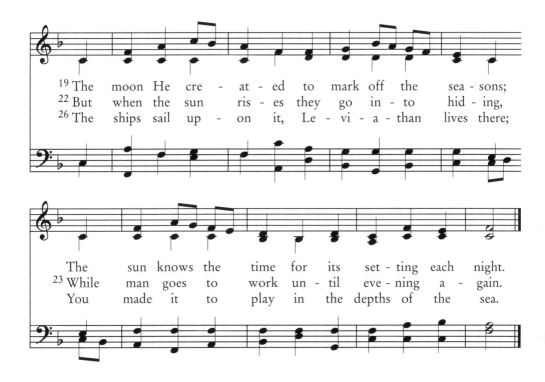

19 The moon He cre - at - ed to mark off the sea - sons;
22 But when the sun ris - es they go in - to hid - ing,
26 The ships sail up - on it, Le - vi - a - than lives there;

The sun knows the time for its set - ting each night.
23 While man goes to work un - til eve - ning a - gain.
You made it to play in the depths of the sea.

Traditional Welsh melody

ASH GROVE 12.11.12.11.12.11

104D
Psalm 104:24-30

How Many Works, Lord

He who was seated on the throne said,
"I am making everything new!" —Revelation 21:5

11. ²⁴How many works, LORD, in wisdom You've made.
12. ²⁶Where ships sail the deep and sea monsters play;
13. ²⁹When You hide Your face, bewildered they yearn.

How fully on earth, Your wealth is displayed.
²⁷These all look to You to give food each day.
When You take their breath, to dust they return.

²⁵Consider the ocean, how great and how wide,
²⁸Whatever You give them they gather for food;
³⁰When You send Your Spirit, created are they.

Where small and great creatures unnumbered abide.
When Your hand You open You fill them with good.
The face of the ground You renew every day.

John K. Robb, 1950

BRADFORD 10.10.11.11

Forevermore May the LORD's Glory Stand

The creation waits in eager expectation
for the sons of God to be revealed. —Romans 8:19

104E

Psalm 104:31-35

14. ³¹ For - ev - er - more may the LORD's glo - ry stand;
15. ³³ As long as I live, the LORD I will praise;
16. ³⁵ Con - sumed from the earth let sin - ners then be;

The LORD will en - joy the works of His hand.
To God I will sing through - out all my days.
The wick - ed in life no more let us see.

³² He looks at the earth and it trem - bles in fear;
³⁴ May my med - i - ta - tion be pleas - ing to Him;
And now, O my soul, bless - ing give to the LORD!

He touch - es the moun - tains, the smoke then ap - pears.
My heart in the LORD then with glad - ness will brim.
Let glad hal - le - lu - jahs ring; O praise the LORD!

William Croft, 1708

HANOVER 10.10.11.11

105A O Thank the LORD (Call on His Name)

Psalm 105:1-8

Abraham...is the father of all who believe.
—Romans 4:11

1. ¹O thank the LORD, call on His name; His deeds declare to all. ²O sing to Him, sing praise to Him; His wondrous works recall.
2. ³Let hearts that seek the LORD rejoice, His holy name adore. ⁴O seek the LORD, and seek His strength; His face seek evermore.
3. ⁵Remember all His wondrous deeds, The works that He has done, The righteous judgments of His mouth, His miracles each one—

4. ⁶O you, the seed of Abraham,
   God's servant—you, his sons,
   And all who sons of Jacob are,
   His own, His chosen ones.

5. ⁷He surely is the LORD our God,
   His judgments fill the land;
   ⁸He keeps in mind His covenant,
   That it may always stand.

Sylvanus B. Pond, 1841

HENRY Cℎ

God's Covenant Stays

Blessed are the poor in spirit, for theirs is the kingdom of heaven.
— Matthew 5:3

105B

Psalm 105:8-15

6. [8]God's cov-e-nant stays for-ev-er se-cure;
7. [9]The cov-e-nant He with A-bra-ham made;
8. [11-12]This prom-ise He made, though they were yet few:
9. [13]As they wan-dered from one realm to the next,

He brings it to mind, so shall it en-dure.
His oath He in turn to I-saac re-layed;
"Be-hold, Ca-naan's land I give un-to you
[14]He did not al-low that they be op-pressed.

His word to a thou-sand de-scen-dants shall stand;
[10]To Ja-cob con-firmed it, a cer-tain de-cree;
To be your in-her-i-tance where you may dwell."
He warned kings, [15]"Touch not those a-noint-ed by Me;

Through all gen-er-a-tions, so did He com-mand.
To Is-r'el, a cov-e-nant per-ma-nent-ly.
Said while they were few and were strang-ers as well.
Do not on My proph-ets in-flict in-ju-ry."

Henry J. Gauntlett, 1861   HOUGHTON 10.10.11.11

105C

Psalm 105:16-22

He Called for Famine

God has made this Jesus, whom you crucified,
both Lord and Christ. —Acts 2:36

10. ¹⁶ He called for fam-ine on the land, He broke the staff of bread.
11. ²⁰ The king who ruled the peo-ple sent To loose and set him free.

¹⁷ And Jo-seph, though sold as a slave, He thus sent on a-head.
²¹ He made him lord of all his house, To rule his prop-er-ty.

¹⁸ They bound his feet in i-ron chains; In fet-ters he was held.
²² He gave to Jo-seph pow'r to bind The princ-es of the land,

¹⁹ The LORD's word there-by test-ed him Un-til it was ful-filled.
That he might make his el-ders wise, That they would un-der-stand.

William Croft, 1708

ST. MATTHEW CMD

Then Isr'el Came to Egypt's Land

Christ, our Passover lamb, has been sacrificed.
—1 Corinthians 5:7

12. ²³ Then   Is - r'el came to   E-gypt's land; When Ja - cob jour-neyed west,
13. ²⁶ He   sent His ser - vant Mo - ses then, And Aar - on whom He chose.
14. ³⁰ He caused their land to swarm with frogs, Kings' cham-bers filled with them.
15. ³⁴ He spoke, and count-less lo-custs came,³⁵ Their fruits and leaves de-voured.

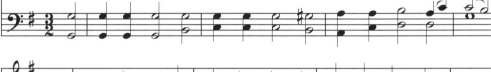

They set - tled in the   land of Ham.²⁴ The LORD His peo - ple   blessed.
²⁷ In   Ham they did His   mir - a - cles; His signs a - mong their   foes.
³¹ He spoke, and swarms of flies and gnats Through-out their coun-try came.
³⁶ He   killed each first-born in their land, The princ - es   of   their   pow'r.

He made them strong-er than their foes,²⁵ Whose hearts He filled with hate
²⁸ He   sent deep dark-ness   on the land,   His word was not de - fied.
³² He   gave them hail in - stead of rain,   Their land with light-ning flashed.
³⁷ He brought His peo-ple out en-riched   With sil - ver and with gold;

That made them hunt His peo-ple out,   His   ser-vants trick and   bait.
²⁹ He turned their wa - ters   in - to blood, And caused their fish to   die.
³³ He struck their fig trees and their vines, By Him their trees were slashed.
And   there was none a - mong His tribes Who stum - bled, young or old.

André Grétry, 1741–1831; arr. William J. Kirkpatrick, 1891   LANDAS CMD

105E

Psalm 105:38-45

How Glad Was Egypt

*They drank from the spiritual rock that accompanied them,
and that rock was Christ. —1 Corinthians 10:4*

16. ³⁸ How glad was E-gypt when they left, For Is-'rel was their dread.
17. ⁴² For He re-called His ho-ly word Which He to Ab-rah'm vowed.

³⁹ By night a fire shone bright for them, By day a cloud He spread.
⁴³ He brought His cho-sen peo-ple forth, With joy they cheered a-loud.

⁴⁰ At their re-quest He brought them quail, From heav-en bread be-stowed.
⁴⁴ The na-tions' lands and oth-er's toil, He gave them for their own,

⁴¹ He split the rock and wa-ter gushed, Through des-ert lands it flowed.
⁴⁵ So that they would o-bey His law. O praise the LORD a-lone!

Irish melody; arr. Robert M. Copeland, 1972

CLONMEL CMD

O Praise the Lord! O Thank the Lord

Consider therefore the kindness and sternness of God.
—Romans 11:22

1. ¹ O praise the LORD! O thank the LORD, For
2. ² O who can ful - ly praise the LORD, Or
3. ⁴ Re - mem - ber me with fa - vor, LORD, Which
4. ⁵ That with Your cho - sen ones I may En -

boun - ti - ful is He; Be - cause His lov - ing -
count His deeds of might? ³ How blessed are they who
You Your peo - ple show. O come to me, draw
joy pros - per - i - ty, And may with Your in -

kind - ness lasts Through all e - ter - ni - ty.
jus - tice keep, And al - ways do what's right.
near that I May Your sal - va - tion know;
her - i - tance In You boast joy - ful - ly.

William B. Bradbury, 1844

BROWN CM

106B

Psalm 106:6-15

With All Our Fathers

This is My body given for you; do this in remembrance of Me.
—Luke 22:19

5. ⁶With all our fa-thers we have sinned; We have done wick-ed-ly.
6. ⁹The Red Sea dried at His re-buke; He led them on dry land.
7. ¹³His peo-ple soon for-got His works, Did not wait for His will;

⁷Our fa-thers did not un-der-stand Your signs in E-gypt seen;
¹⁰He saved them from their hos-tile foes, Re-deemed them from their hand.
¹⁴But lust-ed in the wil-der-ness, And God they test-ed still.

Though they Your acts of love for-got, And at the Sea re-belled,
¹¹The wa-ters drowned their en-e-mies, Not one of them re-mained.
¹⁵So then He lis-tened to their pleas, And heard their sad la-ment;

⁸He saved them still, for His name's sake; His pow-er they be-held.
¹²His peo-ple then be-lieved His words, His praise in song pro-claimed.
But He, while grant-ing their re-quest, A dead-ly sick-ness sent.

Samuel Walter, b. 1916

HIGH POPPLES CMD

They Envied Moses

Father, forgive them, for they do not know what they are doing.
— Luke 23:34

106C

Psalm 106:16-23

8. [16] They envied Moses in the camp, His
leadership they shunned; They envied Aaron's
priestly rank, The LORD's anointed one.

9. [17] The opened earth on Dathan closed, A-
biram's kin entombed. [18] A fire blazed in their
company And wicked ones consumed.

10. [19] And they at Horeb forged a calf, Be-
fore its image kneeled; [20] Exchanged their Glory
for an ox That grazes in the field.

11. [21] Then God their Savior they forgot,
In Egypt His great deeds;
[22] His wonders in the land of Ham,
Signs by the Sea of Reeds.

12. [23] And so He said He would destroy
If Moses, His elect,
Stood not before Him in the breach,
His anger to deflect.

William Robert Broomfield, 1826–1888

ST. KILDA CM

106D
Psalm 106:24-31

Then They Despised

If we judged ourselves, we would not come under judgment.
—1 Corinthians 11:31

13. 24 Then they de - spised the pleas - ant land, Did
14. 26 He there - fore vowed to cast them down, There
15. 28 With Ba - al Pe - or they had joined, Ate
16. 30 The plague was stopped when Phin - e - has A -

not be - lieve His word. 25 In - stead they grum - bled
in the des - ert sands, 27 A - mong the na - tions
of - f'rings to the dead. 29 They stirred His an - ger
rose and in - ter - vened. 31 This was ac - count - ed

in their tents, And dis - o - beyed the LORD.
cast their seed, And scat - ter through the lands.
with their deeds; The plague a - mong them spread.
righ - teous - ness Through all e - ter - ni - ty.

Scottish Psalter, 1615

MARTYRS CM

At Meribah

But now you are light in the Lord. Live as children of light.
— Ephesians 5:8

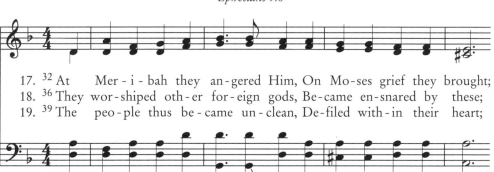

17. ³² At   Mer - i - bah they an-gered Him, On Mo-ses grief they brought;
18. ³⁶ They wor-shiped oth-er for-eign gods, Be-came en-snared by   these;
19. ³⁹ The   peo-ple thus be-came un-clean, De-filed with-in their   heart;

³³ For   they pro-voked his   spir - it there, His   speech was rash and hot.
³⁷ They gave their sons and daugh-ters up That   de - mons be ap-peased.
For   in their deeds and prac - tic - es They played the har-lot's part.

³⁴ They did not heed the LORD's com-mand That peo-ples should be slain;
³⁸ The   blood of daugh-ters and of sons— Blood of the guilt-less child—
⁴⁰ And   so a-gainst His   peo-ple burned The   an - ger of the LORD;

³⁵ In - stead they min-gled in their land, Learned prac - tic - es pro-fane.
Was   sac - ri - ficed to Ca-naan's gods; The   land be-came de-filed.
Then His own peo-ple He de-spised, His   her - i - tage ab-horred.

dward Hamilton, 1812–1870   LEVEQUE CMD

106F God Put His Tribes

Psalm 106:41-48

"Those whom I love I rebuke and discipline."
— Revelation 3:19

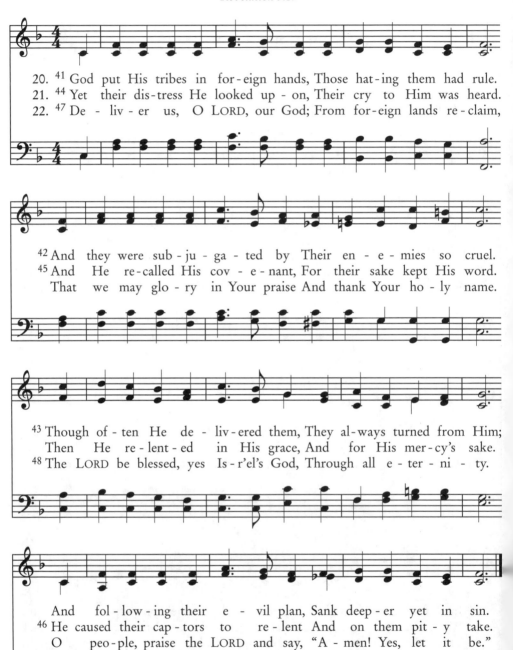

20. ⁴¹God put His tribes in for-eign hands, Those hat-ing them had rule.
21. ⁴⁴Yet their dis-tress He looked up-on, Their cry to Him was heard.
22. ⁴⁷De-liv-er us, O LORD, our God; From for-eign lands re-claim,

⁴²And they were sub-ju-ga-ted by Their en-e-mies so cruel.
⁴⁵And He re-called His cov-e-nant, For their sake kept His word.
That we may glo-ry in Your praise And thank Your ho-ly name.

⁴³Though of-ten He de-liv-ered them, They al-ways turned from Him;
Then He re-lent-ed in His grace, And for His mer-cy's sake.
⁴⁸The LORD be blessed, yes Is-r'el's God, Through all e-ter-ni-ty.

And fol-low-ing their e-vil plan, Sank deep-er yet in sin.
⁴⁶He caused their cap-tors to re-lent And on them pit-y take.
O peo-ple, praise the LORD and say, "A-men! Yes, let it be."

George F. Root, 1871

ALPENA CM

48 Bless - ed be the LORD, The God of Is - ra -
el From ev - er - last - ing to
ev - er - last - ing. Let all the
peo - ple say, "A - men." O praise the LORD!

Eleanor Hutcheson, 1972   DELTA (Irr.)

106H

Psalm 106:48

Book Four Doxology

48 The LORD be blessed, The God of Is-ra-el

From ev-er-last-ing to ev-er-last-ing.

Let all the peo-ple say, "A-men." O

Hal-le-lu-jah! Hal-le-lu-jah!

Brian E. Coombs, 2008

HOMEWOOD (Irr.

O Thank the LORD

*Many will come from the east and west and recline at the table
with Abraham, Isaac, and Jacob. — Matthew 8:11*

1. ¹O thank the LORD for He is good, His love en-
2. ⁴They wan-dered through the wil-der-ness, No cit-y
3. ⁷Then to a cit-y forth they went; He led them

dures e-ter-nal-ly! ²So let the LORD's re-deemed de-
found in which to dwell. ⁵Their hun-ger and their thirst in-
on a path-way straight. ⁸So let them to the LORD give

clare, The ones He from their foes set free; ³He gath-ered
creased, Their souls with-in grew faint as well. ⁶So to the
thanks For all His love and won-ders great. ⁹The thirst-y

them and brought them forth From east and west, from south and north.
LORD they cried, hard-pressed, He res-cued them from their dis-tress.
soul He sat-is-fies; With good the hun-gry He sup-plies.

Dmitri Bortniansky, 1825   ST. PETERSBURG 88.88.88

107B

Psalm 107:10-16

In Death's Dark Shadow

If the Son makes you free, you will be free indeed.
—*John 8:36*

4. ¹⁰ Some in death's dark shad - ow dwelled;
5. ¹² So He hum - bled them with toil;
6. He re - lieved their mis - er - y.
7. ¹⁵ Let them thank the LORD a - bove

Grieved, by chains in pris - on held.
No one helped them when they fell.
¹⁴ They from dark - ness He re - leased,
For His won - ders and His love!

¹¹ They a - gainst God's word re - belled,
¹³ To the LORD they cried for help
From death's gloom He set them free,
¹⁶ He de - mol - ished gates of bronze,

Spurned the Most High's coun - sel.
When they were in trou - ble.
Broke a - part their fet - ters.
Cut through bars of i - ron.

Medieval Plainsong melody; arr. Andrew K. Schep, 2008

DIES IRAE 77.76

The Foolish Suffered for Their Sins

Wretched man that I am!…Who will set me free?…Jesus Christ.
—Romans 7:24-25

107C
Psalm 107:17-22

8. ¹⁷The fool - ish suf - fered for their sins And
9. ¹⁹In trou - ble to the LORD they cried; He
10. ²¹Let them give thanks un - to the LORD For
11. ²²And let them of - fer thanks to Him, The

their re - bel - lious ways. ¹⁸Re - vil - ing ev - ery
saved them from dis - tress; ²⁰He sent His word to
all His kind - ness shown, And for His works so
sac - ri - fice of praise; His works let them de -

kind of food, They drew near to death's gates.
make them whole And lift from wretch - ed - ness.
won - der - ful Which He to men makes known.
clare a - broad, In songs their voic - es raise.

William Horsley, 1774–1858

HORSLEY CM

107D

Psalm 107:23-32

To Those Who Sail the Seas

Who then is this, that even the wind and the sea obey Him?
— Mark 4:41

12. ²³ To those who sail the seas in ships And on great wa-ters trade,
13. ²⁶ The ships were lift-ed to the sky, Then down to depths they dropped.
14. ²⁹ The storm He changed in-to a calm By His com-mand and will,
15. ³¹ Let them give thanks un-to the LORD For all His kind-ness shown.

²⁴ The works and won-ders of the LORD Are in the deep dis-played.
The sail-ors' cour-age dis-ap-peared, And they be-came dis-traught.
And so the waves which raged be-fore Now qui-et were and still.
And for His works so won-der-ful Which He to men makes known.

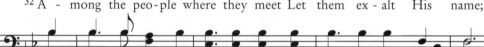

²⁵ By His com-mand the wind was stirred That with a tem-pest blows;
²⁷ They stag-gered just like drunk-en men, And could no an-swer see;
³⁰ Then they were glad, be-cause at rest And qui-et was the sea.
³² A-mong the peo-ple where they meet Let them ex-alt His name;

It lift-ed wa-ters of the sea; Great roll-ing waves a-rose.
²⁸ The LORD, when they cried out to Him, From trou-ble set them free.
He led them to the ha-ven thus Where they de-sired to be.
And where the el-ders are con-vened, Let them His praise pro-claim.

Lowell Mason, 1830

FOUNTAIN CMD

He Changes Streams to Wilderness

Blessed are those who mourn, for they shall be comforted.
— Matthew 5:4

16. ³³ He chang-es streams to wil-der-ness, And springs to thirst-y ground,
17. ³⁷ They plant their vine-yards, sow their fields; Rich har-vests there they grow;
18. ⁴⁰ For He con-tempt on princ-es pours; He lets them go a - stray
19. ⁴² When this the up-right ones ob-serve, They great-ly shall re - joice,

³⁴ A fruit-ful land to salt-y waste, When peo-ples' sins a - bound.
³⁸ His bless-ing makes them mul-ti-ply, Their herds no de-crease know.
And wan-der in the wil-der-ness Where there is not a way.
And all un-righ-teous-ness, a-shamed, Shall cease to raise its voice.

³⁵ He turns the des-ert to a lake, Dry land to wa-ter springs,
³⁹ A-gain they much di-min-ished are And brought to low es - tate
⁴¹ But He from trou-ble lifts the poor By set-ting them on high,
⁴³ Is an-y wise? He'll heed these things Which vers-es here re - cord;

³⁶ And that they may pre-pare a home The hun-gry there He brings.
Through sor-row and ad - ver-si-ty And through op-pres-sion great.
And like a flock in fam-i-lies He makes them mul-ti-ply.
And he'll con-si-der well the love And kind-ness of the LORD.

Thomas E. Perkins, 1831–1912

CANAAN CMD

107F

Psalm 107:1-9

O Glorify Him

Blessed are those who hunger and thirst for righteousness,
for they shall be satisfied. —Matthew 5:6

1. ¹O glo - ri - fy Him, for the LORD, He is good;
2. ⁴They wan-dered through wil - der - ness, des - ert and waste;
3. ⁷A right way He led them un - til they had found

For - ev - er is His cov - 'nant love.
No cit - y to live in was found.
A cit - y, a true dwell - ing place.

²Let those that the LORD has re - deemed make it known—
⁵They suf - fered from hun - ger, they suf - fered from thirst;
⁸For this rea - son let them give thanks to the LORD,

Re - deemed from the hand of the foe.
Their soul grew ex - haust - ed and weak.
Be - cause of His cov - e - nant love—

3 For He took them out of the lands where they were,
6 And then in their trou - ble they cried to the LORD
Be - cause of the great things that He brings a - bout,

And brought them to - geth - er a - gain,
Be - cause of the per - il they faced;
Things done for the sons of man - kind.

From re - gions that lay to the east and the west,
And out from the dan - gers and trou - bles they knew
9 For He quenched the thirst of the soul that was parched,

From those to the north and the south.
He brought them to safe - ty at last.
The hun - ger - ing soul filled with good.

G. Duncan Lowe, 2005

GLORIFY 11.8.11.8 D

107G

Psalm 107:10-16

Some Lived in Darkness

Thanks be to God, that though you were slaves of sin,
you became obedient. —Romans 6:17

4. ¹⁰ Yet some lived in dark - ness, in shad - ow of death,
5. ¹⁴ From dark - ness He brought them, from shad - ow of death;

As pris - on - ers wretch - ed and chained,
And He broke their shack - les a - part.

¹¹ Be - cause they re - belled a - gainst what God had said;
¹⁵ For this rea - son let them give thanks to the LORD,

The Most High's good coun - sel they spurned.
Be - cause of His cov - e - nant love,

12 And so He has hum-bled their heart with hard toil;
Be - cause of the great things that He brings a - bout,

They stum-bled but no one would help.
Things done for the sons of man - kind.

13 Then they in their trou - ble cried out to the LORD;
16 For He broke the might - i - est gates made of bronze,

He res - cued them from their dis - tress.
And cut through their strong i - ron bars.

G. Duncan Lowe, 2005

SHADOW 11.8.11.8 D

107H

Psalm 107:17-22

Fools Were Afflicted

While we were yet sinners, Christ died for us.
—Romans 5:8

6. ¹⁷ Yet   fools were af - flict - ed be - cause they re - belled,
7. ¹⁹ In   trou - ble se - vere they cried out   to   the LORD;
8. ²¹ O   let them give thanks for the LORD's gra - cious love,

Be - cause   of   their   un - god - ly   ways.
He   res - cued   them   from   their   dis - tress.
The   won - ders   He   does   for   man - kind.

¹⁸ Their   soul   felt   ab - hor - rence for   all   kinds   of   food,
²⁰ He   sent   forth   His   word   and   re - stored them   to   health,
²² So   let   them   pre - sent   sac - ri - fic - es   of   thanks,

And   up   to   death's   gates   they   drew   near.
And   saved   them   from   ru - in   and   death.
And   tell   of   His   deeds   in   glad   song.

John K. Robb, 1949

CONWELL 11.8.11.8

All Those Who Go Down to the Sea

He rebuked the wind and said to the sea, "Hush. Be still."
— Mark 4:39

9. [23] All those who go down to the sea in their ships, Who
10. [25] He spoke and com-mand-ed a great storm of wind That
11. [27] They reeled and they stag-gered like men who were drunk. Their

sail the great wa-ters for trade, [24] They too have be-held what the
lift-ed the waves of the sea. [26] They rose to the heav'ns, then dropped
wis-dom had all fled a-way. [28] Then they in their trou-ble cried

LORD has done there, His won-der-ful acts in the deep.
down to the depths. The souls of men melt-ed with fear.
out to the LORD; He res-cued them from their dis-tress.

12. [29] The storm wind He settled and caused to be still;
The waves of the sea became calm.
[30] The men became glad when the waves had died down,
And to a safe haven He led.

13. [31] O let them give thanks for the LORD's gracious love,
The wonders He does for mankind.
[32] When people are gathered, O let them give praise,
And hail Him where elders convene.

Michael Tabon, 2005   SHIPS 11.8.11.8

107J

Psalm 107:33-43

Some Rivers He Changes

He will receive a hundred times as much now…
and in the age to come, eternal life. —Mark 10:30

14. ³³ Some riv - ers He chang - es to des - ert and waste,
15. ³⁷ They then may sow seeds and plant vine - yards and fields,
16. ⁴¹ But safe from af - flic - tion He rais - es the poor,

And wa - ter - springs to ar - id ground.
And gath - er a plen - ti - ful yield.
To set them se - cure - ly on high.

³⁴ A land that is fruit - ful He turns in - to salt,
³⁸ He bless - es them great - ly, their num - bers in - crease;
And fam - i - lies, too, He will treat with His care,

For e - vil were those liv - ing there.
He'll not let their cat - tle de - crease.
And make them to be like a flock.

35 Yet wil-der-ness then He can make in-to pools, From
39 But when they were few, they were bowed and brought low From
42 The up-right will see this, and as they re-joice, All

dry dust can make wa-ter-springs. 36 He makes such a place for the
hard-ship, op-pres-sion, and grief; 40 On princ-es He pours out His
wrong-do-ing clos-es its mouth. 43 Is an-y-one wise? Let him

hun-gry to dwell, To set up a cit-y as
scorn, so they roam In waste-lands with-out an-y
hold to these things, And think on the LORD's gra-cious

home, To set up a cit-y as home.
path, In waste-lands with-out an-y path.
love, And think on the LORD's gra-cious love.

William J. Kirkpatrick, 1890   KIRKPATRICK 11.8.11.8 D

108A

Psalm 108:1-6

God, My Heart Is Steadfast

Seek first His kingdom and His righteousness.
— Matthew 6:33

1. [1]God, my heart is stead - fast; I will sing prais - es.
2. LORD, a - mong the peo - ples I'll sing Your prais - es,
3. [5]God, a - bove the heav - ens O be ex - alt - ed,

And with all my be - ing to You my song I'll sing.
From a - mong the na - tions my praise to You will rise.
And a - bove all earth may Your glo - ry lift - ed be;

[2]Wak - en harp and psal - t'ry; dawn I will a - wak - en,
[4]For Your lov - ing - kind - ness is a - bove the heav - ens,
[6]So that Your be - lov - ed then may be de - liv - ered,

[3]With ma - ny peo - ples, LORD, I thanks will bring.
Your faith - ful - ness ex - tends in - to the skies.
Save with Your right hand; an - swer give to me.

John B. Dykes, 1861

NICAEA 11.12.12.10

God Spoke in Holiness

The God of peace will soon crush Satan under your feet.
—Romans 16:20

108B
Psalm 108:7-13

4. ⁷God spoke in ho-li-ness: "I will ex-ul-tant stand;
5. ⁹"In Mo-ab I will wash, My shoe on E-dom throw;
6. ¹¹Have You not cast us off, O God, in Whom we boast?

I'll meas-ure Suc-coth's val-ley and Ap-por-tion Shech-em's land.
I will a-bove Phi-lis-ti-a With shouts of tri-umph go.
Will You no more, O God, go out In bat-tle with our host?

⁸For Gil-e-ad is Mine; Mine are Ma-nas-seh's fields;
¹⁰O who will bring me to The cit-y for-ti-fied?
¹²A-gainst the foe give help; No help can man be-stow.

Yes, Eph-ra-im My hel-met is; My scep-ter Ju-dah wields."
O who is he that to the land Of E-dom will me guide?"
¹³In God we'll gain the vic-to-ry, For He'll tread down our foe.

George W. Martin; arr. Arthur S. Sullivan, 1862

LEOMINSTER SMD

108C

Psalm 108:1-6

With Steadfast Heart, O God

Give thanks in everything, for this is God's will for you
in Christ Jesus. —1 Thessalonians 5:18

1. ¹With stead - fast heart, O God, My soul will sing Your praise. ²A - wak - en lyre, a - wak - en harp; I'll wake the dawn's first rays.

2. ³I will give thanks to You, A - mong the peo - ples, LORD, A - mong the na - tions I will sing Your praise to all the world.

3. ⁴Your stead - fast love is great, A - bove the heav - ens high. Your truth and faith - ful - ness ex - tend And reach up to the sky.

4. ⁵May You be lifted high
Above the heavens, God;
And may Your glory also be
Above the earth abroad.

5. ⁶That Your beloved ones
Deliverance may see;
O save us by Your strong right hand,
In mercy answer me.

H.A. Cesar Malan, 1787–1864

SILCHESTER SM

God Spoke in Holiness

If God is for us, who is against us?
— Romans 8:31

108D
Psalm 108:7-13

6. ⁷God spoke in ho-li-ness: "I will ex-ul-tant stand;
7. ⁹"In Mo-ab I will wash, My shoe on E-dom throw;
8. ¹¹Have You not cast us off, O God, in whom we boast?

I'll meas-ure Suc-coth's val-ley and Ap-por-tion Shech-em's land.
I will a-bove Phi-lis-ti-a With shouts of tri-umph go.
Will You no more, O God, go out In bat-tle with our host?

⁸For Gil-e-ad is Mine; Mine are Ma-nas-seh's fields;
¹⁰O who will bring me to The cit-y for-ti-fied?
¹²A-gainst the foe give help; No help can man be-stow.

Yes, Eph-ra-im My hel-met is; My scep-ter Ju-dah wields."
O who is he that to the land Of E-dom will me guide?"
¹³In God we'll gain the vic-to-ry, For He'll tread down our foe.

George J. Elvey, 1868

DIADEMATA SMD

109A

God of My Praise

Psalm 109:1-15

If anyone does not love the Lord, he is to be accursed.
—1 Corinthians 16:22

1. ¹God of my praise, O do not be si - lent.
2. ⁶Or - der a wick - ed man to op - press him.
3. ¹¹Let lend - ers take back all his be - long - ings.

²They've slan - dered me with wick - ed, ly - ing mouths.
Let an ac - cus - er stand at his right hand.
Let strang - ers plun - der all for which he worked.

³They've cir - cled me with their words of ha - tred, And
⁷When he is judged, let him be found guilt - y, And
¹²No mer - cy show to him or his chil - dren. ¹³Cut

fought a - gainst me with - out a cause.
look up - on his prayer as a sin.
off his off - spring; blot out their names.

4 In re-turn for my love they rath-er would ac-cuse,
8 Let his days be few; let an-oth-er take his place.
14 Let his fa-ther's sin be re-mem-bered by the LORD.

But I still am in prayer for them.
9 Let his chil-dren be fa-ther-less.
Do not blot out his moth-er's sin.

5 So they have re-paid me Such e-vil for my good-ness, And
Make his wife a wid-ow,10 His wan-d'ring chil-dren beg-gars Who
15 Let the LORD re-mem-ber The sins they've done, for-ev-er. Re-

they gave ha-tred for all my love.
seek food far from their ru-ined homes.
move their mem-'ry from all the earth.

Franki Fuhrman, 2004

JACKI'S 2ND LAMENT (Irr.)

109B
Psalm 109:16-21

Never Thinking to Show Kindness

The Lord will repay him....But the Lord stood with me.
—2 Timothy 4:14, 17

4. [16]Never thinking to show kindness,
He pursued the poor to death; He the needy persecuted, Broken-hearted ones oppressed.

5. [17]He loved cursing; curses on him;
He loathed blessing; give him none. [18]Cursing was his daily clothing; And on him it now has come.

6. May he soak up his own cursing,
Let it penetrate his bones. [19]May it be a belt around him, Let it cover him like clothes.

7. [20]May this be to my accusers
What they're given from the LORD;
Those who evil speak against me,
Let this be their just reward.

8. [21]But, O LORD, my Lord, for Your name
Will You kindly deal with me?
For the goodness of Your mercy,
May You my deliv'rance be.

Johann Thommen, *Erbaulicher Musicalischer Christenschatz*, 1745   BATTY 87.87

Never Thinking to Show Kindness

The Lord will repay him....But the Lord stood with me.
—2 Timothy 4:14, 17

4. ¹⁶Nev - er think - ing to show kind - ness,
5. ¹⁷He loved curs - ing; curs - es on him;
6. May he soak up his own curs - ing,

He pur - sued the poor to death; He the need - y
He loathed bless - ing; give him none. ¹⁸Curs - ing was his
Let it pen - e - trate his bones. ¹⁹May it be a

per - se - cut - ed, Bro - ken - heart - ed ones op - pressed.
dai - ly cloth - ing; And on him it now has come.
belt a - round him, Let it cov - er him like clothes.

7. ²⁰May this be to my accusers
What they're given from the LORD;
Those who evil speak against me,
Let this be their just reward.

8. ²¹But, O LORD, my Lord, for Your name
Will You kindly deal with me?
For the goodness of Your mercy,
May You my deliv'rance be.

Traditional Russian melody; arr. Brian E. Coombs, 2001   KATUSHKA 87.87

109D
Psalm 109:22-31

I Am Very Poor and Needy

Blessed are the poor in spirit, for theirs is the kingdom of heaven.
— Matthew 5:3

9. 22 I am ver - y poor and need - y;
10. 26 Help me, LORD, my Lord; O save me
11. Clothed with shame be my ac - cus - ers,

I am wound - ed in my heart.
In ac - cord - ance with Your love.
Wrapped up in their own dis - grace.

23 My life pass - es like a shad - ow,
27 Let them know this is Your do - ing;
30 With my mouth then I will of - fer

Like a lo - cust shak - en off.
That Your hand, LORD, did this all.
Great thanks - giv - ing to the LORD.

24 Both my knees are weak from fast - ing;
28 Bless me e - ven though they curse me;
In the mul - ti - tude I'll praise Him;

Gaunt my bod - y has be - come.
When they strike, they're put to shame.
31 For He stands be - side the poor

25 I am scorned by my ac - cus - ers;
But may glad - ness fill Your ser - vant,
At their right hand; and He'll save them

See - ing me, they shake their heads.
29 While dis - hon - or cov - ers them.
From those who con - demn his soul.

Traditional Welsh melody; arr. Thomas J. Williams, 1890   EBENEZER (Ton-y-Botel) 87.87 D

110A

Psalm 110

The Lord Has Spoken to My Lord

...Within the veil, where Jesus has entered as a forerunner for us,
having become a high priest. —Hebrews 6:19-20

1. ¹The Lord has spo - ken to my Lord:
2. ³Your peo - ple, in Your day of pow'r,
3. ⁵And when His day of wrath has come;

"At My right hand take Your seat
Free - ly give them - selves to You;
Then the Lord at Your right hand

Un - til I make Your en - e - mies
Your youth, all clothed in ho - li - ness,
Will crush great kings and na - tions judge,

In - to a foot - stool for Your feet."
Ap - pear each day like morn - ing's dew.
With fall - en bod - ies fill the land.

2 The LORD from Zi - on will ex - tend
4 The LORD has sworn a sol - emn oath
6 Just - ly con - demned be - neath His rule

The might - y scep - ter in Your hand:
From which He'll nev - er be re - leased:
Will heads of ma - ny na - tions die;

"Rule in the midst of en - e - mies,
"In th'or - der of Mel - chi - ze - dek
7 But from the brook He'll stop to drink,

Sub - due each un - der Your com - mand."
For - ev - er - more You are a priest."
And His own head He'll lift up high.

C. Hubert H. Parry, 1848–1918; arr. Brian E. Coombs; Andrew K. Schep, 2004   JERUSALEM 8788.8888

110B
Psalm 110

The LORD Has Spoken to My Lord

He sat down at the right hand of the Majesty...
having become as much better than the angels. —Hebrews 1:3-4

1. ¹ The LORD has spo-ken to my Lord: "Sit here at My right hand
2. ³ When You dis-play Your might-y pow'r Your peo-ple come to You;
3. ⁵ The Lord at Your right hand will strike Earth's rul-ers in His wrath.

Un - til I make Your foes a stool On which Your feet may stand."
At dawn, ar-rayed in ho-li-ness, Your youth ap-pear like dew.
⁶ A - mong the na-tions He will judge; The slain will fill His path.

² The LORD from Zi-on shall ex-tend The scep-ter of Your pow'r;
⁴ The LORD has sworn, and from His oath He'll nev-er be re-leased:
In ma-ny lands He'll crush their kings, His wrath will be their dread.

"Rule all sur-round-ing en - e-mies, And be their con-quer - or."
"Of th'or-der of Mel - chi - ze-dek, You'll al-ways be a priest."
⁷ And from the way-side brook He'll drink, In vic - t'ry lift the head.

Henry S. Cutler, 1872

ALL SAINTS NEW CMD

The LORD Said to My Lord

He has become such...according to the power of an indestructible life. —Hebrews 7:16

1. [1]The LORD said to my Lord, "At My right take Your seat,
2. [3]Your peo - ple free - ly serve Through-out Your day of pow'r;
3. [4]The LORD has made an oath, And He will not turn back:
4. [6]The na - tions He will judge, Their dead will fill the land;

Un - til I've made Your foes A foot-stool for Your feet."
Ar - rayed in ho - li - ness, Born in the dawn-ing hour,
"You'll al - ways be a priest, And like Mel - chi - ze - dek."
In ma - ny lands He'll strike Their rul - ers in com - mand.

[2]The LORD from Zi - on spreads Your pow'r:
Your youth have now be - come to You
[5]At Your right hand the Lord will stay,
[7]He will drink from the wa - ter - side;

"A - mong Your foes be con - quer - or."
Re - fresh - ing as the morn - ing dew.
He'll crush kings on His wrath - ful day.
Vic - to - rious, lift His head on high.

William H. Havergal, 1853

ST. JOHN 66.66.88

110D

Psalm 110

The Lord Said to My Lord

Having offered one sacrifice for sins for all time, He sat down...
waiting from that time onward. —Hebrews 10:12-13

1. ¹The LORD said to my Lord: "Sit here at My right hand
2. ³Your peo-ple free-ly come Through-out Your day of pow'r;
3. ⁵The Lord at Your right hand Will shat-ter kings in wrath.

Un - til I make Your en - e - mies A foot-stool for Your feet."
From morn-ing's dawn, in ho - ly robes, Your youth are like the dew.
⁶A - mong the na-tions He will judge, And fill them with their dead.

²The LORD from Zi - on sends Your scep-ter in its strength,
⁴The LORD has sworn an oath, And will not change His mind:
Yes, He will smite and crush Chief men in ma - ny lands.

"With might-y pow - er show Your rule A - mong Your en - e - mies."
"In th'or-der of Mel - chi - ze - dek, You ev - er are a priest."
⁷And from the way-side brook He'll drink, And there-fore lift His head.

Franklin L. Sheppard, 1915; arr. Edward Shippen Barnes, 1926

TERRA BEATA SMD

O Praise the LORD

My food is to do the will of Him who sent Me and to accomplish His work. —*John 4:34*

1. ¹O praise the LORD! With all my heart Thanks
2. ²The works ac - com - plished by the LORD Are
3. ³His work is splen - did and dis - plays His

to the LORD I'll bring To - geth - er with the
ver - y great in might; They're stud - ied close - ly
glo - rious maj - es - ty; And His en - dur - ing

up - right ones, And in their gath - er - ing.
by all those Who find in them de - light.
righ - teous - ness For - ev - er - more will be.

4. ⁴He made His wonders lasting signs
   Remembered endlessly;
   The LORD is most compassionate,
   And merciful is He.

5. ⁵Those fearing Him He fills with food
   Provided by His hand.
   He keeps in mind His covenant,
   That it may ever stand.

H.A. Cesar Malan, 1787–1864

BOYNTON CM

111B

Psalm 111:6-10

The Mighty Power of His Works

I glorified You on earth, having accomplished the work
You have given me. —John 17:4

6. ⁶ The might - y pow - er of His works He
7. ⁷ The works He's done are true and just; His
8. ⁹ He saved His peo - ple and or - dained His
9. ¹⁰ The one who fears the LORD has learned The

has His peo - ple shown, By giv - ing them the
pre - cepts all are sure. ⁸ Set up in truth and
cov - 'nant to re - main; His name is to be
first of wis - dom's ways. All who o - bey will

na - tions' lands To be their ver - y own.
up - right - ness, They ev - er shall en - dure.
held in awe, For ho - ly is His name.
un - der - stand; For - ev - er lasts His praise.

Charles Hutcheson, 1832

STRACATHRO CM

O Praise the LORD

They received the word with great eagerness,
examining the Scriptures daily. —Acts 17:11

111C
Psalm 111:1-5

1. ¹O praise the LORD! With all my heart Thanks to the LORD I'll bring To - geth - er with the up - right ones, And in their gath - er - ing.

2. ²The works ac - com - plished by the LORD Are ver - y great in might; They're stud - ied close - ly by all those Who find in them de - light.

3. ³His work is splen - did and dis - plays His glo - rious maj - es - ty; And His en - dur - ing righ - teous - ness For - ev - er - more will be.

4. ⁴He made His wonders lasting signs
Remembered endlessly;
The LORD is most compassionate,
And merciful is He.

5. ⁵Those fearing Him He fills with food
Provided by His hand.
He keeps in mind His covenant,
That it may ever stand.

Thomas A. Arne, 1762; arr. Ralph Harrison, 1784

ARLINGTON CM

111D

Psalm 111:6-10

The Mighty Power of His Works

If anyone is willing to do His will, he will know of the teaching.
—John 7:17

6. ⁶ The might-y pow-er of His works He has His peo-ple shown, By giv-ing them the na-tions' lands To be their ver-y own.

7. ⁷ The works He's done are true and just; His pre-cepts all are sure. ⁸ Set up in truth and up-right-ness, They ev-er shall en-dure.

8. ⁹ He saved His peo-ple and or-dained His cov-'nant to re-main; His name is to be held in awe, For ho-ly is His name.

9. ¹⁰ The one who fears the LORD has learned The first of wis-dom's ways. All who o-bey will un-der-stand; For-ev-er lasts His praise.

Scottish Psalter, 1615

DUNFERMLINE CM

O Praise the LORD

Love your enemies, do good, and lend, expecting nothing in return.
— Luke 6:35

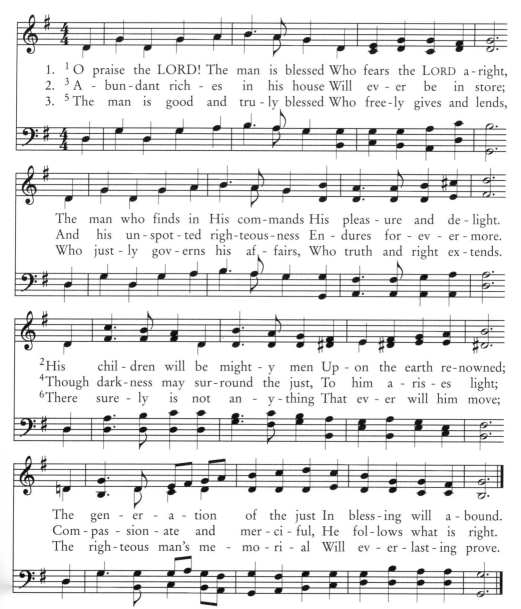

1. [1] O praise the LORD! The man is blessed Who fears the LORD a-right,
2. [3] A-bun-dant rich-es in his house Will ev-er be in store;
3. [5] The man is good and tru-ly blessed Who free-ly gives and lends,

The man who finds in His com-mands His pleas-ure and de-light.
And his un-spot-ted righ-teous-ness En-dures for-ev-er-more.
Who just-ly gov-erns his af-fairs, Who truth and right ex-tends.

[2] His chil-dren will be might-y men Up-on the earth re-nowned;
[4] Though dark-ness may sur-round the just, To him a-ris-es light;
[6] There sure-ly is not an-y-thing That ev-er will him move;

The gen-er-a-tion of the just In bless-ing will a-bound.
Com-pas-sion-ate and mer-ci-ful, He fol-lows what is right.
The righ-teous man's me-mo-ri-al Will ev-er-last-ing prove.

4. [7] And when he hears disturbing news
He will not be afraid;
His heart is fixed; his confidence
Upon the LORD is stayed.
[8] Established firmly is his heart;
He will not fearful be,
Until upon his enemies
He his desire will see.

5. [9] He has dispersed his wealth abroad
And given to the poor;
His horn with honor shall be raised,
His righteousness endure.
[10] The wicked looks on angrily;
He grits his teeth, dismayed,
But melts away, and his desire
Will into nothing fade.

ohn K. Robb, 1949

HETHERTON CMD

112B

Psalm 112

O Praise the LORD

Do not be overcome by evil, but overcome evil with good.
—*Romans 12:21*

1. ¹O praise the LORD! The man is tru-ly blessed
2. ³A-bun-dant rich-es are with-in his house,
3. ⁵The gra-cious man who free-ly lends is blessed,

Who fears the LORD, and in His law de-lights.
His righ-teous-ness en-dures for-ev-er-more.
The one who just-ly gov-erns his af-fairs.

²His chil-dren will be might-y in the earth.
⁴In dark-ness light a-ris-es for the just;
⁶The righ-teous man will sure-ly not be moved,

How blessed the chil-dren of all the righ-teous!
He's full of mer-cy; he's just and gra-cious.
He'll be re-mem-bered through-out the a-ges.

4. ⁷ At evil news he will not be afraid;
His heart is steadfast, trusting in the LORD.
⁸ His heart is firm, he will not live in fear,
Till on his foes he shall look in triumph.

5. ⁹ He helps the poor with generosity;
His good endures, his horn is lifted high.
¹⁰ The wicked sees and grinds his teeth in rage;
But he will vanish, his lust will perish.

Adapt. from Ralph Vaughan-Williams, 1872–1958

SINE NOMINE 10.10.10.10 (Alt

Praise the LORD's Name

He existed in the form of God….He laid aside His privileges…
being made in the likeness of men. —*Philippians 2:6-7*

113A
Psalm 113

1. ¹ Praise the LORD's name, praise the LORD! Praise Him,
2. ³ Dawn to dusk, from east to west, Let the
3. ⁵ Who is like our God a - lone? High in

ser - vants of the LORD. ² May the LORD's name
LORD's great name be blessed. ⁴ O - ver na - tions
heav'n the LORD's en - throned. ⁶ But He con - de -

bless - ed be Now and to e - ter - ni -
lift - ed high, LORD, Your glo - ry crowns the
scends to know Things in heav'n and earth be -

ty! Now and to e - ter - ni - ty!
sky! LORD, Your glo - ry crowns the sky!
low. Things in heav'n and earth be - low.

4. ⁷ From the dust He lifts the poor,
Makes the needy grieve no more.
⁸ Those He's raised up from the pit
With His people's princes sit.

5. ⁹ He the barren woman takes,
And a joyful mother makes;
In her home she finds reward.
Hallelujah! Praise the LORD!

H.A. Cesar Malan, 1827

HENDON 77.77

113B

Psalm 113

O Praise the LORD

...Jesus, because of the suffering of death,
crowned with glory and honor. —Hebrews 2:9

1. ¹O praise the LORD; Sing praise, All ser-vants of the LORD. ²Come praise the LORD's great name, Bless Him for-ev - er - more. ³From dawn to dusk, from east to west, O let the LORD's name there be blessed.

2. ⁴LORD o - ver na - tions all, His glo - ry crowns the sky. ⁵Who's like the LORD our God, En - throned in heav - en high? ⁶Who con - de - scends that He may know All things in heav'n and earth be - low?

3. ⁷He lifts the poor from dust, And from the ash - es' heap. He lifts the need - y high, ⁸A - mong no - bil - i - ty. ⁹The bar - ren wife has joy re - stored With home and chil - dren. Praise the LORD!

Horatio W. Parker, 1894

JUBILATE 66.66.88

Praise the LORD's Name

He raised us up with Him, and seated us with Him in the heavenly places in Christ Jesus. —Ephesians 2:6

113C
Psalm 113

1. [1] Praise the LORD's name, praise the LORD!
2. [3] Dawn to dusk, from east to west,
3. [5] Who is like our God a - lone?

Praise Him, ser - vants of the LORD.
Let the LORD's great name be blessed.
High in heav'n the LORD's en - throned.

[2] May the LORD's name bless - ed be
[4] O - ver na - tions lift - ed high,
[6] But He con - de - scends to know

Now and to e - ter - ni - ty!
LORD, Your glo - ry crowns the sky!
Things in heav'n and earth be - low.

4. [7] From the dust He lifts the poor,
   Makes the needy grieve no more.
   [8] Those He's raised up from the pit
   With His people's princes sit.

5. [9] He the barren woman takes,
   And a joyful mother makes;
   In her home she finds reward.
   Hallelujah! Praise the LORD!

Michael Tabon, 2000

BETH 77.77

114A

Psalm 114

When Isr'el Went Forth

Behold, the veil of the temple was torn in two from top to bottom,
and the earth shook and the rocks were split. — Matthew 27:51

1. ¹ When Is - r'el went forth, and all Ja - cob's house,
2. ³ The sea looked and fled; the Jor - dan turned back.
3. ⁶ You moun - tains, O why do you leap like rams?

To leave E - gypt's land and their for - eign tongues,
⁴ Like rams moun - tains leapt, and hills skipped like lambs.
And why, all you hills, do you skip like lambs?

² Then Ju - dah be - came His own ho - ly place,
⁵ What ails you, O sea? And why do you flee?
⁷ O earth, quake be - fore the Lord, Ja - cob's God.

And His do - min - ion then be - came Is - ra - el.
O Jor - dan's flow - ing streams, why do you turn back?
⁸ He made the rock a pool, from flint made a spring.

Brian E. Coombs, 2004 ERIE 10.10.10.11

When from Egypt Isr'el Parted

114B
Psalm 114

Behold, a severe earthquake had occurred, for an angel of the Lord descended…and rolled away the stone. —Matthew 28:2

1. ¹When from E - gypt Is - r'el part - ed,
2. ³When it saw, the sea fled quick - ly,
3. ⁵Sea, what made you flee so quick - ly?
4. ⁷Trem - ble, earth, be - fore the Mas - ter;

Ja - cob's house left for - eign tongues,
Riv - er Jor - dan made re - treat;
Jor - dan, why did you turn back?
Here, be - hold, is Ja - cob's God—

²Ju - dah was His sanc - tu - ar - y,
⁴Moun - tains then like rams were leap - ing;
⁶O why leap like rams, you moun - tains?
⁸Who turned rock to pools of wa - ter,

1. 2. 3. | **4.**

His do - min - ion Is - ra - el.
Hills were skip - ping just like lambs.
Hills, why do you skip like lambs?
Hard flint rock to gush - ing springs.

Andrew K. Schep, 2004

IN EXITU ISRAEL 87.87

115A

Psalm 115:1-8

Not unto Us, LORD

Worthy is the Lamb who was slain, to receive...glory.
—Revelation 5:12

1. [1] Not un-to us, LORD, no, not us, But to Your name a-bove, Bring glo-ry for Your faith-ful-ness And for Your stead-fast love.

2. [2] Why should the hea-then na-tions say, "Why does their God keep still?" [3] For our God lives in heav-en high, And car-ries out His will.

3. [4] Of gold and sil-ver are their gods, Which men craft care-ful-ly, [5] And give them mouths that can-not speak And eyes that can-not see.

4. [6] Though they have ears, they cannot hear;
   Their nose no scent has found.
   [7] Their hands can't feel, their feet can't walk;
   Their throats can make no sound.

5. [8] Whoever makes these lifeless gods—
   These idols which are vain—
   Whoever puts his trust in them
   In time becomes the same.

William Croft, 1708

ST. ANNE CM

O Israel, Trust in the LORD

115B

Psalm 115:9-18

Blessed be the God and Father of our Lord Jesus Christ, who has blessed us with every spiritual blessing. — Ephesians 1:3

6. [9] O Is - ra - el, trust in the LORD, He is their help and shield.
7. [12] The LORD has kept us in His thoughts; And He will bless us still.
8. [15] May you have bless-ing from the LORD, Who made the skies and land.

[10] O house of Aar - on trust the LORD, He is their help and shield.
He'll bless the house of Is - ra - el, Bless Aar-on's house as well.
[16] The high - est heav - ens are the LORD's, But earth He gave to man.

[11] O all of you who fear the LORD, He is their help and shield;
[13] He'll bless all those who fear the LORD, The great as well as small.
[17] The dead are si - lent in the grave, They can-not praise the LORD;

Put all your trust up - on the LORD, He is their help and shield.
[14] O may the LORD still pros-per you, You and your chil-dren all.
[18] But we'll for - ev - er bless the LORD. Give prais-es to the LORD!

John K. Robb, 1949

SCOTT CMD

116A How Fervently I Love the LORD

Psalm 116:1-9

Jesus as Lord...Lord of all, abounding in riches
for all who call on Him. —Romans 10:9, 12

1. ¹How fer-vent-ly I love the LORD— My cries for help He hears!
2. ⁴Up-on the LORD's name then I called, In my ex-trem-i-ty:
3. ⁷O now, my soul, re-turn a-gain To your own qui-et rest,

²So, all my life I'll call on Him Who turned to me His ear.
"O LORD, I beg You, spare my life; And let my soul go free."
Be-cause the LORD a-bun-dant-ly Has caused you to be blessed.

³The ropes of death en-tan-gled me And wrapped them-selves a-round;
⁵The LORD our God is kind and just; Com-pas-sion-ate is He.
⁸You freed from death; You dried my tears, My stum-bling feet re-stored.

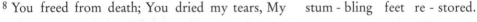

The ter-rors of the grave took hold— I grief and trou-ble found.
⁶The LORD pre-serves the meek in heart; From depths He res-cued me.
⁹And there-fore in the land of life I'll walk be-fore the LORD.

William Croft, 1708

ST. MATTHEW CMD

I Still Believed

When He had taken a cup and given thanks, He gave it to them, saying, "Drink from it, all of you." — Matthew 26:27

116B

Psalm 116:10-19

4. ¹⁰I still be-lieved, al-though I said, "How sore-ly I am tried!"
5. ¹³I'll lift sal-va-tion's cup, O LORD, And on the LORD's name call;
6. ¹⁷My gifts of thanks I'll of-fer You, And on the LORD's name call;

¹¹In my a-larm I cried a-loud, "All men are but a lie!"
¹⁴My vows I will pay to the LORD Be-fore His peo-ple all.
¹⁸The vows I prom-ised to the LORD, I'll keep and pay them all

¹²What can I ren-der to the LORD? What shall my of-f'ring be
¹⁵The LORD counts pre-cious in His sight The death of all His saints.
Be - fore the peo-ple of the LORD, ¹⁹With-in His tem-ple courts,

For all the gra-cious ben - e - fits That He has giv-en me?
¹⁶LORD, I'm Your slave, Your hand-maid's son; You freed me from my chains!
There, in Your midst, Je - ru - sa - lem. Give prais-es to the LORD!

Lowell Mason, 1792–1872

OSTEND CMD

116C

Psalm 116:1-8

I Love the LORD

In the days of His flesh, He offered up prayers...to the One
able to save Him from death. —Hebrews 5:7

1. ¹I love the LORD be - cause He hears my plead - ing.
2. ⁵Our God, the LORD, is mer - ci - ful and righ - teous;

²He's heed - ed me; through life I'll call on Him.
⁶Gra - cious, the LORD pre - serves the sim - ple ones.

³Bound by the ropes of death and She - ol's ter - rors;
When I was low, to me He gave sal - va - tion.

In deep dis - tress I grief and trou - ble found.
⁷Turn back a - gain, my soul, and be at rest;

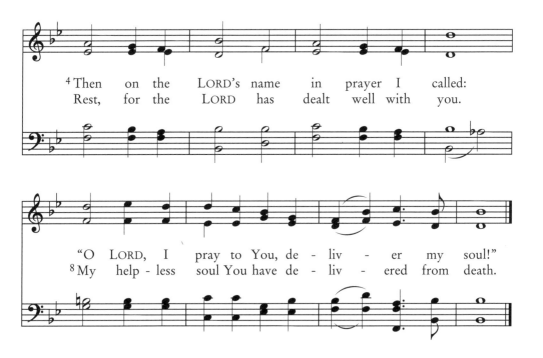

4 Then on the LORD's name in prayer I called:
Rest, for the LORD has dealt well with you.

"O LORD, I pray to You, de - liv - er my soul!"
8 My help - less soul You have de - liv - ered from death.

James Walch, 1889

116D

Psalm 116:8-19

My Crying Eyes

"Blessed are the dead who die in the Lord." "Yes," says the Spirit,
"that they may rest from their labors." —Revelation 14:13

3. ⁸ My cry - ing eyes, my stum - bling feet, You res - cued.
4. ¹³ Sal - va - tion's cup I'll lift, and call the LORD's name,
5. ¹⁷ I'll bring to You an of - f'ring of thanks - giv - ing;

⁹ In lands of life, I'll walk be - fore the LORD.
¹⁴ Vows to the LORD be - fore His peo - ple pay.
With sac - ri - fice I'll call up - on the LORD.

¹⁰ I have be - lieved and said, "I am af - flict - ed."
¹⁵ Ob - served by Him, and pre - cious in the LORD's sight,
¹⁸ I'll pay the LORD the vows that I have prom - ised;

¹¹ I said in my dis - may, "All men are false!"
Is ev - ery death a - mong His god - ly ones.
This I will do where all His peo - ple meet,

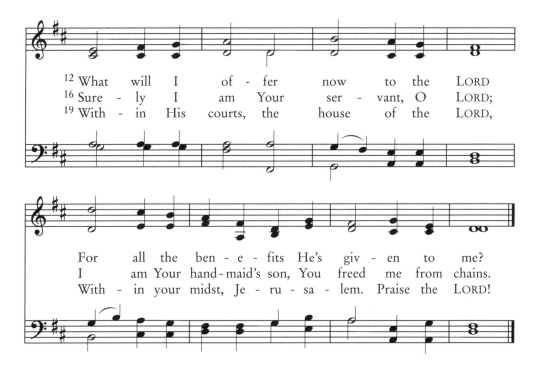

12 What will I of - fer now to the LORD
16 Sure - ly I am Your ser - vant, O LORD;
19 With - in His courts, the house of the LORD,

For all the ben - e - fits He's giv - en to me?
I am Your hand - maid's son, You freed me from chains.
With - in your midst, Je - ru - sa - lem. Praise the LORD!

Henry Smart, 1868   PILGRIMS 11.10.11.10.9.11

117A
Psalm 117

O All You Nations of the Earth

Jesus as Lord...abounding in riches for all who call upon Him.
—Romans 10:9, 12

1. ¹O all you na - tions of the earth, Give prais - es to the LORD. O all you peo - ples mag - ni - fy His name with one ac - cord. His name with one ac - cord.

2. ²Be - cause His love for us is strong— His lov - ing - kind - ness - es. The LORD is faith - ful ev - er - more; Praise to the LORD ex - press! Praise to the LORD ex - press!

George F. Handel, 1728

CHRISTMAS CM

Praise the LORD

117B
Psalm 117

The grace of our Lord was more than abundant, with the faith
and love which are in Christ Jesus. —1 Timothy 1:14

1 Praise the LORD! Praise the LORD! All you na-tions, ex-

tol Him; Ex-tol Him, all you peo-ples; 2 For

great is His love toward us, And the faith - ful - ness

of the LORD En - dures for-ev - er.

Timothy McCracken, 1997   MISSION 6.7.7.7.8.5

117C

Psalm 117

Praise the LORD

In every nation the man who fears Him and does what is right is welcome to Him. —Acts 10:35

1 Praise the LORD! Praise the LORD! O all you
Al - a - bad a J'ho - vah! Na - cio - nes

peo - ple, ev - ery na - tion, shout His prais - es;
to - das, pueb - los to - dos, a - la - bad - le;

2 For so great, yes, so mag - ni - fi - cent
Por - que ha en - gran - de - ci - do

Has been the lov - ing - kind - ness He has shown to us.
So - bre no - so - tros su mi - se - ri - cor - di - a.

118A

Psalm 118:1-9

O Thank the LORD, for He Is Good

But the Lord stood with me and strengthened me.
—2 Timothy 4:17

1. ¹O thank the LORD, for He is good, His
2. ³O let the house of Aar - on say, "His
3. ⁵In an - guish to the LORD I cried; The

gra - cious love en - dures. ²O let all Is - ra-
gra - cious love en - dures." ⁴Let those who fear the
LORD then set me free. ⁶The LORD's with me, I

el now say, "His gra - cious love en - dures."
LORD now say, "His gra - cious love en - dures."
will not fear. What harm can man do me?

4. ⁷The LORD supports me at my side,
   He gives His help to me;
   And so in triumph I will look
   On all those hating me.

5. ⁸O better far to trust the LORD
   Than on man's help rely.
   ⁹Yes, better far to trust the LORD
   Than men whose rank is high.

Michael Tabon, 1999

WHITE LAKE CM

Because He's Good

118B
Psalm 118:1-9

I thank Christ Jesus our Lord, who has strengthened me.
—1 Timothy 1:12

1. [1]Be - cause He's good, O thank the LORD; His
2. [3]Let Aar - on's house this tri - bute pay: "His
3. [5]When to the LORD, dis - tressed, I cried, The

love en - dures for - ev - er! [2]Let Is - r'el say with
love en - dures for - ev - er!" [4]Let those who fear the
LORD re - plied and freed me. [6]Be - cause the LORD is

one ac - cord, "His love en - dures for - ev - er!"
LORD now say: "His love en - dures for - ev - er!"
on my side, From fear I have been set free.

4. Why should I fear what man can do?
    [7]The LORD stands by to help me.
    I'll look in triumph on all those
    Who hated and opposed me.

5. [8]In men place not your confidence;
    [9]To trust the LORD is better.
    Instead of hoping in a prince,
    Find in the LORD your shelter.

John B. Dykes, 1868   DOMINUS REGIT ME 87.87 (Iambic)

118C All Earth's Nations Joined Together

Psalm 118:10-14

*I saw the beast and the kings of the earth and their armies
assembled to make war against Him. —Revelation 19:19*

6. ¹⁰All earth's na-tions joined to-geth-er
7. ¹¹They sur-round-ed and en-closed me,
8. ¹²Though like bees they swarmed a-round me,
9. ¹³Strik-ing me, you caused my down-fall;

They en-cir-cled me a-round.
Yes, from ev-ery side they came;
Soon they died like thorns a-flame;
But the LORD gave help to me.

But I cut off in the LORD's name
But I cut them off com-plete-ly
For I cut them off com-plete-ly
¹⁴So the LORD's my song and pow-er,

All those who did me sur-round.
In the LORD— by His great name.
In the LORD— by His great name.
He's be-come my vic-to-ry.

William Boyce, 1710–1779

SHARON 87.87

Loud Shouts of Joy

He disciplines us for our good, so that we may share His holiness.
—Hebrews 12:10

Psalm 118:15-18

10. ¹⁵ Loud shouts of joy and vic-t'ry fill The just's en-camp-ment site.
11. ¹⁷ I will not pass a-way in death; No, I will sure-ly live;

"The right hand of the LORD per-forms Great deeds of val-iant might!
And to the works the LORD has done My tes-ti-mo-ny give.

¹⁶ The LORD's right hand is lift-ed up, A-bove the high-est height.
¹⁸ The LORD se-vere-ly chas-tened me, And stern cor-rec-tion gave;

The right hand of the LORD per-forms Great deeds of val-iant might."
But He with-held the stroke of death, And spared me from the grave.

ohn K. Robb, 1949   HETHERTON CMD

118E

Psalm 118:19-29

Now Open Wide the Gates

…Christ Jesus Himself being the cornerstone.
—*Ephesians 2:20*

12. ¹⁹ Now o-pen wide the gates for me, The gates of righ-teous-ness, And I will en-ter in through them; With thanks the LORD I'll bless.

13. ²⁰ This is the gate that is the LORD's, The righ-teous en-ter in. ²¹ I'm thank-ful You have an-swered me; My Sav-ior You have been.

14. ²² That stone is now the cor-ner-stone That build-ers once de-spised. ²³ This is the do-ing of the LORD, And won-drous in our eyes.

15. ²⁴ This is the day the LORD has made; Let us be glad and sing. ²⁵ Ho-san-na, LORD! O give suc-cess! O LORD, sal-va-tion bring!

16. ²⁶ O blessed is the one who comes,
Comes in the LORD's great name.
A blessing from the LORD's own house
Upon you we proclaim.

17. ²⁷ The LORD is God and He to us
Has made the light arise.
With cords bind to the altar's horns
The festal sacrifice.

18. ²⁸ You are my God, I'll give You thanks;
My God, I'll give you praise.
²⁹ O thank the LORD, for He is good;
His love lasts endless days.

Thomas Jackson, *Twelve Psalm Tunes*, 1780

JACKSON CM

How Blessed Are Those Above Reproach

Which one of you convicts Me of sin?
—John 8:46

119A

Psalm 119:1-8

1. ¹How blessed are those a - bove re - proach, The LORD's law guid - ing all they do. ²Blessed those who seek Him ear - nest - ly And keep His tes - ti - mo - nies true. ³They prac - tice no un - righ - teous - ness, But in His ways they on - ward press.

2. ⁴Your pre - cepts You have giv - en us With dil - i - gence to be o - beyed. ⁵May all my ways be firm - ly fixed To keep the stat - utes You have made. ⁶For I will not be put to shame When Your com - mands are all my aim.

3. ⁷Then I will give my thanks to You With all sin - cer - i - ty of heart, When I with grat - i - tude have learned The righ - teous judg - ments You im - part. ⁸I'll keep Your stat - utes faith - ful - ly; Do not for - sake me ut - ter - ly.

Ernest R. Kroeger, 1862–1934

CHRISTINE 88.88.88

119B

Psalm 119:9-16

How Can a Young Man Cleanse His Way?

Be diligent to present yourself approved to God.
—2 Timothy 2:15

4. [9] How can a young man cleanse his way?
5. [11] Your word I've treas-ured in my heart
6. [13] I have re-peat-ed with my lips
7. [15] I on Your pre-cepts med-i-tate,

Let him with care Your word o-bey.
So that from You I will not turn.
All of the laws Your mouth has told.
And I will pon-der all Your ways.

[10] With all my heart I seek for You;
[12] That I'll not sin, O bless-ed LORD,
[14] I have re-joiced in Your com-mands
[16] I will de-light in Your de-crees,

From Your com-mands let me not stray.
Your stat-utes teach, that I may learn.
As one de-lights in pur-est gold.
Your word re-mem-b'ring all my days.

Henry Baker, 1866

HESPERUS LM

That I May Live and Keep Your Word

119C

"These are My words which I spoke to you"....Then He opened their minds to understand the Scriptures. — Luke 24:44-45

Psalm 119:17-24

8. 17 That I may live and keep Your word,
9. 19 I am a strang - er here on earth;
10. 21 The proud, ac - cursed, You have re - buked,
11. 23 Princ - es a - gainst me have con - spired;

Deal with Your ser - vant gra - cious - ly.
Hide Your com - mand - ments not, I pray!
From Your com - mand - ments they have strayed.
Your ser - vant pon - ders Your de - crees.

18 O - pen my eyes to know Your law,
20 Your or - di - nanc - es I de - sire,
22 Re - move con - tempt and scorn from me;
24 Your tes - ti - mo - nies are my joy,

That all its won - ders I may see.
And ache with yearn - ing ev - ery day.
Your tes - ti - mon - ies I've o - beyed.
They are the ones who coun - sel me.

H. Percy Smith, 1874

MARYTON LM

119D

Psalm 119:25-32

My Soul Clings to the Dust

I commend you to God and to the word of His grace
which is able to build you up. —Acts 20:32

12. ²⁵ My soul clings to the dust— re - vive;
13. ²⁷ I'll pon - der all Your won - drous works;
14. ²⁹ A life of false - hood take from me;
15. ³¹ LORD, let me not be put to shame;

And as You prom - ised, let it be.
And Your com - mands O help me see.
Your law now give me in Your grace.
Your tes - ti - mo - nies I hold fast.

²⁶ When I re - count my ways, You hear;
²⁸ My soul is shed - ding tears of grief;
³⁰ I chose the life of faith - ful - ness;
³² I'll run the way of Your com - mands;

Your or - di - nanc - es teach to me.
As You have prom - ised, strength - en me.
Be - fore me I Your judg - ments place.
My mind You will en - large at last.

William Bradbury, 1853

OLIVE'S BROW LM

That I May Keep Your Statutes

When Christ came into the world, He said…"I have come to do Your will, O God." —Hebrews 10:5, 7

119E
Psalm 119:33-40

16. 33 That I may keep Your stat - utes, LORD,
17. 35 Lead me to walk in Your com - mands;
18. 37 A - vert my eyes from worth - less things;
19. 39 O take a - way my feared dis - grace;

In - struct me in their way.
They bring me joy in - deed.
Con - firm Your word to me.
Your laws are good in - deed.

34 Yes, make me wise to keep Your law;
36 In - cline my heart to seek Your law
38 That I Your ser - vant be re - vived
40 Re - vive me in Your righ - teous - ness;

Whole - heart - ed, I'll o - bey.
And turn a - way from greed.
To serve You rev - 'rent - ly.
I long for Your de - crees.

William Wheale, 1729

BEDFORD CM

119F O Let Your Lovingkindnesses Now Come

Psalm 119:41-48

In your hearts regard Christ the Lord as holy, always
being prepared to make a defense. —1 Peter 3:15

20. [41] O let Your lov - ing - kind - ness - es Now
21. [42] Then I shall an - swer him who taunts, For
22. [44] For - ev - er con - stant to the end, I'll

come to me, O LORD; May Your sal - va - tion
in Your word I trust. [43] Take not the true word
keep the law You speak. [45] And I will walk at

al - so come, Ac - cord - ing to Your word.
from my mouth; I trust Your judg - ments just.
lib - er - ty, For I Your pre - cepts seek.

23. [46] Your testimonies kings will hear,
I'll speak them unashamed.
[47] Yes, I delight in Your commands;
For they my love have claimed.

24. [48] I love Your statutes and decrees,
To them I lift my hands,
And with my mind consider them,
And ponder Your commands.

C.E. Leslie

CITY OF OUR GOD CM

Keep Your Promise to Your Servant

Yours they were, and You gave them to Me,
and they have kept Your word. —John 17:6

119G
Psalm 119:49-56

25. [49] Keep Your prom - ise to Your ser - vant;
26. [51] Though the ar - ro - gant de - ride me,
27. [53] I was an - gered by the wick - ed;
28. [55] In the night, Your name re - mem - b'ring,

I rest in the hope You give.
I have not turned from Your word.
They for - sake Your law di - vine.
LORD, I'll keep Your stat - utes' way.

[50] This my com - fort in af - flic - tion,
[52] Pon - der - ing Your an - cient pre - cepts,
[54] But I make my song Your stat - utes
[56] Sure - ly this to me was giv - en,

That Your prom - ise makes me live.
I find com - fort in them, LORD.
In this pil - grim tent of mine.
Since Your pre - cepts I o - bey.

Amos Pilsbury, *U.S. Sacred Harmony*, 1799; harm. Robert M. Copeland, 1972 CHARLESTOWN 87.87

119H

Psalm 119:57-64

My Portion Is the Lord

*About midnight Paul and Silas were praying and
singing hymns of praise to God. —Acts 16:25*

29. ⁵⁷My por - tion is the LORD Him - self.
30. ⁵⁹I viewed my ways and turned my feet
31. ⁶¹The wick - ed wrapped me round with cords,
32. ⁶³I'm friend of all who rev - 'rence You,

"I'll keep Your words," my vow will be.
Un - to Your tes - ti - mon - ies' way.
But I Your law did not for - get;
Of those Your stat - utes who o - bey.

⁵⁸I've sought Your face with all my heart;
⁶⁰I has - tened Your com - mands to keep;
⁶²Be - cause Your stat - utes righ - teous are,
⁶⁴O LORD, Your love fills all the earth!

Be gra - cious as You prom - ised me.
I kept Your law with - out de - lay.
I'll rise at night and thank You yet.
In - struct me in Your stat - utes' way.

Traditional Gaelic melody

TEANN A NALL LM

According to Your Word, O Lord

1191

Psalm 119:65-72

If what I said is wrong, bear witness about the wrong; but if what I said is right, why do you strike Me? —John 18:23

33. ⁶⁵Ac - cord - ing to Your word, O Lord,
34. ⁶⁷I strayed be - fore You hum - bled me;
35. ⁶⁹The proud have smeared me with their lies;
36. ⁷¹Af - flic - tion has been good for me,

You have Your ser - vant blessed.
Your word I now o - bey.
Your pre - cepts are my choice.
Your laws I've learned to hold

⁶⁶Teach me good judg - ment, knowl - edge give;
⁶⁸For You are good; Your deeds are good.
⁷⁰Their hearts, en - closed in fat, are dull;
⁷²As far more pre - cious than great stores

On Your com - mands I rest.
Teach me Your stat - utes' way.
I in Your law re - joice.
Of sil - ver and of gold.

George M. Allen, 1846

MAITLAND CM

119J

Your Hands Created and Established Me

Psalm 119:73-80

*They were astonished at His teaching, for He taught them
as one who had authority. — Mark 1:22*

37. ⁷³ Your hands cre - at - ed and es - tab - lished me.
38. ⁷⁵ O LORD, I know how right Your judg - ments are;
39. ⁷⁷ Let Your com - pas - sion come to give me life,
40. ⁷⁹ May all of those who fear You turn to me,

Give un - der - stand - ing; Your com - mands I'll learn.
In faith - ful - ness You have af - flict - ed me.
For in Your law my joy is ver - y great.
Those who Your tes - ti - mon - ies know and claim.

⁷⁴ May those who fear You see me and be glad
⁷⁶ As to Your ser - vant You once gave Your word,
⁷⁸ Shamed be the proud who wrong me with their lies;
⁸⁰ May my heart keep Your stat - utes blame - less - ly

When they have seen how to Your word I turn.
May Your un - fail - ing love my com - fort be.
But on Your pre - cepts I will med - i - tate.
So that I nev - er may be put to shame.

William H. Monk, 1861

EVENTIDE 10.10.10.10

My Soul Is Fainting

So they took Jesus, and He went out, bearing His own cross.
—John 19:17

119K

Psalm 119:81-88

41. ⁸¹ My soul is faint - ing to see Your sal - va - tion;
42. ⁸³ I'm like a wine - skin that smoke has now with - ered;
43. ⁸⁵ Proud men have dug hid - den pits to en - snare me;
44. ⁸⁷ Here on the earth they have al - most de - stroyed me.

Yet do I put all my hope in Your word.
Yet all Your stat - utes I do not for - get.
Such things are not what Your law jus - ti - fies.
Yet from Your pre - cepts I nev - er will swerve.

⁸² My eyes grow dim as I look for Your prom - ise;
⁸⁴ How ma - ny days now re - main for Your ser - vant?
⁸⁶ All Your com - mand-ments are faith - ful for - ev - er.
⁸⁸ My soul re - vive in Your great lov - ing - kind - ness;

When will You give me Your com - fort de - ferred?
When will my foes with Your judg - ment be met?
Help me, for men per - se - cute me with lies.
Your tes - ti - mo - nies I then will ob - serve.

Alexis F. Lvov, 1833

RUSSIAN HYMN 11.10.11.10 (Alt.)

119L

Psalm 119:89-96

Evermore, O Lord

The chief priests and the scribes were seeking how to
seize Him by stealth and kill Him. —Mark 14:1

45. ⁸⁹ Ev - er - more, O LORD, in heav - en
46. ⁹³ I will not for - get Your pre - cepts,

There Your word for - ev - er stands.
You by them my life re - new.

⁹⁰ You are faith - ful through all a - ges;
⁹⁴ I be - long to You. O save me!

Earth stands firm, set by Your hands.
I have sought Your pre - cepts true.

91 All things stand as You de-ter-mine;
95 Though the wick-ed plot to kill me;

Do-ing all that You de-cide.
On Your words I med-i-tate.

92 If Your law had not en-thralled me,
96 I've seen bounds to all per-fec-tion;

In dis-tress I would have died.
Your com-mand-ment's breadth is great.

Wolfgang Mozart, 1756–1791; arr. Joshua Leavitt, *The Christian Lyre*, 1831   ELLESDIE 87.87 D

119M

Psalm 119:97-104

O How I Love Your Law!

I seek not My own will but the will of Him who sent me.
—John 5:30

47. ⁹⁷ O how I love Your law! It is My stud-y all the day.
48. ¹⁰¹ I've kept my feet from e-vil ways, That I might keep Your word.

⁹⁸ It makes me wis-er than my foes; Its pre-cepts with me stay.
¹⁰² Since I've been taught by You, I from Your pre-cepts did not turn.

⁹⁹ More than my teach-ers or the old, I've come to un-der-stand;
¹⁰³ How sweet in taste Your prom-is-es, Than hon-ey far more sweet!

¹⁰⁰ For on Your words I med-i-tate, And fol-low Your com-mands.
¹⁰⁴ Your pre-cepts un-der-stand-ing give; I there-fore hate de-ceit.

John H. Tenney, 1840–1918

PERFECT WAY CMD

Your Word's a Lamp

...Having the eyes of your hearts enlightened.
—Ephesians 1:18

119N

Psalm 119:105-112

49. 105 Your word's a lamp to guide my feet,
50. 107 I've suf - fered much; re - new my life,
51. 109 My life in con - stant dan - ger is;
52. 111 Your tes - ti - mo - nies thrill my heart;

A light to shine up - on my way.
O LORD, ac - cord - ing to Your word.
But I do not Your law for - get.
This last - ing her - i - tage is mine.

106 I now con - firm this vow I swore:
108 Ac - cept the of - f'rings of my mouth,
110 I have not from Your pre - cepts strayed,
112 I turn my heart now to Your law,

Your righ - teous judg - ments I'll o - bey.
In - struct me in Your judg - ments, LORD.
De - spite the traps the wick - ed set.
To keep it till the end of time.

Thomas Tallis, c. 1505-1585

TALLIS' CANON LM

1190

People of Double Mind I Hate

Psalm 119:113-120

I will declare to them, "I never knew you; depart from Me,
you workers of lawlessness." — Matthew 7:23

53. ¹¹³ Peo - ple of dou - ble mind I hate;
54. ¹¹⁵ Let wick - ed ones de - part from me;
55. Keep me from shame; ful - fill my hope.

Your law my love has stirred. ¹¹⁴ You are my shield and
Then God's com - mands I'll heed. ¹¹⁶ Keep me, ac - cord - ing
¹¹⁷ In safe - ty hold me high; Then will Your stat - utes,

hid - ing place; My hope is in Your word.
to Your word, That I may live in - deed.
con - stant - ly, My think - ing oc - cu - py.

56. ¹¹⁸ Those straying from Your statutes' way —
   All their deceit is vain.
   These You reject ¹¹⁹ and purge from earth;
   Like dross they'll not remain.

57. So I Your testimonies love,
   Yes, how I love Your law!
   ¹²⁰ My flesh is trembling, fearing You;
   Your judgments fill with awe.

Cuthbert Howard, 1856–1927

LLOYD CM

People of Double Mind I Hate

*I will declare to them, "I never knew you; depart from Me,
you workers of lawlessness." — Matthew 7:23*

119P
Psalm 119:113-120

53. ¹¹³ Peo - ple of dou - ble mind I hate; Your
54. ¹¹⁵ Let wick - ed ones de - part from me; Then
55. Keep me from shame; ful - fill my hope. ¹¹⁷ In

law my love has stirred. ¹¹⁴ You are my shield and
God's com - mands I'll heed. ¹¹⁶ Keep me, ac - cord - ing
safe - ty hold me high; Then will Your stat - utes,

hid - ing place; My hope is in Your word.
to Your word, That I may live in - deed.
con - stant - ly, My think - ing oc - cu - py.

56. ¹¹⁸ Those straying from Your statutes' way —
All their deceit is vain.
These You reject ¹¹⁹ and purge from earth;
Like dross they'll not remain.

57. So I Your testimonies love,
Yes, how I love Your law!
¹²⁰ My flesh is trembling, fearing You;
Your judgments fill with awe.

William Arnold, 1768–1832

ALEXANDRIA CM

119Q
Psalm 119:121-128

I've Judged Rightly

*Do not judge according to appearance, but judge with
righteous judgment. —John 7:24*

58. 121 I've judged right - ly and with jus - tice; Leave me
59. 125 I'm Your ser - vant; give me in - sight That Your

not lest foes op - press. 122 Guar - an - tee good for Your
stat - utes I may know. 126 LORD, it is Your time for

ser - vant, Lest the proud cause me dis - tress.
ac - tion, For Your law they o - ver - throw.

123 Your just prom - ise, Your sal - va - tion, My eyes,
127 But I love all Your com - mand - ments More than

fail - ing, long to see. 124 With Your ser - vant deal in

gold, the fin - est gold. 128 So Your pre - cepts I deem

mer - cy, And Your stat - utes teach to me.

up - right, All that's false in ha - tred hold.

Traditional American melody; John Wyeth, *Repository of Sacred Music, II*, 1813

NETTLETON 87.87 D

119R

Your Testimonies I Have Kept

Psalm 119:129-136

Jesus Christ, who gave Himself for us to redeem us...His own possession who are zealous for good works. —Titus 2:13-14

60. 129 Your tes - ti - mo - nies I have kept,
61. 131 I o - pen wide my mouth and pant
62. 133 Make firm my foot - steps by Your word,
63. 135 Up - on Your ser - vant shine Your face;

For they are won - drous in my eyes.
For all com - mand - ments You pro - claim.
And let no sin rule o - ver me.
136 Teach me to know Your stat - utes' way.

130 The op - 'ning of Your word gives light
132 O turn to me! Deal gra - cious - ly,
134 Re - deem me from op - pres - sive pow'r,
The tears in streams flow from my eyes,

And makes the sim - ple - heart - ed wise.
As with all those who love Your name.
That all Your pre - cepts I may keep.
For they Your law do not o - bey.

Thomas Hastings, 1842

RETREAT LM

O, Lord, You Are the Righteous One

119S
Psalm 119:137-144

…The sacred writings, which are able to make you wise for salvation through faith in Christ Jesus. —2 Timothy 3:15

64. 137 O LORD, You are the right - teous
65. 139 My zeal con - sumes me ut - ter -
66. 141 Though I am low - ly and de -
67. 143 Though grief and trou - ble come to

One; Just judg - ments come from You.
ly; Your words my foes have shunned.
spised, Your laws I'll not for - get.
me, Your law is my de - light.

138 Your tes - ti - mo - nies You com -
140 Be - cause Your words are ver - y
142 E - ter - nal is Your righ - teous -
144 Your laws for - ev - er righ - teous

mand In righ - teous - ness and truth.
pure, Your ser - vant loves each one.
ness; In Your law truth is set.
are; Through wis - dom give me life.

Traditional English melody, 1591; harm. Martin Fallas Shaw, 1875–1958   COVENTRY CAROL CM

119T I Cry With My Whole Heart

Psalm 119:145-152

I do know Him and keep His word.
—John 8:55

68. 145 I cry with my whole heart; O LORD, an-swer me!
69. 147 Be-fore dawn I rise and I cry out for help,
70. 149 O LORD, in Your love hear my voice when I call;
71. 151 O LORD, You con-tin-ue to be near to me;

The things You com-mand I will do.
My hope by Your prom-is-es stirred.
Re-vive me as Your judg-ments say.
How truth-ful is all You com-mand!

146 I cry out to You; give sal-va-tion to me;
148 My eyes still are o-pen as night watch-es pass,
150 Those fol-low-ing e-vil are gain-ing on me;
152 From Your tes-ti-mo-nies I al-ways have known

And I to Your law will be true.
That I may re-flect on Your word.
They've strayed from Your law far a-way.
That You set them al-ways to stand.

John Wyeth, *Repository of Sacred Music, II,* 1813; harm. Austin C. Lovelace, b. 1919   DAVIS 11.8.11.8

My Grief Regard

All Scripture is breathed out by God and profitable.
—2 Timothy 3:16

119U
Psalm 119:153-160

72. 153 My grief re - gard, and res - cue me,
73. 155 Res - cue is far from wick - ed ones,
74. 157 Ma - ny are my tor - ment - ing foes;
75. 159 See how I love Your pre - cepts' way!

For I do not Your law for - get.
For they Your stat - utes do not seek.
Yet from Your law I will not turn.
LORD, in Your love, give life to me.

154 My cause de - fend; re - deem my soul;
156 Your mer - cies, LORD, how great they are!
158 I see and loathe the treach - er - ous,
160 The sum of all Your words is truth;

Your prom - ise keep; re - vive me yet.
As You have judged, new life give me.
For they Your word for - ev - er spurn.
Your judg - ments stand e - ter - nal - ly.

Gregorian Chant; arr. Lowell Mason, 1824

HAMBURG LM

119V
Though Princes Hunt Me Without Cause

Psalm 119:161-168

The large crowd enjoyed listening to Him.
—Mark 12:37

76. 161 Though princ - es hunt me with - out cause,
77. 163 I hate all lies with bit - ter hate;
78. 165 Great peace have those who love Your law;
79. 167 My soul Your tes - ti - mo - nies keeps;

Your words I tru - ly have re - vered.
But in Your law I take de - light.
And noth - ing caus - es them to fall.
168 I love them with such great de - light.

162 I am re - joic - ing at Your word
164 I praise You sev - en times a day
166 I hope for Your sal - va - tion, LORD,
I keep Your pre - cepts and Your laws;

As one who is by treas - ure cheered.
Be - cause Your judg - ments all are right.
And Your com - mands— I'll keep them all.
My ways are all be - fore Your sight.

Katholisches Gesangbüch, Vienna, c. 1774

HURSLEY LM

80. 169 LORD, let my cry be-fore You come; True to Your word, en-light-en me. *(tenor)* 170 Be-fore You let my plead-ing come; True to Your prom-ise, res-cue me.

(bass) 170 Be-fore You let my plead-ing come; True to Your prom-ise res-cue me.

(soprano) 170 Be-fore You let my plead-ing come; True to Your prom-ise, res-cue me.

(alto) 170 Be-fore You let my plead-ing come; True to Your prom-ise, res-cue me.

81. 171 Since You in-struct me in Your law, O let my lips Your praise ex-press. 172 My tongue will sing a-bout Your word, For Your com-mands are righ-teous-ness.

82. 173 Be ready with Your hand to help,
Because Your precepts are my choice.
174 I long for Your salvation, LORD,
And in Your law do I rejoice.

83. 175 That I may praise You, let me live;
And let Your judgments bring me aid.
176 Your servant won't forget Your laws;
Seek me, who, like a sheep, has strayed.

Daniel Read, 1786

RUSSIA LM

120A
Psalm 120

I Cried in Trouble to the Lord

If possible, so far as it depends on you, be at peace with all men.
—Romans 12:18

1. ¹I cried in trou-ble to the LORD, And He has an-swered me. ²From ly-ing lips and craft-y tongue, O LORD, my soul set free.

2. ³What shall be giv-en you, false tongue; What add-ed to your doom? ⁴Sharp ar-rows from a war-rior's bow, And red-hot coals of broom!

3. ⁵A-las for me that I've so-journed So long in Me-shech's land, That I have made my dwell-ing where The tents of Ke-dar stand!

4. ⁶Too long my soul has made its home With those who peace ab-hor. ⁷I stand for peace, but when I speak, They then pre-pare for war.

Kenneth G. Finlay, 1936

AYRSHIRE CM

I Cried in Trouble to the Lord

Pray for those who persecute you.
— Matthew 5:44

Descant

4. 6 Too long my soul has made its home With

1. 1 I cried in trou - ble to the LORD, And
2. 3 What shall be giv - en you, false tongue; What
3. 5 A - las for me that I've so - journed So
4. 6 Too long my soul has made its home With

those who peace ab - hor. I stand for peace, but

He has an - swered me. 2 From ly - ing lips and
add - ed to your doom? 4 Sharp ar - rows from a
long in Me - shech's land, That I have made my
those who peace ab - hor. 7 I stand for peace, but

when I speak, They then pre - pare for war.

craft - y tongue, O LORD, my soul set free.
war - rior's bow, And red - hot coals of broom!
dwell - ing where The tents of Ke - dar stand!
when I speak, They then pre - pare for war.

Hugh Wilson, 1766-1824; arr. Robert A. Smith, 1825-1861; desc. Alan Gray, 1855-1935

MARTYRDOM CM

121A

Psalm 121

I Lift My Eyes and See the Hills

Now to Him who is able to keep you from stumbling...
be glory, majesty, dominion and authority. —Jude 1:24-25

1. ¹ I lift my eyes and see the hills;
2. ³ He'll not al - low your foot to slip,
3. ⁵ The LORD will keep you, He's your shade;
4. ⁷ The LORD will keep you from all harm;

From where will come my aid?
Nor rest while you He keeps.
The LORD stands at your right.
He'll keep your life se - cure.

² My help comes on - ly from the LORD
⁴ The One pre - serv - ing Is - ra - el,
⁶ The sun will do no harm to you,
⁸ Your go - ing out and com - ing in

Who heav'n and earth has made.
He slum - bers not, nor sleeps.
Nor will the moon at night.
The LORD keeps ev - er - more.

Lowell Mason, 1841

HEATH CM

I Lift My Eyes and See the Hills

*To Him who is able to establish you according to my gospel
and the preaching of Jesus Christ.* —Romans 16:25

121B

Psalm 121

1. ¹I lift my eyes and see the hills; From where will come my aid? ²My help comes on-ly from the LORD Who heav'n and earth has made. Who heav'n and earth has made.

2. ³He'll not al-low your foot to slip, Nor rest while you He keeps. ⁴The One pre-serv-ing Is-ra-el, He slum-bers not, nor sleeps. He slum-bers not, nor sleeps.

3. ⁵The LORD will keep you, He's your shade;
The LORD stands at your right.
⁶The sun will do no harm to you,
Nor will the moon at night.

4. ⁷The LORD will keep you from all harm;
He'll keep your life secure.
⁸Your going out and coming in
The LORD keeps evermore.

William Bradbury, 1816–1868

ABBEYVILLE CM

121C

Psalm 121

Unto the Hills I Lift My Longing Eyes

*The Lord will rescue me from every evil deed, and will bring
me safely to His heavenly kingdom.* —2 Timothy 4:18

1. ¹ Un-to the hills I lift my long-ing eyes; Whence comes my
2. ⁴ He who keeps Is-r'el slum-bers not nor sleeps By night or
3. ⁷ You will be safe, pro-tect-ed by the LORD, By His con-

aid? ² The LORD's my help, the heav-ens and the earth By
day. ⁵ The LORD keeps you, a shade on your right hand The
trol. From ev-ery e-vil that may come your way He'll

Him were made. ³ Your foot from stum-bling He will al-ways
LORD will stay. ⁶ Through-out the day the sun will nev-er
keep your soul. ⁸ While you go dai-ly out and in your

keep; The One who guards your life will nev-er sleep.
smite, Nor will the moon af-flict you in the night.
door, The LORD will keep you now and ev-er-more.

Charles H. Purday, 1860

SANDON 10.4.10.4.10.10

I Lift My Eyes and See the Hills

121D

May your spirit and soul and body be preserved complete.
—1 Thessalonians 5:23

Psalm 121

1. ¹ I lift my eyes and see the hills;
2. ³ He'll not al - low your foot to slip,
3. ⁵ The LORD will keep you, He's your shade;
4. ⁷ The LORD will keep you from all harm;

From where will come my aid?
Nor rest while you He keeps.
The LORD stands at your right.
He'll keep your life se - cure.

² My help comes on - ly from the LORD
⁴ The One pre - serv - ing Is - ra - el,
⁶ The sun will do no harm to you,
⁸ Your go - ing out and com - ing in

Who heav'n and earth has made.
He slum - bers not, nor sleeps.
Nor will the moon at night.
The LORD keeps ev - er - more.

D. Bruce Martin, 1920

HOPE CM

122A
Psalm 122

I Was Filled with Joy and Gladness

Beloved, I pray that in all respects you may prosper and
be in good health, just as your soul prospers. —3 John 2

1. [1] I was filled with joy and glad - ness
2. [3] In Je - ru - s'lem, built se - cure - ly,
3. [6] For Je - ru - sa - lem's well - be - ing
4. [8] I will say, "May peace be with you!"

When I heard them say to me:
[4] There the tribes— the LORD's tribes— go.
In - ter - cede and pray for peace:
For my friends' and broth - ers' sake.

"Let us make our pil - grim jour - ney,
This is Is - r'el's ob - li - ga - tion,
"All the ones who tru - ly love you,
[9] For the LORD's house, our God's tem - ple,

Then the LORD's house we will see."
To the LORD's name thanks they show.
May they pros - per and in - crease.
This my pur - pose I will make:

2 We were stand - ing! We were stand - ing!
5 There, for jus - tice, there, for jus - tice,
7 Peace and safe - ty, peace and safe - ty
Your well - be - ing, your well - be - ing,

In your gates, Je - ru - sa - lem! *(Sa - lem)*
Stand the thrones of Da - vid's house, *(Da - vid's house)*
Be with - in your walls and towers, *(walls and towers)*
I will seek with all my heart, *(all my heart)*

In your gates, Je - ru - sa - lem!
Stand the thrones of Da - vid's house.
Be with - in your walls and towers."
I will seek with all my heart.

John Hughes, 1907   CWM RHONDDA 87.87.47

122B   Now to the LORD's House Let Us Go!

Psalm 122

*...Not forsaking our own assembling together, as is the habit of
some, but encouraging one another.* —Hebrews 10:25

1. ¹ "Now to the LORD's house let us go!" These
2. ⁶ Pray for Je - ru - s'lem's peace, and may They

words made me re - joice. ² Our feet are stand - ing
pros - per who love you. ⁷ Peace be with - in your

in your gates, ³ Je - ru - sa - lem the strong! ⁴ There
might - y walls! Your for - tress - es have rest! ⁸ Then

do the LORD's own tribes go up— This
for my broth - ers and my friends I'll

is   the   rule   in   Is - ra - el—   The   LORD's   great   name   to

say,   "May   peace   be   found   in   you; [9] And   for   the   LORD   our

glo - ri - fy [5] Where Da - vid's thrones of judg - ment stand.

God's   own   house,   Your   good   I   ev - er   will   pur - sue."

Armenian folk song   DZOVE 86.86.8888

123A
I Lift My Eyes to You

Psalm 123

*...Fixing our eyes on Jesus...who for the joy set before Him,
endured the cross, despising the shame.* —Hebrews 12:2

1. [1] I lift my eyes to You En-throned a-bove the skies. [2] As slaves look to their mas-ter's hand, To You I lift my eyes.

2. As to her la-dy's hand A slave girl turns her face, So we look to the LORD our God That He might show us grace.

3. [3] Show us Your grace, O LORD, Let us Your fa-vor know; For we are filled with their con-tempt, And all the scorn they show.

4. [4] Our souls have had their fill Of scoff-ing and con-tempt, From those who live a life of ease, And from the ar-ro-gant.

French-Genevan Psalter, 1551

ST. MICHAEL SM

I'm Lifting Up My Eyes to You

Grace and peace to you from God our Father and
the Lord Jesus Christ. — Romans 1:7

123B

Psalm 123

1. ¹I'm lift - ing up my eyes to You, In
2. So our eyes, wait - ing, now at - tend Up -
3. For we are bur - dened with con - tempt. ⁴Our

heav - en is Your throne. ²As ser - vants watch their
on the LORD our God, Un - til He shows His
soul is great - ly filled With all the scoff - ing

mas - ter's hand, Or as a maid's eyes
grace to us. ³Be gra - cious to us,
in - so - lence Of those who live at

wait Up - on her mis - tress' hand,
LORD, Be gra - cious un - to us;
ease, And with the proud's con - tempt.

LEAF 86.866

124

Psalm 124

Unless the LORD Had Been There

…The Lord Jesus Christ, who gave Himself for our sins
to deliver us from the present evil age. —Galatians 1:3-4

Descant

3. ⁶Blessed be the LORD who snatched us from their teeth!

1. ¹"Un - less the LORD had been there on our side!"
2. "And when a - gainst us they with an - ger burned,
3. ⁶Blessed be the LORD who snatched us from their teeth!

⁷For, as a bird would from its trap - per flee,

Let Is - ra - el now tes - ti - fy to this:
⁴Swept by fierce wa - ters, we would all have drowned;
⁷For, as a bird would from its trap - per flee,

Our snare is torn and from it we are free!

²"Un - less the LORD had been there on our side
Swift streams en - gulf - ing, tor - rents pull - ing down,
Our snare is torn and from it we are free!

8 Yes, in the LORD's name is our only aid,

When cru - el men a - gainst us rose to strive,
5 Flood - wa - ters rag - ing with their might - y waves
8 Yes, in the LORD's name is our only aid,

By whom the heav - ens and the earth were made.

3 They would in - deed have swal - lowed us a - live."
Would then have dragged us down as to the grave."
By whom the heav - ens and the earth were made.

Louis Bourgeois, 1551; desc. Thomas C. L. Pritchard, 1885–1960   OLD 124TH 10.10.10.10.10

125

All, Like Mount Zion, Unmoved Shall Endure

Psalm 125

The God of all grace...will Himself perfect, confirm,
strengthen and establish you. —1 Peter 5:10

1. ¹All, like Mount Zi - on, un - moved shall en - dure
2. ³No wick - ed rul - er for long will re - main
3. ⁴LORD, to the good and the up - right in heart,

Whose con - fi - dence in the LORD is se - cure.
O - ver the righ - teous ones' cho - sen do - main,
Show good - ness; ⁵but make the crook - ed de - part.

²Like hills en - cir - cling Je - ru - s'lem a - round,
Lest righ - teous men yield to e - vil too strong,
All who do e - vil the LORD will ex - pel;

Al - ways the LORD will His peo - ple sur - round.
Put - ting their hands to com - mit what is wrong.
O let Your peace rest up - on Is - ra - el.

Traditional Irish melody; adapt. from Erik Routley, 1917–1982 and David Evans, 1874–1948

SLANE 10.10.10.10

The Lord Brought Zion's Exiles Back

Report to them what great things the Lord has done for you, and how He had mercy on you. —Mark 5:19

126A
Psalm 126

1. ¹ The LORD brought Zi - on's ex - iles back—
2. "The LORD has done great things for them,"

The LORD brought Zi-on's ex-iles back—
"The LORD has done great things for them,"

We were like dream-ing men:
The na-tions were a-greed.

² Our tongues were filled with
³ The LORD has done great

² Our tongues were filled with
³ The LORD has done great

shouts of joy And laugh-ter once a - gain.
things for us, And we re - joice in - deed!

3. ⁴ As streams revive the desert, LORD,
   Our exiles now restore.
   ⁵ Then those who sow their seed in tears
   Shall reap with joy once more.

4. ⁶ Though sowing seeds is weary toil,
   And he who scatters weeps,
   He'll come again and shout for joy
   With sheaves of grain he reaps.

John Cole, 1810

GENEVA CM

126B

Psalm 126

When Zion's Captive Ones Returned

He who supplies seed to the sower...will supply and multiply your seed for sowing and increase the harvest. —2 Corinthians 9:10

1. ¹ When Zi-on's cap-tive ones Had, by the LORD, re-turned— How like a dream!
2. In Gen-tile lands they said, "Great things the LORD has done, Great things for them!"
3. ⁵ Those who now sow in tears Will reap at har-vest time, And shout for joy.

² Our mouth was filled with joy, With laugh-ter and de-light; Our tongue then o-ver-flowed With shouts of joy.
³ How the LORD made us glad! Great things He's done for us! ⁴ Bring back our ex-iles, LORD, Like des-ert streams.
⁶ That one who sows with tears Bear-ing his bag of seed, Will come with shouts of joy, Bring-ing his sheaves.

Felice de Giardini, 1769

ITALIAN HYMN 664.666

Unless the Lord Build Up the House

127A
Psalm 127

Believe in the Lord Jesus, and you will be saved,
you and your household. —Acts 16:31

1. ¹Un - less the LORD build up the house,
2. ²How vain to work long days, late hours—
3. ³One's sons are gifts, the LORD's re - ward;
4. ⁵How hap - py is the one who has

Its build - ers build in vain;
To eat with toil and cares;
By Him the womb bears fruit.
His quiv - er filled with these!

Un - less the LORD the cit - y guards,
For e - ven so, His loved ones sleep;
⁴The chil - dren of one's youth are like
They'll bear no shame when, at the gates,

Its watch - men watch in vain.
This gift with them He shares.
The ar - rows war - riors shoot.
They speak with en - e - mies.

John K. Robb, 1949

SYRACUSE CM

127B

Unless the Lord Is He Who Builds the House

Psalm 127

I will build My church, and the gates of Hades
will not overpower it. — Matthew 16:18

1. [1] Un - less the LORD is He who builds the house,
2. [2] Your ear - ly ris - ing sure - ly is in vain,
3. [3] See how the LORD gives chil - dren as a gift,
4. [4] Who - ev - er has his quiv - er full of them,

Those build - ing it do all their work in vain.
And your de - lay in ly - ing down a - gain,
And fruit - ful wombs are sure - ly His re - ward.
Let him be count - ed as a hap - py man.

Un - less the LORD will keep the cit - y safe,
Your eat - ing bread that comes through pain - ful toil—
Like ar - rows read - y in a war - rior's hand,
They will not be a - shamed be - fore their foes,

Those keep - ing watch have stayed a - wake in vain.
For af - ter all, He gives His loved ones sleep.
So are the chil - dren one con - ceives in youth.
When speak - ing with them in the cit - y gate.

Brian E. Coombs, 2004

CHAMBERSBURG 10.10.10.10

How Blessed Are All Who Fear the LORD

The promise is for you and your children.
— Acts 2:39

African-American melody; adapt. Henry T. Burleigh, 1939; desc. Warren Sturlaugson, 2006

McKEE CM

128B Blessed Are All Who Fear the Lord's Name

Psalm 128

Who plants a vineyard without eating any of its fruit?
—1 Corinthians 9:7

1. ¹ Blessed are all who fear the Lord's name,
2. ⁴ So the man who fears the Lord shall

And who walk with - in His ways.
In this way great bless - ing know.

² When you eat of your hands' la - bor,
⁵ May the Lord from out of Zi - on

You'll be blessed through - out your days.
Bless - ings rich on you be - stow.

3 In your house your wife will pros - per
May you see Je - ru - s'lem pros - per

Like a vine whose fruits a - bound;
All your days, un - til they cease.

And like ol - ive plants, your chil - dren
6 May you see your chil - dren's chil - dren.

At your ta - ble gath - er 'round.
On all Is - ra - el be peace!

William Moore, 1825   HOLY MANNA 87.87 D

129

Time and Again They Greatly Did Oppress Me

*Alexander the coppersmith did me much harm; the Lord
will repay him according to his deeds. —2 Timothy 4:14*

1. [1] "Time and a-gain they great-ly did op-press me
2. [3] "They plowed my back like farm-ers plow-ing fur-rows;
3. [5] Let them be shamed and turned back in con-fu-sion,
4. [7] With these the reap-er can-not get his hand full,

From my youth up," let Is-ra-el de-clare,
So they have made their goug-es deep and long."
All those who bear toward Zi-on bit-ter hate.
Nor can the bind-er fill his arms with sheaves.

[2] "Time and a-gain they great-ly did op-press me
[4] But yet the LORD is right-teous in His deal-ings;
[6] Let them be-come like grass up-on the house-tops
[8] None pass-ing says, "The LORD give you His bless-ing,"

From my youth up, yet they did not pre-vail."
The ropes of law-less men He cut a-part.
That shriv-els up be-fore it is full grown.
None calls out, "In the LORD's name we bless you."

Louis Bourgeois, 1551; arr. Lois Schafer, 1972

OLD 110TH 11.10.11.10

Lord, From the Depths to You I Cried

...Christ Jesus, who gave Himself for us to redeem us from every lawless deed. —Titus 2:14

130A

Psalm 130

1. ¹ LORD, from the depths to You I cried. ² My
2. ³ LORD, who could stand if You, my Lord, Marked
3. ⁵ I wait, my soul a - waits the LORD; My
4. ⁷ O Is - ra - el hope in the LORD; The

Lord, give ear to me; O hear my voice and
each in - iq - ui - ty? ⁴ But You are one who
hope is in His word. ⁶ Yes, more than watch - men
LORD saves gra - cious - ly, ⁸ And Is - ra - el He

lis - ten to My sup - pli - ca - ting
par - dons sin, That You may rev - 'renced
wait for dawn, My soul a - waits my
shall re - deem From all in - iq - ui -

plea, My sup - pli - ca - ting plea.
be, That You may rev - 'renced be.
Lord, My soul a - waits my Lord.
ty, From all in - iq - ui - ty.

S.A. Sterrett Metheny, 1911

EVADNA CM

130B

Psalm 130

LORD, From the Depths I Cried to You

The Son of Man did not come to be served, but to serve,
and to give His life a ransom for many. —Matthew 20:28

1. 1 LORD, from the depths I cried to You.
2. 3 Lord, who could stand if You, O LORD,
3. 5 I wait, my soul a - waits the LORD,
4. 7 O Is - ra - el, hope in the LORD;

2 O let my voice be heard, my Lord;
Marked each in - frac - tion of Your law?
And from His word my hope is drawn.
Re - deem - ing love a - bounds with Him.

O make Your ears at - ten - tive now,
4 But par - don can be found with You
6 My soul a - waits my Lord far more
8 The LORD will ran - som Is - ra - el

And lis - ten to my plead - ing word.
So that You're feared with rev - 'rent awe.
Than watch - men wait and wait for dawn.
To set him free from all his sin.

Emrys Jones, 1965; arr. Brian E. Coombs, 2005

MORTE CRISTE LM

My Heart Is Not Exalted, LORD

Whoever wishes to be great among you shall be your servant.
— Matthew 20:26

131A

Psalm 131

1. ¹My heart is not ex - alt - ed, LORD, Nor haugh - ty is my eye. I do not deal in mat - ters great, Or things for me too high.

2. ²I have com - posed and calmed my soul, I'm like a lit - tle child; Now weaned, he on his moth - er rests, With soul sub - dued and mild.

3. Yes, like a child who has been weaned, My soul is calmed in me. ³Hope in the LORD, O Is - ra - el, Now and e - ter - nal - ly.

S.A. Sterrett Metheny, 1910

HUMILITY CM

131B

Psalm 131

My Heart Is Not Exalted, Lord

I am among you as the One who serves.
—Luke 22:27

1. ¹ My heart is not ex - alt - ed, LORD, Nor haugh - ty is my eye; I'm not in - volved with mat - ters great, Or things that are for me too high. ² Yes, I've com - posed my soul And now it qui - et lies.

2. My soul be - comes now like a child Weaned from his moth - er's breast; Yes, like a child who has been weaned, And on his moth - er finds his rest. ³ O Is - r'el, in the LORD For - ev - er put your trust.

C. Hubert H. Parry, 1848–1918; arr. Brian E. Coombs, 2001

REPTON 86.88.66

For the Sake of David

*Christ did not enter a holy place made with hands...but into heaven
itself, now to appear in the presence of God for us.* —Hebrews 9:24

132A

Psalm 132:1-9

1. [1] For the sake of Da-vid, Turn Your thoughts, O LORD,
2. [3] "My house I'll not en-ter, There I'll not re-pose;
3. [6] It was first in Eph-rath We heard news re-sound:
4. [8] LORD, now rise and en-ter With Your ark of might

To the things he suf-fered, Hard-ships he en-dured.
[4] I'll not let my eyes sleep, Nor my eye-lids close,
In the field of Ja-ar, There it had been found.
To that place of rest-ing, Pleas-ing in Your sight.

[2] Then he made a prom-ise, Vow-ing to the LORD—
[5] Till I find a dwell-ing Where the LORD would live—
[7] At His place of dwell-ing, Let us en-ter in;
[9] Let Your priest-hood serve You, Clothed in righ-teous-ness;

Might-y One of Ja-cob— Un-to Him he swore:
Might-y One of Ja-cob— Him a house I'll give."
Gath-ered at His foot-stool, Let us wor-ship Him.
Let Your saints with sing-ing Joy-ful-ness ex-press.

John B. Dykes, 1868

ST. ANDREW OF CRETE 65.65 D

132B

Psalm 132:10-12

For Your Servant David

We have such a high priest, who has taken His seat at the right
hand of the throne of the Majesty in the heavens. —Hebrews 8:1

5. [10] For Your ser - vant Da - vid,
6. [11] For the LORD to Da - vid
7. "I will have your off - spring
8. If they hold My teach - ings,

For his sake, I pray: From Your own a -
Sol - emn vows once spoke; Mak - ing him a
Sit up - on your throne [12] If they keep My
If they will o - bey, Then their sons for -

noint - ed, Do not turn a - way.
prom - ise He will not re - voke:
cov - 'nant, Mak - ing it their own.
ev - er On your throne will stay."

Kenneth G. Finlay, 1882; alt. harm. Andrew K. Schep, 2005   GLENFINLAS 65.65

For the Lord Has Chosen Zion

*Christ Jesus the cornerstone…in whom you also are being
built together into a dwelling of God. —Ephesians 2:20, 22*

132C

Psalm 132:13-18

9. ¹³ For the Lord has cho - sen Zi - on;
10. ¹⁵ I'll bless her pro - vi - sion rich - ly;
11. ¹⁷ I'll make Da - vid's pow - er flour - ish,

There He has de - sired to be: ¹⁴ "This My rest - ing
I'll her poor with bread sus - tain, ¹⁶ Clothe her priests with
My a - noint - ed's lamp pre - pare; ¹⁸ I with shame his

place for - ev - er; Here I'll stay, it pleas - es Me.
My sal - va - tion, Then her saints for joy will sing.
foes will cov - er; He a shin - ing crown will wear."

John Stainer, 1887

WYCLIF 87.87

133A

Psalm 133

Behold How Very Good It Is

*The glory which You have given Me I have given to them,
that they may be one, just as We are one. —John 17:22*

1. ¹Be - hold how ver - y good it is, A pleas - ant thing to see; When broth - ers join to live as one In peace and u - ni - ty!

2. ²Yes, it is like the pre - cious oil Poured out up - on the head, Which, run - ning down from Aar - on's beard, Up - on his gar - ments spread.

3. ³It is as though Mount Her - mon's dew On Zi - on's hills de - scends; For there the LORD be - stowed the gift Of life that nev - er ends.

Carl G. Glaser, 1839

AZMON CM

Behold How Very Good It Is

I in them and You in Me, that they may be perfected in unity.
—John 17:23

1. ¹Be - hold how ver - y good it is, A pleas - ant thing to see; When broth - ers join to live as one In peace and u - ni - ty!

2. ²Yes, it is like the pre - cious oil Poured out up - on the head, Which, run - ning down from Aar - on's beard, Up - on his gar - ments spread.

3. ³It is as though Mount Her - mon's dew On Zi - on's hills de - scends; For there the LORD be - stowed the gift Of life that nev - er ends.

Aaron Chapin, 1813

DUNLAPS CREEK CM

134A

Psalm 134

Come, Bless the LORD

You also, as living stones, are being built up as a spiritual house
for a holy priesthood to offer up spiritual sacrifices. —1 Peter 2:5

1 Come, bless the LORD now all you ser-vants of the LORD.

You serv-ing night-ly in the LORD's house, 2 come and bless the LORD,

While to His ho - ly place you lift your hands up high.

3 The LORD from Zi-on bless you, He who made the earth and sky.

Edward Woodall Naylor, 1867–1934

FROM STRENGTH TO STRENGTH 12.14.12.14

Bless the LORD, All You His Servants

They themselves report... how you turned to God from idols
to serve a living and true God. —1 Thessalonians 1:9

134B

Psalm 134

1. [1] Bless the LORD, all you His ser - vants,
2. [2] Lift your hands with - in His tem - ple;

As you serve with one ac - cord; Bless the LORD in
Bless the LORD, and raise them high. [3] May the LORD bless

your night watch - es In the dwell - ing of the LORD.
you from Zi - on, He who made both earth and sky.

Christian F. Witt, *Psalmodia Sacra*, 1715   STUTTGART 87.87

135A

Psalm 135:1-12

Hallelujah! Praise the LORD's Name

We have obtained an inheritance, having been predestined according to His purpose. —Ephesians 1:11

1. ¹ Hal - le - lu - jah! Praise the LORD's name!
2. ⁵ For I know how great the LORD is;
3. ⁸ He killed all of E - gypt's first - born;

Praise Him, ser - vants of the LORD,
Our Lord is a - bove all gods.
⁹ E - gypt, He sent signs to you,

² You that in the LORD's house serve Him,
⁶ Yes, the LORD does what He pleas - es
Signs to Phar - aoh and his ser - vants.

In God's court - yard stand - ing guard.
In the skies, earth, seas, and floods.
¹⁰ He struck na - tions, kings He slew;

3 Praise the LORD! How good the LORD is!
7 He it is who lifts the va - pors
11 Might - y Si - hon, Og of Ba - shan—

Sing His name— how sweet its tone!
From the ends of earth and sea,
All of Ca - naan's king - doms fell!

4 For the LORD has cho - sen Ja - cob,
Who with light - ning brings the rain down,
12 He their land gave to His peo - ple,

Is - ra - el to be His own.
From His store the wind sets free.
Willed it all to Is - ra - el.

Franz. J. Haydn, 1797

AUSTRIA 87.87 D

135B

Psalm 135:13-21

Your Name, LORD, Endures Forever

Therefore, my beloved, flee from idolatry.
—*1 Corinthians 10:14*

4. ¹³ Your name, LORD, en-dures for-ev-er; LORD, Your
5. ¹⁵ Heath-en i-dols, gold and sil-ver, Work of
6. ¹⁷ Hav-ing ears, they nev-er lis-ten; In their

fame each age has known; ¹⁴ For the LORD ac-
hu-man art-ist-ry; ¹⁶ Hav-ing mouths, they
mouth no breath has been. ¹⁸ Those who make them

quits His peo-ple, Has com-pas-sion on His own.
speak of noth-ing; Hav-ing eyes, they do not see;
will be like them— Ev-ery-one who trusts in them.

7. ¹⁹ Bless the LORD, O house of Isr'el!
House of Aaron, bless the LORD!
²⁰ Bless the LORD, O house of Levi!
All who fear Him, bless the LORD!

8. ²¹ Blessings to the LORD be given!
Blessed from Zion be the LORD,
In Jerusalem His dwelling.
Hallelujah! Praise the LORD!

Henry J. Gauntlett, 1805-1876

TRIUMPH 87.87

Your Name, LORD, Endures Forever

135C

Therefore, my beloved, flee from idolatry.
—1 Corinthians 10:14

Psalm 135:13-21

4. [13] Your name, LORD, en - dures for - ev - er; LORD, Your fame each age has known; [14] For the LORD ac - quits His peo - ple, Has com - pas - sion on His own.

5. [15] Heath - en i - dols, gold and sil - ver, Work of hu - man art - ist - ry; [16] Hav - ing mouths, they speak of noth - ing; Hav - ing eyes, they do not see;

6. [17] Hav - ing ears, they nev - er lis - ten; In their mouth no breath has been. [18] Those who make them will be like them— Ev - ery - one who trusts in them.

7. [19] Bless the LORD, O house of Isr'el!
House of Aaron, bless the LORD!
[20] Bless the LORD, O house of Levi!
All who fear Him, bless the LORD!

8. [21] Blessings to the LORD be given!
Blessed from Zion be the LORD,
In Jerusalem His dwelling.
Hallelujah! Praise the LORD!

Isaac B. Woodbury

DORRNANCE 87.87

136A

Psalm 136

Thank the LORD For Good Is He

*Moses and Elijah...speaking of His departure which He was
about to accomplish at Jerusalem. —Luke 9:30-31*

1. [1] Thank the LORD for good is He,
2. [5] He with skill has made the skies,
3. [10] E - gypt's first - born He did smite
4. [15] He drowned Phar - aoh and his men

For His stead - fast love en - dures.

[2] To the God of gods, thanks be,
[6] From the seas made land a - rise, For His stead-fast
[11-12] Brought out Is - r'el by His might,
[16] Led His own through des - erts then,

love en - dures.
[3] Prais - es give the King of kings,
[7] He has made great shin - ing lights,
[13] He the Red Sea split in two,
[17] Kings of splen - dor then He slew,

For His stead-fast love en-dures.
4 He a - lone does
8-9 Sun rules day; moon,
14 He made Is - r'el
18 Might - y kings He

won - drous things,
stars rule night,
pass on through,
o - ver - threw:
For His stead - fast love en - dures.

5. 19 Sihon, king of Amorites,
    For His steadfast love endures,
  20 Og, the king of Bashanites;
    For His steadfast love endures.
  21 He willed Israel their land,
    For His steadfast love endures.
  22 As His servant, heirs they stand,
    For His steadfast love endures.

6. 23 He remembered us when low,
    For His steadfast love endures.
  24 Gave deliv'rance from our foe,
    For His steadfast love endures.
  25 He gives food to all that live,
    For His steadfast love endures.
  26 Thanks to God of heaven give,
    For His steadfast love endures.

136B

Psalm 136:1-9

O Thank the Lord For He Is Good

One Lord, Jesus Christ, by whom are all things.
—1 Corinthians 8:6

1. ¹O thank the LORD for He is good,
2. ⁵With skill - ful - ness He made the skies,

His love en - dures for - ev - er!
His love en - dures for - ev - er!

²Thanks of - fer to the God of gods,
⁶From wa - ter He made land a - rise,

His love en - dures for - ev - er!
His love en - dures for - ev - er!

3 Give thanks un - to the Lord of lords,
7 Great lights He made— 8 the sun rules day,

His love en - dures for - ev - er!
His love en - dures for - ev - er!

4 Great won - ders He a - lone per - forms,
9 The moon and stars make night o - bey,

His love en - dures for - ev - er!
His love en - dures for - ev - er!

Arthur S. Sullivan, 1875

CONSTANCE 87.87 D (Iambic)

136C

All Egypt's Eldest Sons He Struck

Psalm 136:10-26

*The Lamb will overcome them, because He is Lord of lords
and King of kings. —Revelation 17:14*

3. ¹⁰ All E - gypt's el - dest sons He struck,
4. ¹⁴ He brought all Is - r'el through the Sea,
5. ¹⁹ First, Si - hon of the Am - o - rites,
6. ²³ He thought of us when we were low,

His love en - dures for - ev - er!

¹¹ And from their midst He Is - r'el took,
¹⁵ Struck Phar - aoh's ar - my vio - lent - ly,
¹² Then Og who ruled the Bash - a - nites,
²⁴ And res - cued us from ev - ery foe,

His love en - dures for - ev - er!

George F. Root, 1820–1895

SHINING SHORE 87.87 D (Iambic)

136D

Psalm 136:1-26

Thank the LORD for Good is He

We know and rely on the love God has for us.
—1 John 4:16

1. ¹ Thank the LORD for good is He,
2. ⁵ He with skill has made the skies,
3. ⁹ Moon and stars rule o - ver night,
4. ¹³ He the Red Sea split in two,

For His love lasts al - ways.

² To the God of gods, thanks be,
⁶ From the seas He made land rise,
¹⁰ E - gypt's first - born He did smite,
¹⁴ He made Is - r'el pass on through,

For His love lasts al - ways.

3 Prais - es give the King of kings,
7 He has made great shin - ing lights,
11 He brought Is - r'el from their land,
15 He drowned Phar - aoh and his men

For His love lasts

4 He a - lone does won - drous things,
8 Sun rules day by shin - ing bright,
12 With a strong out - stretched arm's hand,
16 Led His own through de - serts then,

al - ways.

For His love lasts al - ways.

5. 17 Kings of splendor then He slew,
    For His love lasts always.
18 Mighty kings He overthrew:
    For His love lasts always.
19 Sihon, king of Amorites,
    For His love lasts always.
20 Og, the king of Bashanites;
    For His love lasts always.

6. 21 He willed Israel their land,
    For His love lasts always.
22 As His servant, heirs they stand,
    For His love lasts always.
23 He remembered us when low,
    For His love lasts always.
24 Gave deliv'rance from our foe,
    For His love lasts always.

* 7. 25 He gives food to all that live,
    For His love lasts always.
26 Thanks to God of heaven give,
    For His love lasts always.

Robert Williams, 1781–1821; harm. by John Roberts, 1822–1877

LLANFAIR 77.77 ref.

137A

Psalm 137

In Babylon We Thought of Zion

A stone of stumbling, and a rock of offense. They stumble because
they disobey the word, as they were destined to do. —1 Peter 2:8

1. [1] In Bab-y-lon we thought of Zi-on; Sit-ting be-side the streams, we wept. [2] We hung our harps up-on the wil-lows. [3] By cru-el men as cap-tives kept; They called for mirth and sing-ing thus: "Sing one of Zi-on's songs for us."

2. [4] Sing the LORD's song? How can we sing it Here in this hos-tile for-eign land? [5] If I for-get you, O Je-ru-s'lem, May pow-er flee from my right hand, [6] And may my tongue be ren-dered mute If I do not re-mem-ber you.

3. Woe un-to me if I es-teem not Je-ru-sa-lem a-bove all else. [7] O LORD, re-call the sons of E-dom, Words spo-ken when Je-ru-s'lem fell: "To its foun-da-tion tear it down! Bring it, de-mol-ished, to the ground!"

4. [8] Daugh-ter of Bab-y-lon, ac-curs-ed! Blessed is that one who then will find How to re-pay you for your ac-tions. Hap-py the one who is as-signed [9] To take up in-fants of your own Who then a-gainst the rock are thrown.

Georg Neumark, 1657

NEUMARK 98.98.88

By Babylon's Rivers

137B
Psalm 137

*He who falls on this stone will be broken to pieces; but on
whomever it falls it will scatter him like dust. —Matthew 21:44*

1. ¹By Bab-y-lon's riv-ers we sat down with weep-ing
2. Our cap-tors made sport: "Sing to us songs of Zi-on!"
3. ⁵Je-ru-sa-lem, if I should ev-er for-get you,

When-ev-er we Zi-on re-called. (re-called.)
"Sing cheer-ful-ly!" was their de-mand. (de-mand.)
My right hand be use-less and lame! (and lame!)

²And there, though we hung up our harps on the wil-lows,
⁴But how can the LORD's song be sung while in ex-ile,
⁶O make my tongue help-less un-less I re-mem-ber

³Our cap-tors de-mand-ed a song.
By for-eign-ers in a strange land?
Je-ru-s'lem with high-est ac-claim.

4. ⁷O LORD, now remember the malice of Edom,
   Who said at Jerus'lem's defeat:
   "Destroy it and raze it to its bare foundation,
   And make its destruction complete!"

5. ⁸O daughter of Babylon—destined to ruin—
   He's blessed who repays as you've done.
   ⁹How blessed is the one who will seize on your infants
   And hurl them to smash on the stone.

ewish folk song; harm. Brian E. Coombs, 2005   RAKEFET 12.8.12.8

138A

Psalm 138

With All My Heart My Thanks I'll Bring

We are His workmanship, created in Christ Jesus for good works, which God prepared beforehand. —Ephesians 2:10

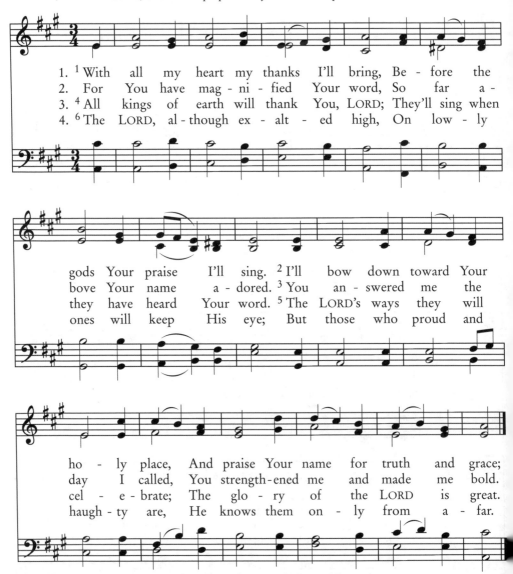

1. [1] With all my heart my thanks I'll bring, Be - fore the gods Your praise I'll sing. [2] I'll bow down toward Your ho - ly place, And praise Your name for truth and grace;

2. For You have mag - ni - fied Your word, So far a - bove Your name a - dored. [3] You an - swered me the day I called, You strength-ened me and made me bold.

3. [4] All kings of earth will thank You, LORD; They'll sing when they have heard Your word. [5] The LORD's ways they will cel - e - brate; The glo - ry of the LORD is great.

4. [6] The LORD, al - though ex - alt - ed high, On low - ly ones will keep His eye; But those who proud and haugh - ty are, He knows them on - ly from a - far.

5. [7] Through trouble though my pathway be,
My life You will preserve for me;
With outstretched hand You will oppose
The wrath and anger of my foes.

6. Your right hand, LORD, will set me free
[8] And work out what pertains to me.
Your love, O LORD, forever stands;
Leave not the works done by Your hands.

William Gardiner, *Sacred Melodies II*, 1815

WALTON LM

With All My Heart My Thanks I'll Bring

He who began a good work in you will perfect it
until the day of Christ Jesus. —Philippians 1:6

138B

Psalm 138

1. [1] With all my heart my thanks I'll bring, Be - fore the gods Your praise I'll sing. [2] I'll bow down toward Your ho - ly place, And praise Your name for truth and grace;

2. For You have mag - ni - fied Your word, So far a - bove Your name a - dored. [3] You an - swered me the day I called, You strength - ened me and made me bold.

3. [4] All kings of earth will thank You, LORD; They'll sing when they have heard Your word. [5] The LORD's ways they will cel - e - brate; The glo - ry of the LORD is great.

4. [6] The LORD, al - though ex - alt - ed high, On low - ly ones will keep His eye; But those who proud and haugh - ty are, He knows them on - ly from a - far.

5. [7] Through trouble though my pathway be,
   My life You will preserve for me;
   With outstretched hand You will oppose
   The wrath and anger of my foes.

6. Your right hand, LORD, will set me free
   [8] And work out what pertains to me.
   Your love, O LORD, forever stands;
   Leave not the works done by Your hands.

Isaac B. Woodbury, 1819–1858

WESLEY LM

139A

You Searched Me, Lord

Psalm 139:1-6

"Lord, You know all things; You know that I love You."
—John 21:17

1. ¹You searched me, Lord, and You per - ceive.
2. ³My ly - ing down, each way I go—
3. ⁵You hem me in, here where I stand,

²You know when I sit down or leave;
All that I do You search and know.
And on me You have laid Your hand.

And from a - far You rec - og - nize
⁴E - ven be - fore I speak a word—
⁶Such won - drous knowl - edge is too vast—

Thoughts and de - sires that in me rise.
all I would say— You know, O Lord.
It is too high, be - yond my grasp.

George Hews, 1835

HOLLEY LM

Where Can I from Your Spirit Flee?

139B

Psalm 139:7-12

No one will snatch them out of My hand...out of the Father's hand; I and the Father are one. —John 10:28-30

4. [7] Where can I from Your Spir - it flee,
5. [9] If I the wings of morn - ing take,
6. [11] "Could dark - ness blot me out of sight?

Or from Your pres - ence hid - den be?
And farth - est sea my dwell - ing make,
Could light a - round me turn to night?"

[8] You are in heav'n, if there I'd fled,
[10] Your hand will guide me e - ven there,
[12] No! Dark - ness is not dark to You;

And in the grave, were that my bed.
Your right hand hold me in its care.
The night shines bright - ly in Your view.

H. Percy Smith, 1874

MARYTON LM

139C

You Formed My Mind within the Womb

Psalm 139:13-18

If anyone loves God, he is known by Him.
—1 Corinthians 8:3

7. ¹³You formed my mind with - in the womb,
8. My soul knows well that this is true!
9. ¹⁶You on my un - born self did gaze,
10. ¹⁷How pre - cious, God, Your thoughts for me;

My in - ward parts as on a loom.
¹⁵My bones were not con - cealed from You—
While in Your book were set my days—
How vast in their to - tal - i - ty!

¹⁴I'm made with awe - in - spir - ing skill—
They se - cret - ly be - fore my birth,
Days all in - scribed and formed as done,
¹⁸Their sum ex - ceeds the grains of sand;

Your won - drous work! I praise You still!
Were craft - ed in the depths of earth.
Al - though as yet there was not one.
I wake— and still I'm in Your hand.

William Bradbury, 1849

WOODWORTH LM

O That You'd Slay the Wicked, God!

139D

This you have: You hate the works of the Nicolaitans,
which I also hate. —Revelation 2:6

Psalm 139:19-24

11. ¹⁹ O that You'd slay the wick - ed, God!
12. ²¹ Do I not hate Your hat - ers, LORD?
13. ²³ Search me, O God, my heart dis - cern;

De - part from me, you men of blood!
Those fight - ing You I have ab - horred.
Test me my trou - bling thoughts to learn.

²⁰ Your foes, O God, with words pro - fane,
²² I hate them all most fer - vent - ly;
²⁴ See if my heart toward harm might stray;

Re - bel and take Your name in vain.
I count them as my en - e - my.
O lead me in the last - ing way!

William Knapp, 1698–1768

WAREHAM LM

140A

Psalm 140

Save Me, O Lord

The God of peace will soon crush Satan under your feet.
—Romans 16:20

1. [1] Save me, O Lord, from those of e - vil mind;
2. [4] From pow - er of the wick - ed, keep me, Lord.
3. [6] But to the Lord, I say: You are my God;

Pre - serve me from the men of vi - o - lence.
Pre - serve me from the men of vi - o - lence—
Give heed to these my sup - pli - ca - tions, Lord.

[2] For in their hearts they work out e - vil plans,
From those who work out ways to trip my feet.
[7] O Lord, my Lord, and my sal - va - tion's might—

And stir up wars a - round them cease - less - ly.
[5] The proud have placed a hid - den trap for me;
My head You cov - ered when the bat - tle raged.

3 They make their tongue as sharp as vi - pers' fangs;
With cords they made a net and spread it wide;
8 Now, LORD, grant not the wick - ed their de - sires;

Their lips con - tain the poi - son of a snake.
They set their snares for me a - long my path.
Help not their plans, lest they grow great in pride.

4. 9 But let the heads of those surrounding me
　　Be covered with the troubles they have caused.
　10 Let coals fall on them! Cast them into fire;
　　Or into miry pits, no more to rise!
　11 Let none who slanders be established here;
　　Let utter ruin hunt the violent!

5. 12 But this I know: The LORD will yet maintain
　　The lawful claims of those who are oppressed,
　　And bring about true justice for the poor.
　13 The righteous will give thanks to You indeed;
　　Yes, even to Your name they give their praise,
　　And in Your presence shall the upright dwell.

Mark Maurer, 2006   DIAMOND 10.10.10.10.10.10

140B

Psalm 140

Save Me, O Lord

Fire came down from heaven and devoured them.
— Revelation 20:9

1. 1 Save me, O LORD, from those of e - vil mind;
2. 4 From pow - er of the wick - ed, keep me, LORD.
3. 6 But to the LORD, I say: You are my God;

O keep me from the men of vi - o - lence.
O keep me from the men of vi - o - lence—
Give heed to these my sup - pli - ca - tions, LORD.

2 For in their hearts they work out e - vil plans,
From those who work out ways to trip my feet.
7 O LORD, my Lord, and my sal - va - tion's might—

And stir up wars a - round them cease - less - ly.
5 The proud have placed a hid - den trap for me;
My head You cov - ered when the bat - tle raged.

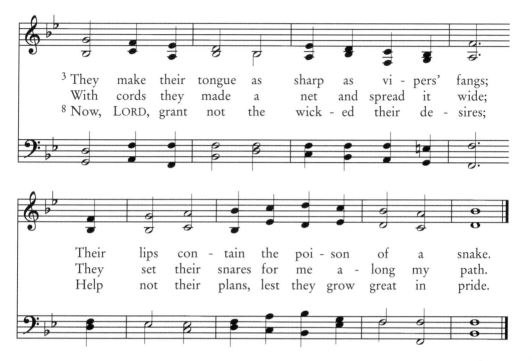

3 They make their tongue as sharp as vi - pers' fangs;
With cords they made a net and spread it wide;
8 Now, LORD, grant not the wick - ed their de - sires;

Their lips con - tain the poi - son of a snake.
They set their snares for me a - long my path.
Help not their plans, lest they grow great in pride.

4. 9 But let the heads of those surrounding me
Be covered with the troubles they have caused.
10 Coals fall on them! and cast them into fire;
Or into miry pits, no more to rise!
11 Let none who slanders be established here;
Let utter ruin hunt the violent!

5. 12 But this I know: The LORD will yet maintain
The lawful claims of those who are oppressed,
And bring about true justice for the poor.
13 The righteous will give thanks to You indeed;
Yes, even to Your name they give their praise,
And in Your presence shall the upright dwell.

John Wainright, 1750   YORKSHIRE 10.10.10.10.10.10

141A

Psalm 141:1-4

I Call You, Lord

In the days of His flesh He offered up both prayers and
supplications with loud crying and tears. —Hebrews 5:7

This tune may be sung as a round, entering at * interval

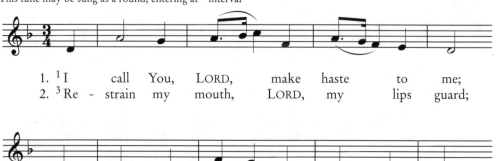

1. ¹I call You, LORD, make haste to me;
2. ³Re - strain my mouth, LORD, my lips guard;

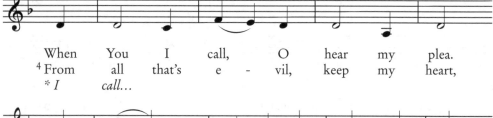

When You I call, O hear my plea.
⁴From all that's e - vil, keep my heart,
* I call...

²And let my prayer as in - cense rise;
From deeds with those who work de - ceit;

Raised hands as eve - ning's sac - ri - fice.
Let me not from their ban - quet eat.

William Billings, 1744–1800

WHEN JESUS WEPT LM

When Just Men Strike Me in Reproof

141B

Do not be deceived: God is not mocked, for whatever one sows,
that will he also reap. —Galatians 6:7

Psalm 141:5-10

3. ⁵When just men strike me in re-proof, Such kind-ness I'll ac - cept.
4. ⁶Down from the side of rock-y cliffs Their lead-ers will be cast;
5. ⁸And so to You, O Sov-ereign LORD, I look with long-ing eyes;

I'll take it as a sooth-ing oil, My head will not re - ject.
The pleas-ant words I speak to them They then will hear at last.
Do not leave me de-fense-less now; On You my soul re - lies.

And yet I will con-tin-ual-ly Cry out in prayer to You
⁷As when the farm-er plows the earth And o-pens up the ground,
⁹O keep me from the traps and snares That wick-ed men have set.

To pro-test all the e-vil deeds That wick-ed peo-ple do.
So at the grave's de-vour-ing mouth Our scat-tered bones are found.
¹⁰While I pass safe-ly, let them fall; Catch them in their own net.

Edward Hamilton, 1812–1870

LEVEQUE CMD

142

To You, O Lord, I Lift My Voice

Cast all your anxiety on Him, because He cares for you.
—1 Peter 5:7

Psalm 142

1. ¹ To You, O Lord, I lift my voice; I
2. ³ For when my soul is o - ver-whelmed, My
3. ⁴ None no - tic - es. Look to my right, No
4. ⁵ I cried to You, O Lord, and said, "You

sup - pli - ca - tion make. ² I pour my thoughts out
ev - ery way You see. Up - on the path on
one re - gards me there. There's no es - cape for
are my ref - uge true; And in the land of

to the Lord, To Him my trou - ble take.
which I walk Their traps were laid for me.
me to take, And none to show me care.
those who live, My por - tion is with You."

5. ⁶ Since I'm brought low in misery,
    O listen to my cry;
    Save me from persecuting foes
    Who stronger are than I.

6. ⁷ So, out of bondage, bring my soul
    That I Your name may praise;
    The righteous then will join with me,
    For You have shown me grace.

Frederick A.G. Ouseley

CONTEMPLATION CM

Lord, Listen to My Prayer

Let us draw near with confidence to the throne of grace, to receive mercy and find grace to help in time of need. —Hebrews 4:16

143A

Psalm 143:1-6

1. 1 LORD, lis-ten to my prayer As I for mer-cy cry.
2. 3 My en-e-my pur-sued And crushed me to the ground;
3. 5 Yet I re-call the past, The works Your hands have done;

In faith-ful-ness re-spond, In righ-teous-ness re-ply.
He has, as those long dead, In dark-ness kept me bound.
And I con-sid-er all Your won-ders, ev-ery one.

2 To judg-ment do not bring Your ser-vant to be tried;
4 There-fore my spir-it faints, I'm o-ver-whelmed with-in;
6 I will reach out for You, To You I'll stretch my hands;

No liv-ing man can stand In Your sight jus-ti-fied.
My heart in me dis-mayed And des-o-late has been.
My soul thirsts af-ter You Like dry and thirst-y lands.

Frederick C. Maker, 1881

INVITATION 66.66 D

143B O Lord, My Spirit Fails

Psalm 143:7-12

I will ask the Father, and He will give you another Helper, that
He may be with you forever, the Spirit of truth. —John 14:16-17

4. ⁷O LORD, my spir - it fails, Your an - swer swift - ly send;
5. I lift my soul to You; Teach me the way to go.
6. ¹¹To glo - ri - fy Your name, O LORD, pre - serve my life.

Hide not Your face from me Lest I to depths de - scend.
⁹In You I ref - uge take; LORD, save me from my foe.
Your righ - teous - ness I claim; De - liv - er me from strife.

⁸Be - cause I trust in You, O grant that I might hear
¹⁰Be - cause You are my God In - struct me to o - bey;
¹²And in Your stead - fast love, Cut off my en - e - my;

Your stead - fast love a - gain As morn - ing light draws near.
Let Your good Spir - it lead Me on the lev - el way.
Since I am serv - ing You, Slay those af - flict - ing me.

Robert Lowry, 1826–1899   I NEED THEE 66.66 D

Lord, Listen to My Prayer

143C

God is the one who justifies....Christ Jesus...
who also intercedes for us. —Romans 8:33-34

Psalm 143:1-6

1. [1] LORD, lis-ten to my prayer; My cry for mer-cy hear.
2. [3] The foe has hound-ed me; My life to earth he crushed.
3. [5] Yet I re-call the past; I muse on all Your deeds;

In righ-teous-ness and truth re-ply.
Shut in the dark as those long dead.
I think of all Your hands have done.

[2] And to Your ser-vant now In judg-ment do not come,
[4] My spir-it there-fore faints, With-in me o-ver-whelmed.
[6] I stretch my hands to You; My soul longs af-ter You

For in Your sight no man is just.
My heart in me is des-o-late.
As thirsts a dry and des-ert land.

Traditional Silesian folk song

ST. ELIZABETH 668.668

143D

LORD, Quickly Answer Me!

Walk by the Spirit, and you will not carry out the desire of the flesh.
—Galatians 5:16

Psalm 143:7-12

4. [7] LORD, quick-ly an-swer me! O how my spir-it fails!
5. [8] O let me hear Your love When morn-ing light ap-pears;
6. [9] O LORD, de-liv-er me From all my en-e-mies;
7. [11] For Your name's sake, O LORD, Save me, pre-serve my life,

O do not hide Your face from me,
For I have placed my trust in You.
[10] Teach me Your will, I hide in You,
And free my soul in righ-teous-ness.

That I may not be-come Like those now in the pit,
Teach me to know the way, Show me where I should walk,
You tru-ly are my God; May Your good Spir-it lead,
[12] True to Your cov-'nant love, Ful-ly con-sume my foes,

O let me not with them de-scend.
For I lift up my soul to You.
Di-rect-ing me on lev-el ground.
Be-cause I ser-vant am to You.

Traditional Silesian folk song

ST. ELIZABETH 668.668

Blessed Be the LORD, My Rock

144A

He must reign until He has put all His enemies under His feet.
—1 Corinthians 15:25

Psalm 144:1-8

1. ¹Blessed be the LORD, my Rock, Who trains my hands for war,
2. ³O LORD, what then is man That You take note of him?
3. ⁵O bow Your heav-ens, LORD, May You Your-self come down!
4. ⁷From heav-en stretch Your hand; Reach down to res-cue me,

My fin-gers for the fight. ²My Stead-fast Love, my Fort,
What is the son of man That You con-sid-er him?
Yes, touch the moun-tain-tops That they may burn with smoke.
And save me from the floods, The grip of for-eign pow'rs,

My Strong-hold, my De-liv-er-er, My Shield in whom I
⁴The life of man is like a breath; The to-tal num-ber
⁶Make light-ning flash and scat-ter them. O may Your ar-rows
⁸The ones whose mouth speaks what is false, The ones whose right hand

ref-uge take, He brings my peo-ple un-der me.
of his days Is like a shad-ow pass-ing by.
be sent forth To trou-ble and dis-qui-et them!
is the same, A right hand of de-ceit-ful-ness.

J.C. Friedrich Schneider, 1839

LISCHER 66.66.888

144B

Psalm 144:9-15

O God, in Praise to You

Peace be to you all who are in Christ.
—1 Peter 5:14

5. ⁹O God, in praise to You, A new song I will sing;
6. ¹¹O res-cue me and save; Grant me de-liv-er-ance

And with a ten-stringed harp Your praise I'll sing a-loud.
From out of a-lien hands, The grip of for-eign pow'rs,

¹⁰For He sal-va-tion gives to kings; His
The ones whose mouth speaks what is false, The

¹⁰For He sal-va-tion gives to kings; His ser-vant Da-vid
The ones whose mouth speaks what is false, The ones whose right hand

ser-vant Da-vid He will help And keep him from the cru-el sword.
ones whose right hand is the same, A right hand of de-ceit-ful-ness.

He will help And keep him from the cru-el sword.
is the same, A right hand of de-ceit-ful-ness.

7. ¹²O may our sons like plants
Grow sturdy in their youth;
And may our daughters be
Like palace cornerstones.
¹³May gathered crops fill up our barns,
And all our flocks be multiplied
By thousands and ten thousands more.

8. ¹⁴O may our herds increase
Without distress or loss;
And may our streets be free
Of outcry and of strife.
¹⁵Behold how blessed such people are!
O happy people who can say
They have the LORD to be their God!

Louis Edson, 1782

LENOX 66.66.888

I'll Give You Praise, My God, O King

"There is another king: Jesus."
—Acts 17:7

145A

Psalm 145:1-7

1. [1] I'll give You praise, my God, O King,
2. [3] Great is the LORD, de-serv-ing praise;
3. [5] I'll con-tem-plate Your won-drous works,
4. [7] Call-ing to mind Your good-ness great,

I will for-ev-er bless Your name;
His great-ness none can com-pre-hend.
Your splen-dor and Your glo-ry great.
Its fame they ea-ger-ly ex-press;

[2] I will ex-tol You ev-ery day,
[4] One gen-er-a-tion to the next
[6] Men will de-clare Your awe-some acts;
And they sing prais-es joy-ful-ly,

And ev-er-more Your praise pro-claim.
Will all Your might-y works com-mend.
Your pow'r and great-ness I'll re-late.
Tell-ing of all Your righ-teous-ness.

John Hatton, 1793

DUKE STREET LM

145B

Full of Compassion Is the LORD

Psalm 145:8-14

*Moved with compassion, Jesus stretched out His hand
and touched him. —Mark 1:41*

5. ⁸Full of com - pas - sion is the LORD,
6. ⁹His mer - cies cov - er all He's made;
7. ¹¹They of Your king - dom's glo - ries speak,
8. ¹³Your king - dom has no end at all,

And He with gra - cious - ness a - bounds;
Good is the LORD to all who live.
And of Your pow - er they will tell.
Through all the ag - es You will reign.

Mov - ing to an - ger He is slow,
¹⁰All of Your works will praise You, LORD;
¹²Peo - ple may then His great works know,
¹⁴All those brought low the LORD lifts up,

Great stead - fast love in Him is found.
Your saints to You will prais - es give.
His king - dom's glo - ries that ex - cel.
And those who fall He will sus - tain.

Lowell Mason, 1850

ERNAN LM

The Eyes of All Are Turned to You

He causes His sun to rise on the evil and the good, and sends
rain on the righteous and the unrighteous. — Matthew 5:45

145C

Psalm 145:15-21

9. ¹⁵ The eyes of all are turned to You;
10. ¹⁷ The LORD is just in all His ways;
11. ¹⁹ Those fear - ing Him He sat - is - fies;
12. ²¹ I'll speak the prais - es of the LORD,

Their food in sea - son You will give;
In all His works His love is shown;
He'll save them for He hears their cry.
His prais - es from my mouth will pour;

¹⁶ You sat - is - fy with o - pened hand
¹⁸ The LORD is near to all who call,
²⁰ The LORD pre - serves those lov - ing Him,
All flesh will bless His ho - ly name

De - sires of ev - ery - thing that lives.
Who call in truth on Him a - lone.
But by His wrath the wick - ed die.
For - ev - er and for - ev - er - more.

Karl P. E. Bach, 1714–1788; arr. Edward Miller, 1790

ROCKINGHAM LM

145D

Psalm 145:1-9

I Will Extol You

...Our Lord Jesus Christ...who is the blessed and only Sovereign,
the King of kings and Lord of Lords. —1 Timothy 6:14-15

1. ¹ I will ex-tol You, my God and Sov-'reign,
2. ⁴ One gen-er-a-tion speaks to an-oth-er,
3. ⁷ They'll cel-e-brate Your good-ness a-bound-ing;

And I will give Your name end-less praise.
Prais-ing the might-y things You have done.
Your righ-teous-ness they'll sing of with joy.

² Day af-ter day my praise I will give You;
⁵ I too will pon-der Your glo-rious splen-dor,
⁸ Gra-cious the LORD is, full of com-pas-sion,

I will ex-alt Your name ev-er-more.
Your maj-es-ty and won-der-ful deeds.
Slow to be an-gered, bound-less in love.

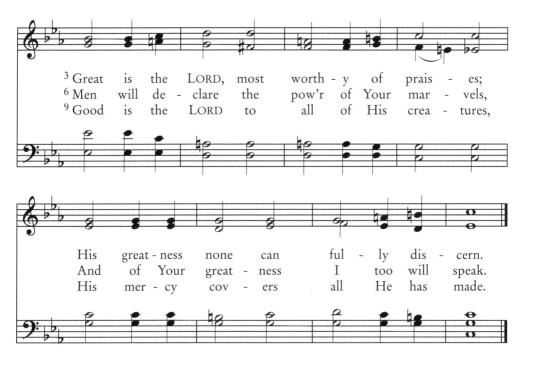

3 Great is the LORD, most worth - y of prais - es;
6 Men will de - clare the pow'r of Your mar - vels,
9 Good is the LORD to all of His crea - tures,

His great - ness none can ful - ly dis - cern.
And of Your great - ness I too will speak.
His mer - cy cov - ers all He has made.

Ludwig van Beethoven, 1770–1827; arr. Andrew K. Schep, 2008   BEETHOVEN'S 7TH 10.9.10.9.10.9

146A

Psalm 146

Praise the LORD

In Him you have been made complete.
—Colossians 2:10

1. ¹ Praise the LORD, let all with - in me
2. ⁵ He who has the God of Ja - cob
3. ⁷ He will al - ways ren - der jus - tice
4. How the LORD loves all the righ - teous!

Of - fer to the LORD His praise.
As his help is tru - ly blessed.
For the sake of those op - pressed.
⁹ He pro - tects the strang - er's stay,

² I will praise the LORD for - ev - er,
On the LORD his God for - ev - er
He gives food to those who hun - ger,
Helps the fa - ther - less and wid - ow,

Praise my God through all my days.
Will his hope se - cure - ly rest.
Sat - is - fies their emp - ti - ness.
But sub - verts the wick - ed's way.

3 Put no trust in earth - ly princ - es—
6 God has made the earth and heav - en,
Cap - tive ones the LORD re - leas - es,
10 Yes, the LORD will reign for - ev - er;

Mor - tal men who can - not save.
And He al - so made the sea;
8 To the blind the LORD gives sight;
Zi - on's God for - ev - er - more,

4 When he dies his thoughts will per - ish,
He made ev - ery - thing with - in them;
Those brought low the LORD will lift up,
Through - out ev - ery gen - er - a - tion;

Bur - ied with him in the grave.
He is faith - ful con - stant - ly.
He re - lieves them from their plight.
Hal - le - lu - jah! Praise the LORD.

Charles C. Converse, 1870

CONVERSE 87.87 D

146B

Psalm 146

Psalm 146

Praise the LORD

Go in peace, and be healed of your disease.
— Mark 5:34

1. ¹ Praise the LORD, let all with - in me
2. ⁵ He who has the God of Ja - cob
3. ⁷ He will al - ways ren - der jus - tice
4. How the LORD loves all the righ - teous!

Of - fer to the LORD His praise.
As his help is tru - ly blessed.
For the sake of those op - pressed.
⁹ He pro - tects the strang - er's stay,

² I will praise the LORD for - ev - er,
On the LORD his God for - ev - er
He gives food to those who hun - ger,
Helps the fa - ther - less and wid - ow,

Praise my God through all my days.
Will his hope se - cure - ly rest.
Sat - is - fies their emp - ti - ness.
But sub - verts the wick - ed's way.

3 Put no trust in earth - ly princ - es—
6 God has made the earth and heav - en,
Cap - tive ones the LORD re - leas - es,
10 Yes, the LORD will reign for - ev - er;

Mor - tal men who can - not save.
And He al - so made the sea;
8 To the blind the LORD gives sight;
Zi - on's God for - ev - er - more,

4 When he dies his thoughts will per - ish,
He made ev - ery - thing with - in them;
Those brought low the LORD will lift up,
Through - out ev - ery gen - er - a - tion;

Bur - ied with him in the grave.
He is faith - ful con - stant - ly.
He re - lieves them from their plight.
Hal - le - lu - jah! Praise the LORD.

Gregorian chant; arr. Lowell Mason, 1839

RIPLEY 87.87 D

147A

Psalm 147:1-11

Sing Hallelujah!

He is before all things, and in Him all things hold together.
— Colossians 1:17

1. ¹ Sing Hal - le - lu - jah! O how good To
2. ² The LORD builds up Je - ru - sa - lem, Brings
3. ⁴ He counts the num - ber of the stars; He

praise our God with song! For it is pleas - ant
Is - r'el's ex - iled sons. ³ He binds up all their
names each one of them. ⁵ Our Lord is great in

and is right; To Him all praise be - longs.
wounds and heals The bro - ken - heart - ed ones.
pow'r and might His wis - dom has no end.

4. ⁶ Those humbled low the LORD will raise;
He casts the wicked down.
⁷ O praise the LORD our God with thanks;
With harp His praises sound.

5. ⁸ He covers all the sky with clouds,
Makes rain for earth below;
He is the One who makes the grass
Upon the mountains grow.

6. ⁹ Food for the cattle He provides,
And all their need supplies;
He also feeds the raven's young,
And hears their hungry cries.

7. ¹⁰ In strength of horse or speed of man,
The LORD takes no delight;
¹¹ But those who fear and trust His love
Are pleasing in His sight.

Source unknown

ONWARD CM

O Praise the Lord, Jerusalem

We know that all things work together for good to those who love God and are called according to His purpose. —Romans 8:28

147B

Psalm 147:12-20

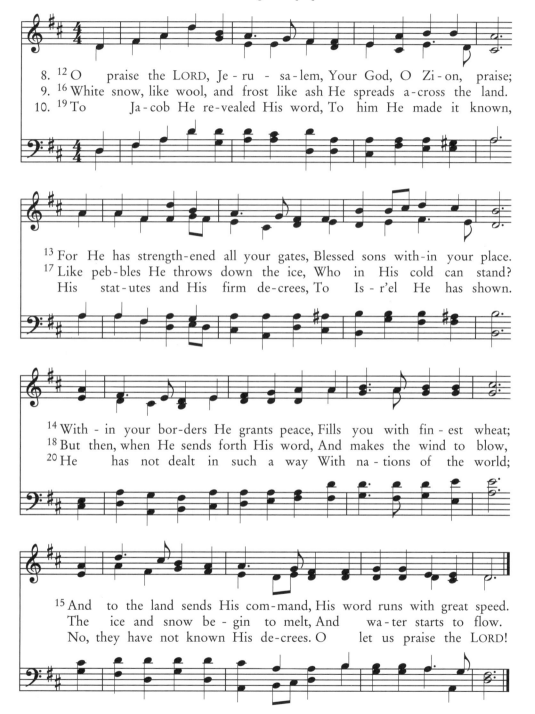

8. 12 O praise the LORD, Je-ru-sa-lem, Your God, O Zi-on, praise;
9. 16 White snow, like wool, and frost like ash He spreads a-cross the land.
10. 19 To Ja-cob He re-vealed His word, To him He made it known,

13 For He has strength-ened all your gates, Blessed sons with-in your place.
17 Like peb-bles He throws down the ice, Who in His cold can stand?
His stat-utes and His firm de-crees, To Is-r'el He has shown.

14 With-in your bor-ders He grants peace, Fills you with fin-est wheat;
18 But then, when He sends forth His word, And makes the wind to blow,
20 He has not dealt in such a way With na-tions of the world;

15 And to the land sends His com-mand, His word runs with great speed.
The ice and snow be-gin to melt, And wa-ter starts to flow.
No, they have not known His de-crees. O let us praise the LORD!

Clement W. Poole, 1875

PETERSHAM CMD

148A

Psalm 148

From Heav'n O Praise the LORD!

...That He Himself will come to have first place in everything.
—Colossians 1:18

1. ¹ From heav'n O praise the LORD! On high the LORD O praise!
2. ⁵ O let them glo - ri - fy The LORD's ma - jes - tic name;
3. ⁷ From earth O praise the LORD You deeps and all be - low.

LORD!
- fy
LORD

LORD! On high the LORD O praise!
- fy The LORD's ma - jes - tic name;
LORD You deeps and all be - low.

² All an - gels, praise ac - cord; Let all His hosts give praise.
When He spoke from on high, They in - to be - ing came.
⁸ Wild winds that do His word; You clouds, fire, hail, and snow;

³ Praise Him on high, Sun, moon, and star
⁶ And He ar - ranged, Where they should stand,
⁹ Hills low and high, And ce - dars tall,

Praise Him on high, Sun, moon, and star
And He ar - ranged, Where they should stand,
Hills low and high, And ce - dars tall,

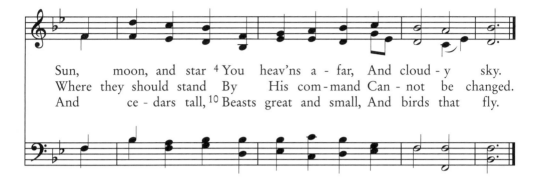

Sun, moon, and star [4] You heav'ns a - far, And cloud - y sky.
Where they should stand By His com - mand Can - not be changed.
And ce - dars tall, [10] Beasts great and small, And birds that fly.

4. [11] Let all the peoples praise,
    And kings of every land;
    Let all their voices raise
    Who judge and give command.
  [12] By young and old,
    By girl and boy,
    By girl and boy,
  [13] His name with joy
    Should be extolled.

5.   The LORD alone be praised
    Above the earth and sky!
  [14] He for His saints has raised
    A king to rule on high;
    So praise accord
    O Israel,
    O Israel,
    Who near Him dwell,
    O praise the LORD!

Horatio R. Palmer, 1834–1907   ST. CATHERINES 66.66.44.44

148B
Psalm 148

Hallelujah! Praise the LORD's Name

The Father loves the Son and has given all things into His hand.
—John 3:35

1. ¹ Hal - le - lu - jah! Praise the LORD's name
2. ⁵ Let them praise the Name, the LORD's name,
3. ⁹ All you hills and loft - y moun - tains,
4. ¹³ Let them prais - es give the LORD's name,

From the heav - ens praise His name.
They were made at His com - mand.
Fruit - ful trees and ce - dars high,
For His name a - lone is high;

In the heights a - bove, O praise Him,
⁶ And, by His de - cree es - tab - lished,
¹⁰ Creep - ing things, wild beasts, and cat - tle,
And His glo - ry is ex - alt - ed

² All His an - gels praise pro - claim.
They for - ev - er - more will stand.
Birds that in the heav - ens fly,
Far a - bove the earth and sky.

All His hosts to - geth - er praise Him.
7 From the earth, O praise the LORD's name:
11 Kings of earth and all its peo - ples,
14 He a horn raised for His peo - ple,

3 Praise Him, sun and moon on high.
All you deeps, sea crea - tures all,
Princ - es, and its judg - es all,
By His saints in praise a - dored;

4 Praise Him, stars; praise Him, O heav - ens.
8 Fire and hail and snow and va - pors,
12 Boys and girls, young men and wom - en,
They are Is - ra - el His peo - ple,

Praise Him, wa - ters in the sky.
Storm - y winds that heed His call,
Old - er ones and chil - dren small.
Near to Him. O praise the LORD!

William J. Kirkpatrick, 1838–1921

PRAISE JEHOVAH 87.87 D

149A

Psalm 149:1-4

Praise the LORD! Hallelujah!

…Those sanctified in Christ Jesus, saints by calling, with all who in every place call on the name of our Lord Jesus Christ. —1 Corinthians 1:2

1. ¹ Praise the LORD! Hal - le - lu - jah!
2. ² May the thought of his Mak - er
3. ³ In ex - u - ber - ant danc - ing
4. ⁴ For the LORD, in His peo - ple,

Sing the LORD a new song!
Joy to Is - ra - el bring;
Let them wor - ship His name;
Finds great joy and de - light;

Sing with fresh thanks - giv - ing
Let the sons of Zi - on
Tam - bou - rine and harp join,
He a - dorns the hum - ble,

Where saints gath - er as one.
Take de - light in their King.
Help them sing of His fame.
Sav - ing them by His might.

Andrew K. Schep, 2004

DANCE OF THE DAWN 76.66

O Praise the Lord, O Sing Aloud

Do you not know that the saints will judge the world?
—1 Corinthians 6:2

1. ¹O praise the LORD, O sing a-loud, A new song to the LORD;
2. ³With danc-ing let them of-fer up Their prais-es to His name;
3. ⁵With glo-ry let the god-ly ones Ex-ult with lift-ed heads;
4. ⁷Up-on the na-tions they shall bring Re-venge and judg-ment just;

Where god-ly peo-ple con-gre-gate, Let them His praise ac-cord.
Let them with sound of harp and drum Sing psalms of praise to Him.
Yes, let them all with glad-ness shout, And sing up-on their beds.
⁸With i-ron chains their kings and chiefs They'll in-to bon-dage thrust.

²With joy in their Cre-a-tor now Let Is-r'el shout and sing;
⁴That peo-ple whom the LORD has claimed Is plea-sant in His eyes;
⁶O let the loft-y praise of God From out their throats be poured,
⁹On them the judg-ment ex-e-cute Found writ-ten in His word;

And so let all of Zi-on's sons Be joy-ful in their King.
And with sal-va-tion's ra-di-ance The meek He beau-ti-fies.
And let them have with-in their hands A sharp two-edg-ed sword.
This hon-or all His god-ly have. Give prais-es to the LORD!

Gottfried W. Fink, 1842; arr. Arthur S. Sullivan

BETHLEHEM CMD

150A

Psalm 150

Praise the LORD!

If there is any excellence and if anything worthy of praise,
dwell on these things. —Philippians 4:8

1 Praise the LORD! Praise God in His sanc - tu - ar - y.

Praise Him in His might - y ex - panse. 2 Praise Him for His

might - y deeds. Praise Him ac - cord - ing to His ex - cel - lent great - ness.

3 Praise Him with the trum - pet sound. Praise Him with the harp and ly - re.

4 Praise Him with tim - brel and danc - ing. Praise
Him with stringed in-stru-ments and pipe. 5 Praise Him with loud
cym - bals. Praise Him with re-sound-ing cym-bals. 6 Let
ev-ery-thing that has breath praise the LORD! Praise the LORD!

Eleanor Hutcheson, 1972

OMEGA (Irr.)

150B
Psalm 150

Book Five Doxology

*Through Him then, let us continually offer up
a sacrifice of praise to God.* —Hebrews 13:15

1. [1]O praise the LORD! Give praise to God With-
2. [2]O praise Him for His val - iant works, His
3. [3]O praise Him with the trum - pet's blast; Praise
4. [5]O praise Him with the cym - bals' crash, With

in His ho - ly place; And in His
acts of prov - i - dence; And give Him
Him with harp and lute. [4]Praise Him with
cym - bals praise ac - cord. [6]Let all things

might - y, vast ex - panse Sing out to Him your praise.
praise ac - cord - ing to His loft - y ex - cel - lence.
tam - bou - rine and dance, Praise Him with strings and flute.
liv - ing praise the LORD; You, al - so, praise the LORD.

Chester G. Allen, 1869

SUNDERLAND CM

Indexes

Copyright Resources

The Book of Psalms for Worship is intended to make the singing of psalms more accessible. The publisher's desire is for everyone to experience the blessings of singing God's Word found in the Psalms. To that end, the following exception to the copyright statement on page ii may be taken:

In the course of a year, an individual or church may make no more than 500 copies each of up to any 12 psalm selections for a not-for-profit use, as long as the copyright for the tune or arrangement is held by this publisher. (If a tune or arrangement is copyrighted by another publisher, there will be a © symbol and name at the bottom of the psalm's page.) The copies should not be kept for more than a year. Each copy must have the following credit line:

Any other use must have express written permission of the publisher. Permission forms can be found at www.crownandcovenant.com. Other copyright holders found in this book can be reached at the following addresses:

Abingdon Press
201 Eighth Avenue South
P.O. Box 801
Nashville, TN 37202

Oxford University Press
200 Madison Avenue
New York, N.Y., 10016

Psalmody Committee of the
Free Church of Scotland
15 North Bank Street
Edinburgh, Scotland EH1 2LS

These musical compositions or arrangements are copyrighted by the named individuals and licensed for exclusive use in *The Book of Psalms for Worship*:

Coombs, Brian E. (b. 1969)....................2D, 3B, 10B, 15B, 23C, 38B, 42C, 58A,67C, 72E, 74A, 81A, 82A, 88A, 102CD,106H, 109C, 110A, 114A, 119H, 127B, 130B, 131B, 137B

Copeland, Robert M. (b. 1945) 14B, 16E, 27D, 105E, 119G

Fuhrman, Franki (b. 1947)................... 41B, 52A, 70B, 78DG, 109A

Hutcheson, Eleanor M. (1920–1990).....41C, 72G, 97C, 100D, 106G, 150A

Lowe, G. Duncan (b. 1935)................. 63A, 69A, 83, 107FG

Martin, D. Bruce (1880–1941) 37A, 73C, 79B, 121D

Maurer, Mark (b. 1974)........................... 140

Metheny, S.A. Sterrett (1869–1921)......24C, 37D, 44C, 130A, 131A

McBurney, Charles (1914–2007) 97C

McCracken, Lori (b. 1961) 42D

McCracken, Paul D. (1898–1989)........ 51B

McCracken, Timothy (b. 1959) 117B

McCrory, Don (b.1952)........................ 16D

Robb, John K. (1868–1960)... 4A, 31D, 46B, 86A, 104BD, 107H, 112A, 115B, 118D, 127A

Schep, Andrew K. (b. 1963) 27A, 62A, 68A, 107B, 110A, 114B, 132B, 145D, 149A

Tabon, Michael (b. 1950)........................13B, 95D, 107I, 113C, 118A

Every effort has been made to trace composers and original sources of the music in this volume and to record these in the alphabetical index of tunes. Permission for the use of copyrighted tunes or harmonizations has been acknowledged on the page with the music. If in any instance proper credit has not been given, the publishers will welcome notice that can lead to the removal of inaccuracies in the future printings or editions.

All versifications (psalm texts) in **The Book of Psalms for Worship** *are copyrighted by* ***The Board of Education & Publication of the Reformed Presbyterian Church (Crown & Covenant Publications).***

Index of Tunes Alphabetically

Index of Tunes, Metrically

Index of Composers, Arrangers, and Sources

Index of First Lines & Phrases Alphabetically

Index of Biblical Topics, Alphabetically

The following biblical topics are followed by the Psalm number and the relevant selection of the Psalm. A related or substitute topic listed after "See" is in capital letters if it is a major heading in the index, and in lower case if it is a sub-heading. In cases where only the Psalm number is referenced, without its selection letter, all selections of that Psalm are relevant to the subject. This index is not intended as an exhaustive concordance, but only as a broad help to locate Psalms that speak of the listed subject.

Index of Psalm Usage in the New Testament

Bold face: Psalm Quotation   Regular face: Psalm Allusion

Psalm Ref., chapter : verse	New Test. Ref.	Psalm Ref., chapter : verse	New Test. Ref.
1:6	1 Cor. 8:3	26:8	Matt. 23:21
2:1–2	**Acts 4:25–26;** Rev. 11:18	27:14	1 Cor. 16:13
2:6	Rev. 14:1	28:4	Rev. 20:12; 22:12
2:7	**Acts 13:33; Heb. 1:5; 5:5**	29:3	Acts 7:2; Rev. 10:3
2:8	Heb. 1:2	31:5	**Luke 23:46**
3:8	Rev. 7:10	31:24	1 Cor. 16:13
4:4	**Eph. 4:26**	32:1–2	**Rom. 4:7–8**
5:5	Rom. 1:30	32:2	Rev. 14:5
5:9	**Rom. 3:13**	32:9	Jam. 3:3
6:8	**Matt. 7:23; Luke 13:27**	33:3	Rev. 5:9; 14:3
7:9	Rev. 2:23	33:12	Tit. 2:14
7:13	Eph. 6:16	33:13–15	Heb. 4:13
7:14	Jam. 1:15	34:2	Luke 1:46
8:2	**Matt. 21:16**	34:8	1 Pet. 2:3
8:4–6	**Heb. 2:6–7**	34:12,16	**1 Pet. 3:10–12**
8:6	**1 Cor. 15:27; Eph. 1:22**	34:14	Rom. 12:18; 14:19; Heb. 12:14; 3 John 11
9:8	Acts 17:31	34:15	John 9:31
10:7	**Rom. 3:14**	34:20	John 19:36
14:1–3	**Rom. 3:10–12**	35:9	**Luke 1:47**
16:8–11	**Acts 2:25–28**	35:19	**John 15:25**
16:10	Acts 13:35	36:1	**Rom. 3:18**
17:15	Rev. 22:4	37:11	**Matt. 5:5**
18:2	Luke 1:69	37:24	2 Cor. 4:9
18:49	**Rom. 15:9**	37:27	3 John 11
19:1,6	Rom. 1:20	38:11	Luke 23:49
19:4	**Rom. 10:18**	38:20	1 John 3:12
19:9	Rev. 16:7; 19:2	39:1	Jam. 1:26
21:3	Rev. 14:14	39:5	Matt. 6:27; Luke 12:25; Jam. 4:14
22:1	**Matt. 27:46; Mark 15:34**	39:5–6	Rom. 8:20
22:5	Rom. 5:5	39:6	Luke 12:20
22:7	**Matt. 27:39**	39:12	Heb. 11:13; 1 Pet. 2:11
22:8	**Matt. 27:43**	40:3	Rev. 5:9; 14:3
22:16,20	Phil. 3:2	40:6–8	**Heb. 10:5,9**
22:18	**Matt. 27:35; Mark 15:24; Luke 23:34; John 19:24**	41:9	**John 13:18**
22:21	2 Tim. 4:17	41:13	**Luke 1:68**
22:22	**Heb. 2:12**	42:2	Rev. 22:4
23:1,2	John 10:11; Rev. 7:17	44:2	Acts 7:45
24:1	**1 Cor. 10:26**	44:22	**Rom. 8:36**
24:2	2 Pet. 3:5	45:5–6	**Heb. 1:8–9**
24:4	Matt. 5:8; 1 Tim. 2:8	45:8	John 19:39
25:9,14	John 7:17	46:3	Luke 21:25
26:2	Rev. 2:23	46:4	Rev. 22:1
		46:6	Rev. 11:18
		47:3	Rev. 3:9
		47:8	Rev. 4:2,9,10; 5:1
		50:6	Heb. 12:23

The Book of Psalms for Worship was typeset and
designed on an Apple Macintosh operating system
using Finale 2009 and Adobe InDesign CS4. All
psalm texts are set in Stempel Garamond, and the
music attributions are set in Gill Sans. *The Book of
Psalms for Worship* is printed on 50# white offset
paper by McNaughton & Gunn, Inc, of Ann Arbor,
MI., certified by the Forest Stewardship Council.

(A colophon like this was first used in the *Mainz
Psalter of 1457.*)

FSC
www.fsc.org
MIX
Paper from
responsible sources
FSC® C011935